Diversity, Violence, and Recognition

Diversity, Violence, and Recognition

How Recognizing Ethnic Identity Promotes Peace

ELISABETH KING AND CYRUS SAMII

OXFORD
UNIVERSITY PRESS

OXFORD
UNIVERSITY PRESS

Oxford University Press is a department of the University of Oxford. It furthers the University's objective of excellence in research, scholarship, and education by publishing worldwide. Oxford is a registered trade mark of Oxford University Press in the UK and certain other countries.

Published in the United States of America by Oxford University Press
198 Madison Avenue, New York, NY 10016, United States of America.

Library of Congress Cataloging-in-Publication Data
Names: King, Elisabeth, 1978– author. | Samii, Cyrus, author.
Title: Diversity, violence, and recognition : how recognizing ethnic identity promotes peace / Elisabeth King and Cyrus Samii.
Description: New York, NY : Oxford University Press, 2020. |
Includes bibliographical references and index.
Identifiers: LCCN 2019047164 (print) | LCCN 2019047165 (ebook) |
ISBN 9780197509456 (hardback) | ISBN 9780197509463 (paperback) |
ISBN 9780197509487 (epub) | ISBN 9780197509494 (online)
Subjects: LCSH: Ethnic groups—Government policy. | Ethnic relations—Government policy. |
Ethnic conflict—Prevention—Government policy. |
Peace building—Social aspects—Government policy.
Classification: LCC JF1061.K56 2020 (print) | LCC JF1061 (ebook) |
DDC 323.11—dc23
LC record available at https://lccn.loc.gov/2019047164
LC ebook record available at https://lccn.loc.gov/2019047165

1 3 5 7 9 8 6 4 2

Paperback printed by Marquis, Canada
Hardback printed by Bridgeport National Bindery, Inc., United States of America

CONTENTS

PART I   FOUNDATIONS

v

PART IV   CONCLUSIONS

ILLUSTRATIONS

Figures

Tables

PREFACE

This book originated in discussions we had about the intricacies of ethnic politics in Burundi and Rwanda and the contrasting approaches that the two countries' governments had taken to address conflict. The conversations started over coffee and tea in cubicles at Columbia University's Institute for Social and Economic Research and Policy and the university's Department of Political Science, where King was a post-doctoral fellow and Samii a graduate student ten years ago. They continued after we both landed as faculty at New York University (NYU). Our discussions were based in our respective research on quota-based integration of the Burundian military and treatment of ethnic identity in Rwanda's education system. The comparison between the two cases was fascinating, but it led us to wonder whether the Burundian or Rwandan approach was more representative of what countries around the world were doing to address ethnically charged violent conflicts and, moreover, what was more effective. We needed data, and so with the help of an impressively multilingual master's student at NYU, Adriana Castro Gonzalez, we started in 2012 to read constitutions and comprehensive settlements (in the original English, French, Spanish, or Portuguese when possible, and then using Google Translate when not) from conflict-affected countries around the world. We wrestled with definitions and case selection criteria for two years, presenting to country and thematic experts, before arriving at the core concept on which this book is based. While our initial focus was on ethnic quotas, we came to realize that quotas were but one way to implement a broader strategy of what we labeled "ethnic recognition." It is an irony that the Dropbox folder in which we work is still called "Ethnic Quotas" seven years later.

Our aim with this book is to establish a set of high-level stylized facts and detailed case study examples that can serve as a foundation for investigating recognition strategies for managing conflict. The book is intended to be accessible to general audiences, including undergraduates, but also to be precise and rigorous enough to serve as a reliable guide for practitioners and scholars in designing conflict management policies and more targeted research on conflict. All of the data and the analysis code used for the cross-national analysis are available through a Harvard Dataverse archive with the same title as the book. While we began this project without knowing what type of story we would ultimately be telling, in the end this is a rather optimistic account of at least one strategy for promoting post-conflict peace, in contrast to the pessimistic analyses that dominate scholarship on governance, development, and peace today.

This book was nearly a decade in the making and was possible only through the support and contributions of many, many friends and colleagues.

When we first began exploring ethnic recognition in contexts around the world, we turned to people who knew them well. Our work benefited from excellent advice from Taisier Ali, Laia Balcells, Gina Bateson, Florian Bieber, Rob Blair, Brittany Danisch, Jesse Driscoll, Omar Garcia Ponce, Guy Grossman, Oded Haklai, David Jandura, Robert O. Matthews, Laura Seay, and Ian Spears. Mathias de Roeck and Filip Reyntjens shared data they collected from Burundi and Rwanda.

Leonardo Arriola, Kanchan Chandra, Frank De Zwart, Lahra Smith, Jack Snyder, Murat Somer, Stef Vandeginste, and Stefan Wolfe carefully read an earlier version of the manuscript in its entirety and offered terrific suggestions that much improved the version you are reading now. Sarah Zukerman Daly, Kimuli Kasara, and Gwyneth McClendon read many revised chapters, also offering invaluable guidance to refine our argument and writing. Anonymous peer reviewers provided positive encouragement and we hope they will recognize their suggestions in these pages.

A large number of talented students enthusiastically offered their time and numerous skills to meaningfully advance this research project and book. These include Adamseged Abebe, Sorana Acris, Reema Badrinarayan, Talin Bagdassarian, Ashley Bertolini, Amanda Blewitt, Adriana Castro Gonzalez, Emily Dunlop, Brittany Gray, Ugurcan Evci, Morissa McQuide, Grace Pai, Cam Skinner, Isa Spoerry, Ally Tritten, and Sidak Yntiso.

Contributions from discussants, co-panelists, and audience members at numerous conferences and workshops also improved this book. These include the American Political Science Association, the Contemporary African Political Economy Research Seminar, the Folke Bernadotte Academy Research Working Group on Peace, the Global Centre for Pluralism, the International Political Science Association, the International Studies Association, and the NYU Politics Department internal workshop. We are grateful to all who asked tough questions or offered ideas and support, including Keith Banting, Will Kymlicka, Brendan O'Leary, Adam Przeworski, and David Stasavage. Of course, the remaining errors are our own.

Thank you to Macartan Humphreys, who was long ago most correct in first suggesting that we might enjoy working together. Séverine Autesserre has been an enduring source of support, friendship, and good advice.

We are grateful to the Folke Bernadotte Academy, and especially the Academy's research directors, Birger Heldt and Mimmi Soderberg Kovacs, for providing generous financial support for the project through two successive grants, and to the NYU Office of Global Initiatives, which underwrote a book workshop that we hosted at NYU's beautiful Florence campus in February 2018.

We also thank our current departments—NYU Politics and Steinhardt's Applied Statistics, Social Science, and Humanities—where we find welcome and thought-provoking homes for research, writing, and teaching about topics about which we are passionate. We are grateful to our many wonderful colleagues, including Dana Burde, Hua-Yu Sebastian Cherng, Mike Gilligan, and Carol Anne Spreen.

From the very first time we met him in our NYU offices, our Oxford editor, David McBride, has been consistently encouraging, enthusiastic, and responsive to us and this project. His editorial team, including Asish Krishna, Harvey Gable, and Emily Mackenzie, has skillfully worked with us and our manuscript.

We often judged our progress on this project not by the data collection, analysis, or writing we had accomplished, but in the growth of our amazing children—none of whom were yet with us when we first began conversations for this project! We thank Cyrus and Nicole Samii's Caspar (age nine) and Soren (age one), and Elisabeth and David Noseworthy's Ella Josephine (age eight); who have encouraged and inspired us in so many ways. Our families—including Ann and Chris Farrell and Nasrin and Siamak Samii—also helped make this book and the long hours of work it took possible. We are grateful always to David and Nicole for their motivation, patience, and enduring support.

ACRONYMS AND ABBREVIATIONS

CNDD	*Conseil national pour la défense de la démocratie*
CUD	Coalition for Unity and Democracy
EPLF	Eritrean People's Liberation Front
EPRDF	Ethiopian People's Revolutionary Democratic Front
EPRP	Ethiopian People's Revolutionary Party
EU	European Union
FARG	*Fonds d'assistance aux rescapés du genocide*
FDD	Forces pour la Défense de la Démocratie
FDLR	*Forces démocratiques de libération du Rwanda*
FDRE	Federal Democratic Republic of Ethiopia
FNL	Forces Nationales de Libération
FRODEBU	Front pour la Démocratie au Burundi
FROLINA	Front pour la Libération Nationale
GAM	Government of Indonesia and the Free Aceh Movement
GDP	gross domestic product
HDI	human development index
MDR	Mouvement Démocratique Républicain
MEISON	All-Ethiopia Socialist Movement
MILC	Managing Intrastate Low-Intensity Conflict
MRND	*Mouvement révolutionaire national pour le développement*
NURC	National Unity and Reconciliation Commission
OAU	Organisation of African Unity
OPDO	Oromo People's Democratic Organization
PALIPEHUTU	Parti pour la Libération du Peuple Hutu
PARMEHUTU	Parti du Mouvement de l'Emancipation Hutu
PL	Parti Libéral
PMPA	*Partis et mouvements politiques armés*
RPF	Rwandan Patriotic Front

TGE	Transitional Government of Ethiopia
TPLF	Tigrayan People's Liberation Front
UK	United Kingdom
UN	United Nations
UNAR	*Union Nationale Rwandaise*
UPRONA	*Union Pour le Progrès National*
US	United States [of America]
VDEM	Varieties of Democracy

Diversity, Violence, and Recognition

PART I

FOUNDATIONS

To Recognize or Not?

The puzzle

This book is about the choice to recognize or not to recognize ethnic identities to manage violence and the implications of this choice around the world today. Consider the case of Rwanda in the aftermath of the 1994 genocide that left, according to government estimates, perhaps 75 percent of the resident ethnic Tutsi minority dead. Ostensibly in the aim of peace, Rwanda's 2003 constitution resolves to "eradicate ethnic, regional and any other form of divisions," and mere reference to Hutu or Tutsi identity can be reason for prosecution under anti-genocide laws. Rwanda's president, Paul Kagame, told Rwandans, "We are working to entrench in your thinking about Rwandan national identity [a view] that transcends the ethnic ideology promoted by previous governments" (Kagame 2014). He remarked to journalists, "We are trying to reconcile our society and talk people out of this nonsense of division" (Pilling and Barber 2017).

Responding to a similarly violent past and nearly identical ethnic and material structural conditions, the neighboring Burundian government has addressed the question of diversity differently. Equally ostensibly in the aim of peace, Burundi's 2005 constitution entrenched public institution quotas for Hutus and Tutsis after the 1993–2004 civil war. Burundi's president, Pierre Nkurunziza, claimed that "today after genocide and civil war we have peace in this country. . . . But before there was exclusion, there was a division, between different groups and the majority was excluded . . . but today, all Burundians are together in the army, police, administration, education, everywhere. So today, we have peace and security" (Nkurunziza 2011).

What can we say about these diametrically opposed choices under such seemingly similar circumstances? The question gets even more complicated when one looks back further in time. Before the genocide, Rwanda's government had a strategy resembling Burundi's today, wherein spots in the public service and secondary schools, for example, were assigned based on ethnic quotas. Before Burundi's civil war, its government took an approach resembling Rwanda's today,

Diversity, Violence, and Recognition. Elisabeth King and Cyrus Samii, Oxford University Press (2020). © Oxford University Press.
DOI: 10.1093/oso/9780197509456.003.0001

wherein one Burundian identity was promoted and reference to ethnic identity was suppressed. Indeed, with our firsthand experiences conducting research in Rwanda and Burundi, where both formal recognition and non-recognition of ethnic identities preceded large-scale violence, we began the research for this book skeptical as to the wisdom of these competing strategies for peace. As political scientists John McGarry and Brendan O'Leary opined, it was "not, in our opinion, possible or desirable to say that either difference-eliminating or difference-managing methods are inherently superior" (1993, 5). Indeed, we realized, our puzzles prompt important questions that reach far beyond central Africa.

We ask: *Under what conditions do governments manage internal violent conflicts by formally recognizing different ethnic identities? Moreover, what are the implications for peace?* To address these questions, we develop a theory, carry out cross-national quantitative analyses, and conduct three qualitative case studies to investigate the adoption and effects of ethnic recognition. The analysis engages long-standing and heated debates between scholars of conflict management who favor "accommodating" or recognizing ethnic identity and assigning group-differentiated rights and those who advocate "integrative" institutions that do not recognize ethnic groups; between classical liberal individualist political philosophers and those of a multiculturalist persuasion; and between ordinary people and leaders grappling with the power of identity and whether to recognize diversity in state institutions. Conflicts over identity are widespread and long-standing (Fukuyama 2018), and there is renewed commitment to conflict prevention worldwide (World Bank and United Nations 2018). Past violent conflict is a robust predictor of future conflict (Collier and Sambanis 2002; Walter 2010). Moreover, conflicts with an ethnic component are nearly twice as likely to recur (Mattes and Savun 2009). These facts make the study of institutional choices regarding ethnicity crucial for peace.

What is ethnic recognition and why should we study it?

Ethnic recognition is the focal concept of this book. By ethnic recognition, we mean public and explicit references to ethnic groups in state institutions. We are interested particularly in the presence (and absence) of positive statements that may be read as affirming groups' existence as part of the body politic. We focus first on such expressions in constitutions and peace agreements, which we deem to have special significance, but then expand our approach to look at other legislation as well as practice. To be considered a recognition regime, a state need not be comprehensive in the sense of recognizing all ethnic groups, or even all "po-litically relevant" (Posner 2004) ethnic groups, nor must it extend that recognition to all institutional domains. We examine these complexities in more detail in the forthcoming chapters. Ethnic recognition must, however, include a clear commitment to publicly acknowledging at least some different ethnic groups as part of the state. Ethnic recognition may consist of such symbolic recognition on its own, or be accompanied by group-differentiated rights (Horowitz 2000; Kymlicka 1995; Kymlicka and Shapiro 1997)—what we call *thin* and *thick* forms of recognition, respectively. Going forward, we use the terms "ethnic recognition" and "recognition" interchangeably and term the absence of such recognition "non-recognition."

Consistent with scholarly consensus, we take ethnicities as socially constructed identities associated with tribe, caste, race, and other descent-based social characteristics that typically define lines of past political or social organization (Chandra 2006, 2012). In analyzing both recognition and non-recognition strategies, we take for granted a core constructivist principle that the salience of ethnicity, or ethnic groups themselves, may change over time. Census data collection, administrative structures, electoral systems, educational systems, and the like can create or change ethnic identities and their political meaning (Chandra 2012; Scott 1995). Recognition and non-recognition thus affect the way ethnicity is understood and implicated in politics. We also appreciate that ethnic identities provide symbolically or instrumentally valuable resources for political entrepreneurs and people themselves (Gagnon 1994; Posner 2005). While some take diversity as a natural threat to solidarity (Huntington 2004; Putnam 2007), the way in which leaders treat and engage with these dynamics is arguably what can lead to positive or negative outcomes for individuals, groups, and states.

Liberal theorists propose that the salience of ethnicity should disappear with modernization (Connor 1972; Deutsch 1966; Snyder 2000), but examples abound of the continued importance of ethnic identity to understanding politics and conflict. In the original preface to his now-canonical 1985 volume *Ethnic Groups in Conflict*, Donald Horowitz asserted that "the importance of ethnic conflict, as a force shaping human affairs, as a phenomenon to be understood, as a threat to be controlled, can no longer be denied. . . . Connections among Biafra, Bangladesh, and Burundi, Beirut, Brussels, and Belfast were at first hesitantly made . . . but . . . [e]thnicity has fought and bled and burned its way into public and scholarly consciousness" (2000, xv). In the preface to the second edition, published fifteen years later, he argued that "ethnic conflict has established itself even more securely as a subject worthy of serious study." Acknowledging not only mass killings in Rwanda and Burundi, Horowitz wrote that "the violent fragmentation of two European and Eurasian pseudofederations [the former

Soviet Union and former Yugoslavia] convinced Western opinion that group loyalty still had a murderous aspect in the heartland of Europe a half century after Hitler" (2000, xi). Now, another fifteen years later, after volumes of work deconstructing the notion of ethnic identity (Appiah 2018; Chandra 2012; Sen 2006), one cannot help but be struck by the continued importance of ethnic conflict in international affairs—from what the UN called "a textbook example" of ethnic cleansing of Rohingya in Myanmar (Malley 2018) to the sectarian cleavages in Syria's civil war and the ongoing cycles of ethnic violence in South Sudan. One could also, of course, point to examples of conflict over diversity, identity, and belonging that have not translated into statewide violence but have nonetheless come to consume domestic affairs. These include the 2016 Brexit referendum through which citizens of the United Kingdom chose to withdraw from the European Union and the 2016 election of Donald Trump in the United States, both at least partially rooted in a rejection of immigration and diversity.

Recent examples illustrate the centrality of the question of ethnic recognition in the negotiation of peace agreements and post-conflict constitutions. According to Larry Diamond, a scholar of democracy who served as senior advisor to the Coalition Provisional Authority in Iraq, interethnic balancing featured prominently in institutional design in Iraq (Diamond 2005), where a federal system with a proportional electoral system and explicit recognition of Kurdish autonomy appeared in the 2005 constitution. As Barnett Rubin, who served as advisor to Afghanistan's 2001 Bonn Agreement, reports in a study with Humayun Hamidzada, ethnic balance—for instance, in the security sector—was likewise an important governance consideration (Rubin and Hamidzada 2007). As former British prime minister Tony Blair writes of his experience with the 1998 Good Friday Agreement to end conflict in Northern Ireland, the key question concerned "on what basis and on what principles would Republicans [who favored unification with Ireland] accept" remaining a part of Britain (2010, 174). As McGarry and O'Leary (1999) describe it, the answer was ultimately based on multiple forms of recognition for each of the two identity groups, one connecting more strongly with Ireland and the other with Britain.

When leaders choose ethnic recognition, they may select one or more of a host of strategies for using recognition to manage differences. Strategies could include consociationalism or ethnically based power sharing, wherein elites representing different ethnic groups share power at the executive level of government (McGarry, O'Leary, and Simeon 2008; O'Leary 2005), as we see in Burundi (Chapter 6). Additional strategies, many of which we also see in Burundi, consist of ethnically preferential policies, or ethnic quotas, that assign privileges in central institutions or markets on the basis of recognized ethnic identities (Horowitz 2000; Sowell 2004; Weiner 1983; Weisskopf 2004). Other approaches include federalism, wherein power is divided between a central government and territorially based—and likely identity-based—units (Forum of Federations n.d.), such as we find in Ethiopia (Chapter 8). Alternatively, recognition may be symbolic, such as including different ethnic groups' symbols on schools and other public institutions. In our reading, ethnic recognition is distinct from non-discrimination clauses that bar differential treatment based on ethnicity. Ethnic recognition goes beyond equal protection or non-discrimination clauses since "the politics of difference" often requires differential treatment (Taylor 1992; see also Banting and Kymlicka 2003). In Chapter 2, we also discuss distinctions between ethnic recognition and factional power sharing.

In other cases, a careful consideration of ethnicity in the aftermath of conflict has resulted in non-recognition—which, like recognition, can manifest in different ways and have effects on peace that similarly merit investigation. Yash Ghai, who advised in the negotiation and writing of constitutions in fifteen countries, noted of the 2008 constitution-drafting process in Kenya, "We wanted to remove ethnicity from politics. We didn't want parties to start squabbling on ethnic lines" (Ismail 2017). A similar logic informed the explicit denial of recognition based on ethnic group identity in Rwanda, as we explore in Chapter 7.

Just as there are multiple strategies to implement recognition, a leader may opt for non-recognition of ethnic groups in a number of ways. Difference may simply be overlooked, although in perusing the sociopolitical landscape, it is not easy to identify cases in which recognition questions have been neglected altogether. The opposite of recognition would be explicit bans on references to ethnic differences within the population. In France, for example, *laïcité*, often translated as "secularism," is the bedrock of French republican values, and expression of religious and cultural difference in state affairs is disallowed. In post-independence Ghana, Kwame Nkrumah made the word "tribe" illegal, and the slogan "for the nation to live, the tribe must die" was widely embraced by left-leaning African liberation movements and especially popularized by Guinea Bissau's Amilcar Cabral (Mhlanga 2013, 282). In Mexico, elites have long disseminated an ideology centered around the country's lack of racism as a strategy to promote national identity and foster solidarity among Mexicans, despite the ongoing presence of racism (Sue 2015). In Turkey as well as many sub-Saharan African countries, one manifestation of non-recognition comprises legal provisions that ban ethnically based parties in the electoral system (Basedau and Moroff 2011; Bogaards, Basedau, and Hartman 2010; Ishiyama 2009).

In Chapter 3, we offer a systematic mapping of when and where ethnic recognition has been adopted in conflict-affected countries since 1990. Our cross-national analysis focuses principally on the high-level decision to recognize ethnicity or not, and in the first instance we do not distinguish between different recognition or non-recognition strategies. Later in the book we study how the basic decision of whether or not to recognize affects policies in various domains—executive, legislative, civil service, security sector, justice, education, and language. The case study chapters then go into more detail on how recognition or non-recognition has been operationalized through additional policies.

One could make the case that we should follow the more common practice of increasing analytic disaggregation to study the specifics of consociational versus centripetal institutions (Horowitz 2014; McCulloch and McGarry 2017), ethnofederalism (Brancati 2006), ethnic quotas (Jarstad 2001), indigenous rights (Joshi and Darby 2013; Multicultural Policy Index 2019), or "territorial self-government" (Csergő, Roseberry, and Wolff 2017), for instance, rather than study "ethnic recognition." Our concept overlaps with certain aspects of these definitions and excludes others, and in Chapter 3, we compare our dataset to others and go into more explicit detail in relating our operationalization of recognition to other existing measures.

Why do we consider rather varied institutional arrangements as all "cases of" the same phenomenon, ethnic recognition? First, we focus on the high-level concept of ethnic recognition because we want a concept that can travel. Ethnofederalism, for example, applies to Ethiopia but not Burundi. Indigenous rights apply to Guatemala but not to Iraq, and so on. Second, the high-level concept allows us to develop a theory in which the nature of the challenges, benefits, and trade-offs in dealing with ethnicity in post-conflict contexts can be posed in similar terms, even if the institutional specifics differ. Third, focusing on only one set of institutions misses interdependencies across institutional domains such as governing institutions and the security sector (McCulloch and McGarry 2017), education and politics (King 2014), and power-sharing and justice (Vandeginste and Sriram 2011). We want to characterize broader strategies and choices across the range of state institutions, from the executive, legislative, and civil service to security, justice, education, and language. Fourth, by concentrating on this higher-level concept, we can make useful connections among scholarly communities that do not often speak to each other, such as those who study ethnic power-sharing and scholars of affirmative action. Finally, the concept of ethnic recognition allows us to address the first-order issue of how people "belong" in a polity, a key question of the twenty-first century (Ignatieff, quoted in Taub 2016).

The post-conflict context and ethnic politics

In this book, we focus especially on diversity and recognition in contexts affected by violent conflict. Whether a war comes to an end through military victory or, more commonly, negotiated settlement (Olson Lounsbery and DeRouen

2016), post-conflict leaders are left facing a common set of core challenges in regard to (re)establishing security, political institutions, economic development, justice, and reconciliation (Ali and Matthews 2004). Reaching across all of these challenges is the issue of how to deal with ethnic identity as part of a peace- and state-building strategy.

The dynamics and circumstances that leaders face in conflict settings are crucial for understanding their strategic choices. Imagine a context in which killing, sexual violence, and displacement occur largely along ethnic lines. Consistent with theoretical analyses of civil conflict that emphasize social polarization as a result of security dilemmas, intergroup fear and mistrust are likely to increase and intergroup social cohesion to decrease in such contexts (Collier et al. 2003; Posen 1993; Snyder and Jervis 1999). While ethnic differences are likely to have been politically relevant before the conflict, it is often conflict itself that further shapes and hardens group identities (Brown and Langer 2010; Kaufmann 1996; Levine and Campbell 1972). Notwithstanding the fact that strong state institutions are sometimes a key part of carrying out violence, such as in Rwanda (Straus 2006), political institutions are often weakened during conflict. In a period of reconstruction, states are arguably guided by the ongoing commitments of major donors and international organizations to liberal internationalism, which is the dominant peace-building paradigm, rooted in the promotion of liberal democracy and a market-oriented economy (Paris 1997). In the ensuing contexts of political competition, people often vote in ways akin to an "ethnic headcount" (Chandra 2004; Kauffman and Haklai 2008). It is in the context of these dynamics that we consider the adoption and effects of recognition.

A focus on institutions

Current political science literature focuses intensely on institutions as the basis of societal harmony (Acemoglu and Robinson 2012), including peace after ethnic conflict (Kuperman 2015; Reilly 2001; Reynolds 2011). Of course, while institutions do not work alone or in a vacuum, their malleability means that they are a focal point for considering the choices that leaders and societies face in addressing social upheaval. For the questions of this book, the institutions of interest define the state's unequivocal public commitments to use or refrain from using ethnic identities in governance. Many believe it is in divided societies that institutional arrangements "have the greatest impact" (Belmont, Mainwaring, and Reynolds 2002, 3).

While there is strong consensus on the importance of institutions, we know too little about how different institutional arrangements to manage ethnic conflict come to be (Horowitz 2014; McGarry 2017b; Sisk 1996). Despite reference to the apparent commonality of ethnic recognition (Krook and O'Brien 2010; Reynolds 2005), we believe there is no systematic mapping of the adoption of recognition in the context of violent conflict. Yet it is important to study the origins of institutions, focusing on critical junctures that follow social upheaval (Acemoglu and Robinson 2012; North, Wallis, and Weingast 2009). In Chapter 2, we consider domestic and international explanations that might explain the adoption of recognition. We also offer our own explanation, focused on ethnic power configurations. Understanding this institutional choice is a crucial first step toward assessing the impact of recognition on peace.

Alongside important gaps in knowledge about the genesis of institutions, there is heated debate over the relative merits of different institutional strategies in building stability and peace. In particular, there are strong arguments both favoring and against recognition as an approach to conflict management. Some of these debates are normative ones—pitting the idea of group-differentiated rights against individualism, for instance (ideas we develop further in Chapter 2). Empirically, too, this choice defines an "enduring debate" among scholars and in policy discussions (McGarry, O'Leary, and Simeon 2008).

The two contending views propose opposite strategies for best dealing with ethnicity after violent conflict. On one side, a growing group of scholars contends that recognizing and guaranteeing rights to ethnic groups builds peace (Cederman et al. 2017; Lijphart 1977, 1985; McGarry and O'Leary 2006). Inequality across ethnic lines has historically provided a cause for violent intergroup conflict (Cederman et al. 2013; Gurr 1993; Stewart 2002; Wimmer et al. 2009; World Bank and United Nations 2018), and such historic disadvantage is not self-correcting through free markets or free elections (Duflo 2005; Dunning 2010; Fryer and Loury 2005; Samii 2013b). Recognition strategies have the potential to redress grievances by granting groups status or allowing for more precise targeting of resources along ethnic lines (Cunningham, Loury, and Skrentny 2002). Recognition, such as in quotas or autonomy arrangements, may also help address minority ethnic group members' concerns over "tyranny of the majority" (McGarry, O'Leary, and Simeon 2008). Such ideas date back to at least the League of Nations, whose approach reflected awareness of the potential connections between minority rights and stability (Kirisci and Winrow 1997).

Other scholars make the case that institutions that avoid reference to ethnic groups—non-recognition—best prevent conflict (Horowitz 1991, 2000; Snyder 2000). Such non-recognition could avoid freezing divisions that emerged in the heat of conflict (Simonsen 2005) and open more space for conflict transformation (Taylor 2001). Likewise, political scientist Jack Snyder, in writing about democratization and nationalist conflict, argues that recognition-based strategies "should be avoided," since they result in centering politics on ethnic difference (2000, 40). Moreover, political scientists Evan Lieberman and Prerna Singh

(2012, 2017), in their study of the consequences of administrative use of ethnic identities, argue that, historically, institutionalizing ethnicity has contributed to ethnic war.

Empirically, it is unlikely that one strategy definitely trumps the other. It is well recognized that there is no one-size-fits-all approach to social or institutional engineering to address ethnic conflict (Wolff 2010, 137). Yet it behooves us to do more to understand the conditions under which one approach or the other might be most effective. By asking questions about the effects of recognition and also the conditions under which leaders choose or avoid recognition strategies, we endeavor to distinguish the effects of the policies from the conditions that brought them about (Brancati and Snyder 2011, 2013; Chandra 2012) and move forward our knowledge of both.

Theoretical argument in brief

In considering leaders' institutional choices in conflict-affected countries, we emphasize a key factor that is often overlooked: the ethnic power configuration—and especially leaders' status as minority or non-minority group members. To motivate this emphasis, we first note that recognition has two types of effects. The first are *assuring effects*, which mitigate mistrust across ethnic cleavages. The second are *mobilization effects*, which come from the fact that ethnic recognition licenses and potentially facilitates mass mobilization along ethnic lines.

With respect to adopting recognition, when these effects reinforce each other in contributing to leaders' political survival, we expect such leaders to adopt recognition. When these two effects clash, we have a "dilemma of recognition" (De Zwart 2005) that makes it less likely that leaders will adopt recognition. We theorize that if a leader comes from a majority or plurality ethnic group—we use the word "plurality" to mean the largest ethnic group, whether or not it makes up more than half of the population—the two effects work together to the leader's benefit. The assuring effects help to manage the mistrust of opposition ethnic group members (and may also assure members of the group in power), while the political mobilization effects lock in a political advantage. If a leader comes from a minority group, the two effects clash; while there may be some benefit from the assuring effects of recognition, the mobilization effects put minority group leaders at a political disadvantage.

With respect to the effects of recognition, we propose that ethnic power configurations also moderate the impact of recognition on peace. In cases of plurality rule, the assuring effects of recognition promote intergroup cooperation, while the absence of a mobilization threat allows the leadership to extend rights without fear of being removed from power. Under minority rule, leaders who adopt recognition must employ measures to counter the mobilization threat, and such measures likely undermine the otherwise assuring effects of recognition. Chapter 2 elaborates these theoretical arguments in more detail. We also consider other explanations and clarify important scope conditions and moderating factors.

Research design

We use a mixed-methods approach to evaluate our theoretical propositions. Our analysis combines quantitative and qualitative approaches. As we detail in Chapter 3, we first draw on a cross-national dataset that includes all cases of conflict from 1990 to 2012 that experienced what we call a "constitutional moment"—that is, cases with comprehensive peace agreements, constitutions, or constitutional amendments that take place amid or within a year following violent conflict. Through an original coding of these documents, we examine the inclusion or exclusion of ethnic recognition at eighty-six constitutional moments in fifty-seven countries. (We address the selection issue arising from cases without constitutional moments in our analysis.) We focus on institutionalized forms of recognition that serve as the state's public commitments to recognizing (or not) ethnic identities in governance. Anticipating questions about how adoption correlates with actual implementation of recognition, we also created and draw upon a large dataset that examines policies, legislation, and informal strategies that take place on the ground in each of the fifty-seven conflict-affected countries. In each case, we surveyed legislation, academic literature, reports, and news to qualitatively examine, then score, the state of recognition in the state's executive and legislative branches of government, civil service, security sector, and institutions of justice, education, and language policy. In Chapters 4 and 5 we combine our original data with existing datasets related to peace and conflict outcomes, and we carry out a cross-national analysis on the conditions under which leaders choose recognition in conflict-affected contexts and the effects of these choices. We expand on the methodology for the cross-national analysis in Part II of the book.

Complementing the cross-national quantitative analysis, we use comparative qualitative case study research to go into more depth to explore if and how the post-conflict decision-making process regarding (non-)recognition and the implications for peace follow the logic of our theory, and whether more convincing alternative accounts emerge (Lieberman 2005; Slater and Ziblatt 2013; Van Evera 1997). This book includes three in-depth case studies that carefully trace processes within countries and study variation over time within each case (George and Bennett 2004). While the case studies stem from Africa, they inform our understanding of other places with similar structural conditions. Throughout the book, we discuss how our argument extends to conflict-affected contexts around the globe.

We first select Burundi and Rwanda as two well-predicted cases on the question of adoption. We trace whether the assumptions and mechanisms of our theory characterize what actually occurred in terms of adoption and effects. Burundi went from minority to plurality leadership after the peace process beginning in 2000 and, correspondingly, went from a non-recognition regime to a recognition regime. Rwanda went from plurality to minority leadership after the 1994 genocide and, correspondingly, went from recognition to non-recognition. We chose Burundi and Rwanda because of the structural similarities between the two cases and because of the changes over time within each case. These factors create an extraordinarily well-controlled set of comparisons.

We also selected Ethiopia as a case because it did not conform to our basic predictions regarding adoption. Ethiopia was, until 2018, always led by a minority regime, yet it embraced recognition starting in 1992 in the form of a post-conflict ethnic federation. For a case like this, we are interested in exploring additional contextual conditions or mechanisms. For instance, Ethiopia's population is divided into a large number of territorially concentrated ethnic groups, and there is not a large difference in the size of the largest and second-largest groups. These features distinguish Ethiopia from Burundi and Rwanda. The logic of our theory suggests that such ethnic fractionalization may be an important moderating factor, and the case study on Ethiopia allows us to assess this possibility. Moreover, including the case of Ethiopia allows us to investigate effects of recognition under a minority-led regime. We elaborate on our methodology for the qualitative case studies in the introduction to Part III.

Findings in brief

Our cross-national data indicate substantial variation in the adoption of recognition: post-conflict governments formally recognize ethnic groups in about 40 percent of constitutions and comprehensive settlements. In line with our theory, the adoption of recognition is closely tied to ethnic power configurations. Under the leadership of a plurality group member, recognition is adopted about 60 percent of the time, whereas under minority leadership, it is adopted only 24 percent of the time. No other factor that we have identified accounts for so much variation in adoption rates, and the strength of this relationship stands up to controlling for a large number of potential confounding variables.

With respect to the effects of recognition, de jure recognition at the constitutional level is strongly associated with implementing recognition-based

provisions in the domains of executive institutions, legislative assemblies, security institutions, the justice sector, civil service, education policies, and language policies. Recognition is also strongly associated with improvements in
de facto assessments of ethnic group inclusion. In general, peace outcomes that
follow constitutions and political settlements are more positive in the cases
where ethnic recognition was adopted. More precisely, though, we find that
ethnic power configurations moderate the effects of recognition. In cases with
plurality leaders, agreements that include recognition generally result in better
outcomes than those that do not, not only for negative peace—lower political
violence—but also for measures of positive peace such as economic vitality and
levels of democracy. For minority-led regimes, we find that recognition tends,
on average, to make things neither better nor worse for peace. Our focused attention on ethnic power configurations may help explain why those who argue
that recognition promotes peace are sometimes right, and why those who argue
the opposite are sometimes right.

The case studies add further insights. In each case study, we show that
viewing the case through the lens of our theory helps us better understand both
the adoption of recognition and its effects. Out of the cases, we develop the ideas
of a "paradox of recognition," wherein the salience of ethnicity can begin to be
overcome through recognition, and a "paradox of non-recognition," in which,
despite non-recognition, ethnicity does not lose its salience. The cases also push
forward our thinking as to how leaders may endeavor to manage what we term
an "institutional mismatch," wherein a minority leader adopts recognition or
a plurality leader chooses a non-recognition approach. The cases further provide examples of how leaders can use both recognition and non-recognition in
a Machiavellian fashion to contain political opponents or use the cover of either
of these strategies to pursue exclusionary aims.

Implications

Our analysis has important implications for scholars and policymakers. For
scholars, we demonstrate the value of the high-level concept of ethnic recognition and the relevance of assuring and mobilization effects. We use these ideas
to provide insight into conflict-affected contexts and ethnic identity around the
world today. We show how important it is to study institutional origins alongside their effects; in fact, we find that similar forces shaped both the adoption
and effects of ethnic recognition. We also demonstrate that the effects of ethnic
recognition on peace are conditional, providing a way forward for reconciling
often contradictory findings in the literature. We elaborate on these implications
for social scientists in the conclusion (Chapter 9) and lay out a research agenda,

with the hope that this book serves as a foundation for a broader research program on institutional strategies to address ethnic conflict.

For policymakers, we illustrate that many countries have contended with the dilemma of recognition, so we first recommend that observers and policymakers consult this history. Our theory, with its emphasis on the ethnic power configuration, provides guidance for determining which countries' histories would be most informative for any new case at hand. Second, the historical record suggests that recognition tends to promote peace in contexts of ethnic division. Our analysis also illustrates that, even in cases where recognition is not adopted, it is naive to think that the salience of ethnicity has disappeared. Third, there are many ways through which recognition might be tailored to a given context, with varying emphasis on different state sectors (e.g., legislature, security sector, etc.) that interact as part of a recognition system. Finally, the recent history of recognition policies highlights some of the challenges of social engineering. This includes the fact that such engineering is highly constrained by political—and, in particular, ethnic—power configurations. It also includes the fact that institutional effects can be paradoxical. We elaborate on these implications in Chapter 9.

The plan for the book

Chapter 2 lays out our theoretical framework for analyzing the adoption of recognition and its effects in conflict-affected contexts. It explains our focus on leaders and the key decisions they face in managing ethnic divisions. It then presents possible explanations for the adoption of recognition, grouped into domestic and international explanations. It highlights what is missing from these accounts—namely, a focus on ethnic power configurations and how they influence leaders' interests. The chapter then details the assuring effects of recognition, on one hand, and its mobilization effects, on the other, illustrating the mechanisms underlying each and the way we predict these effects to influence the adoption or non-adoption of recognition as well as the effects of recognition on peace. We also introduce the concept of "the dilemma of recognition" that arises for minority leaders and theorize the implications for peace of recognition under different ethnic power configurations.

Part II presents our cross-national analysis. Chapter 3 explains how we coded for ethnic recognition in constitutions and peace agreements. The chapter then describes trends in the set of eighty-six constitutional moments we studied across fifty-seven countries. We show that ethnic recognition has been a common strategy over the past decades. While rates of adoption have been consistent over time, we demonstrate important regional differences in rates of recognition, ranging from universal adoption in Europe to quite rare recognition in sub-Saharan Africa.

Chapter 4 tests our theory related to ethnic power configurations and assesses the adoption of recognition under plurality- and minority-led regimes. The cross-national patterns since 1990 are largely consistent with our predictions. Plurality-led regimes are much more likely than minority-led regimes to adopt recognition. This pattern is robust to accounting for various domestic and international factors.

Chapter 5 examines the effects of recognition on peace. We find that de jure recognition at the constitutional level is regularly followed by implementation of recognition policies across seven domains, from the executive and legislative arenas to the civil service, the security and justice sectors, education, and language. Recognition also predicts large reductions in ethnic exclusion from societal power structures. On average, recognition is associated with more positive trends in reduced violence, economic vitality, and democratic inclusiveness. We then examine how these effects vary depending on the ethnic power configuration. After adopting recognition, plurality-led regimes tend to experience significantly less violence, more economic vitality, and improved democracy in the short and medium terms. Minority-led regimes do, on average, neither better nor worse with non-recognition.

Part III of the book consists of our in-depth investigation of three cases where recognition has and has not been adopted. Chapter 6 focuses on Burundi, where, in accordance with our theory, the majority Hutu regime enshrined ethnic recognition in state institutions after the most recent civil war. We first show the relevance of the dilemma of recognition to its adoption in this case, then examine the complex follow-on effects. We show how under recognition in this plurality-led regime factional politics are promisingly no longer defined along ethnic lines, what we term a "paradox of recognition." There are, however, moves toward authoritarianism under the majority Hutu-led government, and this raises questions about the sustainability of the recognition regime, at least in the form that was institutionalized in the 2005 constitution, which emphasized parity between Hutus and Tutsis.

Chapter 7 turns to Rwanda, where the contemporary non-recognition outcome was also consistent with our theory and cross-national trends. We argue that the dilemma of recognition logic offers the most convincing explanation for Rwanda's effort to "eradicate" ethnicity and that consideration of the government's minority status and strategic calculations offers important insights into the effects of the strategy on peace. We find potentially destructive contradictions in the non-recognition policy, its implementation, and the everyday experience of Rwandans that maintain the salience of ethnicity and may thus constitute a "paradox of non-recognition."

Chapter 8 considers Ethiopia, a minority-led regime like Rwanda, but one where the post-conflict constitution enshrined ethnic federalism and even the right of self-determination for ethnic groups. We show that the regime appreciated the assuring effects that recognition could bring, and that it was also very concerned about mobilization against it, although in a different way than our theory suggests. Having allied with other ethnic groups to overthrow the previous regime, and having promised recognition, the new minority leadership needed to grant recognition in order to win power. We examine the impact of the assuring effects of recognition, the strategies that this minority-led regime has used to compensate against the ongoing mobilization risks, and the mixed implications for peace. We also consider the post-2018 transfer of power wherein a plurality now leads Ethiopia for the first time, and the prospects for peace that may be enabled by having overcome an institutional mismatch.

In our conclusion, Chapter 9, we review our main findings as a foundation for implications and next steps. We discuss the implications for policymakers endeavoring to build peace in conflict-affected contexts. We also draw out implications for scholars, concluding the chapter with a series of questions that may serve as a research agenda to continue to push forward our understanding of diversity, violence, and recognition.

2

A Theory of Recognition

Kenya's leaders came together in 2008 to craft a new constitution in the aftermath of electoral violence that was often targeted along ethnic lines. The question of how to deal with ethnicity was a major concern that elicited various arguments. Influential Kenyan author and journalist Binyavanga Wainaina opined that Kenya needed a "constitution that names and recognizes the tribal nations within our nation," arguing that a series of conflict management strategies since independence that did not recognize ethnic groups had failed to reduce the salience of ethnic identities or build national cohesion (cited in Smith 2013, 22). In contrast, as recounted in Chapter 1, others—including Yash Ghai, who chaired the Kenyan Constitution Commission—took a different stance. Ghai asserted, "We wanted to remove ethnicity from politics . . . [and] we didn't want parties to start squabbling on ethnic lines" (Daily Mirror 2017). The point is that the 2010 constitution, which ultimately does not name ethnic groups (but does recognize Kenya's "ethnic diversity"), was not a foregone conclusion at the outset of the constitutional process, but rather a deliberate choice. In this chapter, we present a theory that endeavors to explain the factors that go into the choice to recognize or not to recognize. Moreover, we argue that these same factors are important in explaining the effects of recognition on peace.

To some, the past three decades can be read as reflecting growing regard among political theorists of the value of multiculturalism and the rights of marginalized identity groups *qua* groups (Fraser 1995; Kymlicka 1995; Phillips 1995; Young 1990). Pro-recognition norms are increasingly reflected in the formal norms-defining documents of the United Nations (UN) and regional bodies. While the UN Charter (1945) and Declaration of Human Rights (1948) do not include explicit recognition provisions (in contrast to the League of Nations), the UN International Covenant on Civil and Political Rights (1966), the UN General Assembly Declaration on the Rights of Persons Belonging to National or Ethnic, Religious and Linguistic Minorities (1992), and the UN Declaration on the Rights of Indigenous Peoples (2013) affirm minority rights. The 2015 Sustainable Development Goals target on "quality education" includes

Diversity, Violence, and Recognition. Elisabeth King and Cyrus Samii, Oxford University Press (2020). © Oxford University Press.
DOI: 10.1093/oso/9780197509456.003.0001

"appreciation of cultural diversity and of culture's contribution to sustainable development" (United Nations 2015). There is even a new global institution, the Global Centre for Pluralism, based in Ottawa, Canada, expressly dedicated to promoting respect for diversity in the world, especially ethnic diversity.

Yet there is also strong normative aversion to group-based recognition, particularly among post–World War II liberal theorists who favor instead the promotion of individual rights. In such a view, group-based rights, such as ethnically based power-sharing, subordinates individual rights (Barry 2001; Brass 1991). A prominent example of this logic in practice is the Universal Declaration of Human Rights, whose authors removed all mention of ethnic and national minorities from the document. The idea is that by ensuring the rights of each individual, one does not need further ethnic-group-based protections. Moreover, the aspiration and expectation is that the salience of so-called parochial ethnic group loyalties declines with modernization. Many other groups also critique the idea of ethnically based group-differentiated rights for reasons other than the primacy of individual rights (for an overview, see McGarry 2017b, 268). These include scholars who argue that focusing on ethnicity distracts attention from class, gender, or anti-colonial struggles (Appiah 2005; Song 2017).

Our interest is in laying out a practical framework and using this framework to assemble evidence about the adoption of ethnic recognition and its effects on peace. We want to understand what leads to a decision like the one that was implemented in Kenya versus, say, Iraq, where the post–Saddam Hussein constitutional process enshrined recognition of an autonomous Kurdish region and an executive leadership that includes a Shi'a prime minister, Sunni speaker, and Kurdish president. Understanding the conditions under which recognition is adopted is important for explaining the genesis of institutions, and also so that we can get a better sense of the "adoptability" of different institutional configurations (McGarry 2017a). In addition, such an understanding allows us to disentangle the effects of recognition and non-recognition institutions from the conditions that brought them about. We are ultimately interested in learning empirically about the relative abilities of recognition and non-recognition strategies to contribute to both a negative peace—the elimination of large-scale violence—and positive peace, the building of institutions and practices that help society develop and that avoid a return to violence (Galtung 1969).

This chapter sets up our theory on the adoption of recognition and its effects, which we test quantitatively in Chapters 3 through 5, and through case studies in Chapters 6 through 8. We begin this chapter by reflecting on existing answers to the adoption question. The second part lays out our explanation, which centers on the missing pieces of these explanations—a focus on leaders' interests, especially political survival, and ethnic power configurations. In the third and fourth sections, we present the core of our theory centered around two sets of effects that we expect to influence leaders' incentives and constraints: first, the assuring effects of recognition, and then the mobilization effects. We detail our anticipation that the political implications of these effects play out differently under plurality and minority leadership, influencing both the adoption of recognition and the effects on peace. The fifth section describes the "dilemma of recognition" for minority leaders as it relates to adoption. The sixth part focuses on the implications of the dilemma of recognition as it relates to the consequences of recognition for peace. We then propose ethnic fractionalization and the degree of a leadership's hegemony as important scope conditions of our theory of recognition, address limitations, and conclude the chapter with a discussion of how we use our theory in the rest of the book.

Other explanations for the adoption of recognition

This book focuses on ethnic power configurations. We present a theoretical and empirical case for their importance in explaining the adoption and effects of recognition. Of course, we do not contend that our analysis explains every case, and the mechanisms that we emphasize most certainly exist alongside other mechanisms. Before getting to our theory, in this section we consider other accounts of institutional adoption and how institutions shape politics and conflict. We do so for three reasons. First, we want to acknowledge other theories. Our work complements these other efforts that cast issues pertaining to institutional adoption and ethnic conflict in different terms. Second, reviewing alternative accounts allows us to identify factors that may confound our attempt to study the variables that our theory emphasizes. Third, in our empirical analysis, we can evaluate patterns suggested by our theory and compare them to patterns associated with other accounts. This allows us to gauge the relative importance of the mechanisms central to our theory.

When it comes to the question of how leaders choose institutions, we can classify alternative accounts into two categories: those that focus on conditions internal to the leaders' domestic political system, and those that focus on international factors external to the domestic political system. Turning first to domestic factors, institutional analysis often starts from the basic idea that strategic calculations are different for leaders in democracies and autocracies. "Domestic democratic peace" literatures lead us to believe that democratic governments will be more likely to include minorities (Daly 2013; Davenport 2007). Since recognition, in particular, would seem to require some degree of power-sharing, it stands to reason that leaders in democracies, who are obligated to accept pluralistic competition, may be likelier to adopt recognition. Conversely, many assert that authoritarian leaders tend to enforce group assimilation and thereby choose non-recognition (Barkhof 2011; Kaufmann and Haklai 2008; Rothchild 1997). Or perhaps the choice is determined less by the values or structure of democracy and authoritarianism and more by the degree of hegemony or acceptance of constraints on a leader's autonomy. Insofar as political realists are right that constitutional or peace agreements come at moments of relative weakness on the part of the incumbent (Horowitz 2014; McFaul 2007; O'Donnell and Schmitter 1986; Samuels 2006), it may be that those who "need" to share power with other ethnic groups do and therein adopt recognition, whereas those who are sufficiently strong avoid recognition. In this reasoning, too, autocrats who have a strong grip on the state and citizenry would avoid recognition.

While an attractive explanation, perhaps especially for those committed philosophically to both democracy and recognition, the arguments about democracy and hegemony leave much to be explained about the adoption of ethnic recognition in contexts of diversity and violence. As we discuss in Chapter 4, we find that "free" democracy (as defined by the standards of the Freedom House project) is almost perfectly predictive of a recognition strategy. Yet in the settings upon which we focus, divided post-conflict contexts, most states are "democratizing" (Snyder 2000). Moreover, as political scientist Leonardo Arriola (2013) points out, autocracies and partial democracies tend to have higher levels of ethnic diversity than full democracies, making the choice over recognition particularly salient. In these cases, we find substantial variation in adoption of ethnic recognition. States ranked as "partly free" by the standards of the Freedom House project adopt recognition and non-recognition at relatively equal rates. The same goes for states ranked as "not free." In Chapter 4 we also show that the adoption of recognition occurs at similar rates in contexts where conflicts have been resolved through military victory and in cases of negotiated settlement, a measure of post-conflict political hegemony. Recognition and power-sharing often go together, but sometimes they do not—a distinction we develop in Chapter 3. Finally, there are clear examples of recognition being adopted when there was no resounding threat to the political standing of the dominant group, such as in the case of affirmative action for African Americans in the United States or reservations for marginalized castes in India. Both of these examples reflect recognition (and group-differentiated rights) in instances where minority groups had mobilized to redress inequalities, but where the majority group retained a firm grip on power. While the question of hegemony comes back in our discussion of scope conditions later in this chapter, the implication is that there must be something more to the adoption of recognition beyond considerations of democratic competition or hegemony.

Turning to international factors, scholars point to various processes of "diffusion" as well as geopolitical strategic considerations. For example, norm diffusion can sometimes explain similarities in institutional choices either in functional domains, such as the domains of security policy or environmental standards, or within regions (Finnemore and Sikkink 1998; Howard and Stark 2018). One could extend the argument to the ways in which international norms and multilateral initiatives influence recognition and non-recognition. Such processes also occur at the regional level. In Europe, for example, the promotion of minority rights is an institutionalized tenet of European multilateral initiatives, and national policies on minorities have been fundamentally changed by countries' aspirations for membership in the European Union (EU) coupled with the EU's precondition of a model of minority rights (Johns 2003; Sasse 2005). In Africa, in contrast, the commitment to non-recognition has long been common, based on the logic that colonial powers had used divisions to rule. As political philosopher Frantz Fanon (1963) observed, decolonization often required unifying people on national bases, what Sefa Dei (2005, 268) calls "the strategic radical decision to remove from them their heterogeneity." Political scientist Peter Uvin calls the denial of ethnicity "general African practice" (1999, 259). A related variant on this diffusion explanation might be constitutional mimicry, whether through colonial legacies, drawing lessons from neighbors, or even intervention by external actors who introduce recognition strategies from their own domestic contexts (Vandeginste 2009). Other external factors have to do with geopolitical considerations. For example, when a minority group in a country has co-ethnics in a bordering country, leaders may see recognition as raising the risk of the cross-border mobilization for the group members to unite. Turkish leaders' resistance to Kurdish recognition is sometimes attributed to such strategic concerns (Olson 1996; Somer 2005) since the Kurds in Turkey, together with Kurds in neighboring Iran, Iraq, and Syria, represent a very large ethnic group without their own state.

Such international factors are unlikely to be the whole story. There is a good deal of variation in the adoption of recognition globally, suggesting limited scope for an explanation based on either pro-recognition international norms or liberal individualist norms. In Chapter 3 we show that while regions do vary in the rates at which they adopt recognition, we also see within-region variation that would seem to require consideration of domestic circumstances. The exception, interestingly enough, is Europe, for which all recently conflict-affected countries (namely, the countries of the former Yugoslavia, the countries in the Caucasus region, and the United Kingdom's Northern Ireland) have resulted in the adoption of ethnic recognition. Colonial legacies cannot account for change over time, despite the fact that we often observe such change, nor can they account for differences across countries with the same colonial ties but different recognition outcomes. To name but a few examples, Burundi and Rwanda were both Belgian colonies and India and Kenya both British colonies, but within each pair, leaders have chosen different approaches to recognition. Geopolitical concerns related to cross-border groups may be important at times, but even with the Kurdish example, we see substantial variation across Turkey, Iraq, Syria, and Iran in the nature and extent of ethnic recognition. Finally, focusing on external factors also gives short shrift to the agency of domestic actors who have the most at stake in the institutional choice.

Missing pieces: leaders' strategy amid ethnic power configurations

Going beyond the other explanations described earlier, our theory draws attention to structural factors more immediately relevant to ethnic recognition. We consider how leaders reference the ethnic power configuration, and in particular their group's demographic standing, when strategizing as to whether or not to use recognition to address opposition group demands and manage conflict along ethnic lines (Cederman et al. 2010; Fearon et al. 2007; Posner 2005). Our theory emphasizes strategic choices. As political scientist Abigail Eisenberg and philosopher Will Kymlicka write, "Identity politics is, in the end, like most forms of politics, full of strategic and opportunistic actors attempting to advance their interests in the most effective ways they can" (2011, 18).

The outbreak of conflict is the product of mobilization that creates new concentrations of power, brings foundational institutional choices to the surface, and therefore prompts institutional decisions that go beyond ordinary legislating (King 2007). Our analysis focuses on these contexts of extraordinary political concentration and "constitutional moments." Our way of thinking about constitutional decision-making may be less convincing in cases of usual legislative politics, where power to decide on institutions may require the formation of balanced interethnic coalitions and where leaders from no one group are pivotal. Our analysis likely requires modification to apply to such periods of "normal" politics.

We analyze a very stylized setting that brings strategic dynamics into sharp relief. (We draw here on King and Samii [2018], and a formal game-theoretic model is available in the appendix to that article.) We acknowledge that our focus is elite-centric and that our theory is agent-centered. We build on the important work of others who draw attention to the crucial role of leaders in defining inclusive and exclusive political communities (Straus 2015). Our highest-level theory, and the cross-national analysis that follows from it, does not focus on the diversity of within-group demands that individuals may make of elites, although we consider such demands in the case studies.

We consider situations in which leaders are concerned primarily with their political survival in the political order that will be defined by the terms of a political settlement or constitution. We focus attention on circumstances where such leaders view the creation of a constitutionalized order as a viable means for their political survival, and so they are entertaining options for a transition from a state of war to a state of peace. In concentrating on ethnically diverse and conflict-affected contexts, we consider further a situation where we have a leader who is a member of an ethnic group and faces political opposition consisting of individuals from other ethnic groups. Working from the generalized conflict dynamics we describe in Chapter 1, we also presume that conflict has hardened ethnic identities and generated a situation of interethnic mistrust. Theories of grievance-based ethnic mobilization (e.g., Wimmer, Cederman, and Min 2009) suggest that in such circumstances, members of an opposition ethnic group would contest the rule of the incumbent leader if they felt that the opportunities granted to their group by the regime are sufficiently poor. The opposition's demands and potential to mobilize shape the strategic context. The political survival of the leader might be threatened by a critical mass of opposition group members deciding to contest the leader's authority. In such contexts of mistrust and the potential for renewed conflict, political leaders must make decisions about the institutional structure of the state.

We posit that ethnic demographics are a crucial consideration for leaders calculating how to survive politically in the face of opposition. That ethnic demographics are consequential to leaders is well supported. In 1990s Pakistan, for example, the government postponed the census five times, fearing violence from groups who protested that they were being undercounted (Kertzer and Arel 2002). Another well-known example is ethnic demographics in Lebanon, where a census has not been undertaken for nearly a century given sensitivities regarding the sizes of the country's various religious groups relative to each group's quota-based allocations in national institutions (*The Economist* 2016). While many fears and hopes are vested in ethnic numbers (Horowitz 1985), political demography is largely understudied (Kauffman 2011; Kertzer and Arel 2002).

Our analysis focuses on ethnic power configurations defined in terms of the population share of the incumbent leader's ethnic group (Cederman et al. 2010; Fearon et al. 2007). Thus, minority rule is one ethnic power configuration, while plurality rule is another. When we write about plurality leadership, we use the term to include countries under the leadership of a member of a demographic majority, such as in Burundi, where the current president, Pierre Nkurunziza, comes from the Hutu ethnic group, which accounts for roughly 85 percent of the population. Yet we want to simultaneously account for the possibility that the largest group in society may make up a plurality of the population but not the majority. For instance, Kenya's Kikuyus, whose members have often held power, constitute the plurality at circa 22 percent but are clearly not a demographic majority. In Ethiopia, a leader from the plurality Oromo group, who make up roughly a third of Ethiopians, was elected prime minister in 2018, marking the country's first change from minority to plurality leadership.

The size of ethnic groups is often related to their political influence (Chandra 2004; Strand and Urdal 2014), but minorities are not always subordinate. As Horowitz (2001, 170) cautions, "Numbers often have something to do with political power, but not always, not everywhere, and not everything." Scholars and policy-makers alike often refer to "minorities" as synonymous with small, disadvantaged, marginalized communities. As our case study chapters show, however, in present-day Rwanda, post-Derg Ethiopia, and pre-peace-accords Burundi, not to mention numerous additional examples from around the world such as Alawis in Syria, Sunnis in pre-war Iraq, or whites in apartheid South Africa, minorities can and do often hold disproportionate power and state resources (Chua 2003; Kauffman and Haklai 2008). In this book, when we use the term "minority," we mean it in the numerical sense and do not mean it to be synonymous with subordination. We focus on how a country's leadership by a member of a minority or plurality ethnic group influences post-conflict decision-making, especially with respect to identity. This gets at our questions of the conditions under which leaders adopt ethnic recognition. We also consider how this leadership position may affect the effectiveness of recognition and non-recognition approaches, with important implications for peace.

In the analysis that follows, we explain why ethnic demographics are crucial in shaping leaders' choices to adopt or avoid ethnic recognition. We begin by noting that ethnic recognition can confer certain assuring effects, but that equally, or even more, powerful mobilization effects enter the strategic calculation. Grasping the interplay of these effects is crucial for understanding why leaders may or may not adopt recognition and the effects of these choices on peace.

The critical condition determining the weighting of these two effects is the ethnic power configuration. In particular, the analysis in this chapter demonstrates how leaders from plurality ethnic groups are likely to win from adopting recognition through both effects, but that leaders coming from minority groups face a dilemma of recognition wherein the two effects run against one another. We predict that plurality leaders are thus also likeliest to reap the benefits for peace of recognition, whereas the effects of recognition under minority rule may be quite destabilizing. After elaborating on both the assuring effects and the mobilization effects in the next two sections, we discuss how they affect the adoption question and the effects question.

The assuring effects of recognition

The first set of effects of ethnic recognition is rooted in several potential benefits that may help leaders assure, and begin to gain the trust of, the political opposition, who demand protection of rights as well as access to power, opportunities, and resources. Recognition may also offer assurance to members of the leader's group with respect to protection and access to power or state resources in the long run. These assuring effects transpire via three specific mechanisms, discussed in the literature. We expect these assuring effects to make recognition attractive to leaders of plurality and minority regimes. As we detail in this chapter, we also expect that they should help facilitate peace.

First, the symbolism of being recognized can confer a direct benefit to ethnic groups. As political philosopher Sonia Kruks puts it:

> What makes identity politics a significant departure . . . is its demand for recognition on the basis of the very grounds on which recognition has previously been denied: it is *qua* women, *qua* blacks, *qua* lesbians that groups demand recognition. The demand is not for inclusion within the fold of "universal humankind" on the basis of shared human attributes; nor is it for respect "in spite of" one's differences. Rather, what is demanded is respect for oneself *as* different. (2001, 85)

Recognizing cultural differences can in itself attend to demands for addressing past injustices. It can also help guard against fears that a group will be culturally excluded or even erased in the future. Political theorists confirm that it is, normatively and psychologically, a "vital human need" that identities be confirmed and legitimated by others (Taylor 1992, 26; see also Fraser 1995 and Young 1990). For instance, in the mid-1990s, constitutional claimants in Canada moved not only for specific rights for Québec, the only province with a French-speaking majority, but also for symbolic recognition of the province as "a distinct society within Canada" (Chrétien 1995).

Second, through recognition, a regime can allow for visibility about the allocation of resources along ethnic lines. Ethnic recognition is a precursor to the creation and circulation of ethnic statistics. It grants a license to public debates about the standing of ethnic groups in various domains. As a result, ethnic groups, and especially opposition members, are able to more precisely evaluate how well their demands for protection and access to opportunities or resources are being met. This visibility in turn makes it easier for the regime to win opposition members' trust (Cederman and Girardin 2007; Hartzell et al. 2001, 186; Weisskopf 2004). Visibility therefore serves to mitigate problems that leaders face in convincing a mistrustful opposition about credibility of their promises to address opposition demands (Mattes and Savun 2009, 2010). Providing information about ethnic identities and how the regime is treating them is consequential since the relative status of groups matters for conflict. Horizontal inequalities—inequalities between ethnic, religious, or regional groups—are correlated with the onset of violence (Cederman et al. 2013; Stewart 2002). These inequalities, both real and perceived (Langer and Mikami 2013), exist along interrelated social, economic, political, and cultural lines (Langer 2013; Stewart 2002). Horizontal equity or near-equity, when fewer significant inequalities exist between groups, is thought to be more conducive to peace (Stewart and Brown 2007), and recognition would allow groups to best evaluate their situations in these terms.

Third, as political scientists Håvard Strand and Henrik Urdal explain, "the measuring of ethnic groups may be used to inform policies such as the establishment of social programs based on sizes of ethnic minorities, the establishment of quotas for ethnic representation in parliament or public administration, and the designation and use of official languages in schools and public administration, nationally or locally" (2014, 170). The visibility explained earlier improves the efficiency of efforts by a regime's leadership to placate members of opposition groups through the use of targeted transfers or benefits. Recognition serves as a relatively uncontestable legal basis for institutionalizing opposition group rights. These rights may seek to remedy past injustices and work against future discrimination. Group-differentiated rights can reduce opposition groups' uncertainty about how they will fare in the future. For minority groups, this could entail reducing uncertainty about tyranny of the majority. The idea of ethnic power-sharing is based on the understanding that without (what they perceive to be) sufficient representation, ethnic groups are more likely to act against the regime (Lijphart 1977). Political theorist Hanna Pitkin's classic work (1967) makes related arguments about the importance of representation in providing role models, compensating for historical wrongs, representing minority interests, and improving governance. As political scientist Andrew Reynolds puts it, "One of the most important underlying causes of conflict is the perception (real or imagined) that the wealth of the nation, the resources, and the investments in society are skewed toward the members of one group" (2011, 152).

In sum, these multiple assuring effects should make recognition attractive to leaders interested in gaining the trust of the opposition group so as to promote stability and durable peace. This should be true regardless of whether they are from a minority or plurality group. Moreover, as briefly reviewed in Chapter 1, many opine that opportunities afforded by recognition, such as redressing interethnic inequalities and guaranteeing rights to members of disadvantaged ethnic groups, can contribute to peace (Cederman et al. 2017; Lijphart 1977, 1985; McGarry and O'Leary 2006). It is often argued that explicit recognition and group-differentiated rights—thick recognition—are necessary because accumulated inequalities and prejudices do not correct themselves via free markets or free elections (Duflo 2005; Dunning 2010; Fryer and Loury 2005; Samii 2013). Positive effects on peace are most likely when such proactive assuring measures provide a legal basis for rectifying real and/or perceived injustices or inequality that has historically provided a cause for violent intergroup conflict (Cederman et al. 2013; Gurr 1993; Wimmer et al. 2009). At the same time, the measures must not be so encompassing as to threaten the status of those to whom such measures are not directed (Blumer 1958; Coser 1956; Levine and Campbell 1972). Sometimes measures are also meant to assure members of the group in power.

In parallel to these arguments, it is often argued that non-recognition may be conducive to conflict in ways that align with the idea of failing to attend visibly to the demands of certain groups. Non-recognition may lead to the exclusion of important segments of a population and may foster future conflict (Basedau and Moroff 2011; Hartzell et al. 2001). Scholars of ethnic conflict Andreas Wimmer, Lars-Erik Cederman, and Brian Min, for instance, find convincing evidence that "ethnic exclusion from state power and competition over the spoils of government breed ethnic conflict" (2009, 319). Marginalization or exclusion may lead to suspicion of those in power (Hartzell et al. 2001), and "minorities that are excluded from power will probably remain excluded and will almost inevitably lose their allegiance to the regime" (Lijphart 1985, 18–19). In studying ethnic party bans in Africa, a form of non-recognition, political scientists Matthias Basedau and Anika Moroff conclude that bans are often part of a "menu of manipulation" that marginalize political opponents and do not achieve the aspired pacifying effects (2011; see also Niesen 2010).

While the assuring effects of recognition are promising for peace, it is, of course, possible that recognition does not serve to assure. Symbolic recognition and facilitating interethnic comparisons only contribute to peace when they highlight efforts toward improving the conditions of mistrustful members of opposition groups. When such efforts are not in place, status comparisons would result in resentment (Gurr 1993; Petersen 2002), and groups may resort to violence to counter their marginalization (Horowitz 1985).

Another way in which recognition would not serve to assure would be if it privileges the already powerful. There are many examples of perverted applications of recognition—"recognition to exclude"—that reinforce inequality rather than redress it. South Africa's apartheid regime used recognition based on race to privilege the white minority and to marginalize majority blacks and coloreds (to use South African phrasing). In Israel, ethnic and religious identification requirements often serve to institutionalize the marginalization of minority non-Jewish groups (Cinalli 2005). Sri Lanka's "Sinhala Only Act," formally the 1965 Official Language Act, entrenched political and social dominance of the Sinhala majority, representing approximately 70 percent of the population, over the Tamil minority, about 30 percent of the population (Tambiah 1991). In Côte d'Ivoire, the narrative of *ivoirité* served to exclude many northern Ivorians from citizenship and political participation (Bah 2017). That the UN Charter and Universal Declaration of Human Rights did not include references to minority groups is explained, at least in part, by the Nazi regime's abuse of group-based recognition in the Holocaust and the lead-up to it (Kirisci and Winrow 1997).

So long as leaders put some value on assuring the opposition, we predict that recognition should be (1) attractive to both plurality and minority leaders and (2) conducive to peace. Yet the adoption of recognition and its consequences for peace depend not only on the activation of meaningful assuring effects, but rather on weighing the possible "wins" of these assuring effects against the mobilization effects of recognition.

The mobilization effects of recognition

The second type of effect comes from the possibility that recognition serves to entrench ethnic identities as a political cleavage and effectively licenses ethnic mobilization (Lieberman and Singh 2012; Snyder 2000). This strategy may be appealing to leaders from plurality groups, as it helps such leaders to capitalize on their group's demographic advantage. Of course, minority group leaders are likely to view this effect as threatening. In the same way, these mobilization effects are often understood to be conducive to conflict but are likely to play out differently for plurality and minority leaders interested in both the maintenance of power and peace.

The mobilization effect is associated with two types of mechanisms. First, ethnic recognition differentiates and therein is likely to heighten the salience of ethnic identity. Social identity theory suggests that the mere mention of groups can cause people to think about themselves as different from one another (Tajfel 1982). Citizens may take provisions that distribute power on the basis of ethnicity to signal that ethnic lines are primary lines of conflict, implying that one should be wary of attempts to cooperate across ethnic lines. The differentiation that recognition entails may cultivate a sense of division between "us" and "them" (Wimmer 2013, 27).

Multiple examples illustrate how institutions played an important role in constructing ethnic divides under colonial rule. In Rwanda, for instance, the Belgian administration's introduction of identity cards that listed ethnicity is widely critiqued as having solidified the division between Hutus and Tutsis and decreased social mobility. Some argue that institutionalization of ethnicity today plays the same problematic role as it did historically (Lieberman and Singh 2012). According to Uvin, "the acts of categorizing and measuring become part of society's struggles, both directly—for they set the size of various groups' claims on scarce resources—and indirectly—for they contribute to crystallizing people's identities" (2002, 170).

Second, recognition makes ethnic mobilization easier. If ethnic difference is formally acknowledged by a regime—for example, within the constitution—a license has been granted to use ethnic references in public discourse. Should they wish to do so, political entrepreneurs can take advantage of the opportunity to use ethnic appeals to enhance their political position. For opposition members, this may mean endeavoring to challenge the incumbent regime in pursuing group demands. Ethnic group membership has long been an attractive resource when political leaders seek to coalesce and motivate a group to action in peaceful or violent ways. The current literature is clear in identifying substantial co-ethnic advantages in political mobilization, and recognition lowers the barriers to such mobilization (Bates 1983; Habyarimana et al. 2007; Varshney 2007). While ethnic mobilization is possible without recognition, recognition provides a nudge toward using ethnic appeals and capitalizing on its specific value as a political resource.

With an eye to these mobilization effects, recognition should be especially attractive to leaders of plurality groups. If conditions were to warrant mobilization, this mobilization would likely redound to the benefit of the numerically superior group. By effectively licensing the use of ethnic appeals, recognition clears the way for plurality or majority group political entrepreneurs to mobilize on the basis of their demographic advantage in a range of circumstances, from elections to a return to violence. In contrast, along this mobilization dimension, recognition should be much more worrisome to leaders of minority groups. By avoiding recognition, minority groups may hope to "transcend" ethnicity as the primary line of political competition, thereby overcoming a structural, demographic disadvantage (Smith 1986). Put otherwise, on this mobilization dimension, recognition should be a "win" for a plurality leader interested in maintaining power but a much riskier proposition for a minority leader.

For scholars who argue that recognition is likely to promote conflict, many of their arguments parallel the mechanisms developed as the mobilization effects of recognition. First, there can be implications for peace in the way that recognition entrenches ethnic differentiation. Political scientist Sven Gunnar Simonsen (2005) contends that in post-conflict contexts, various institutional recognition policies such as quotas are based on an "assumption of intransigence" and "freeze the current patterns of conflict in the institutional framework." He argues that such an inflexible approach toward ethnic divides hinders reconciliation and conflict transformation (see also Snyder 2000), whereas non-recognition could open more space for conflict transformation and transcendence of ethnic identities (Taylor 2001). Scholars who are optimistic about non-recognition policies and peace acknowledge that these policies are unlikely to result in the transcendence of ethnicity quickly, yet argue that "over the longer term, categories will become less salient, and to the extent that violence is avoided in the years following deinstitutionalization, the likelihood of violence should continue to decrease" (Lieberman and Singh 2012, 6). The idea is that while group identities often have inherent value, if you change the incentive structure such that ethnic categories do not matter to people for access to the state and resources, individuals may be more likely to change the way they think about themselves and the categories that matter (Chandra 2012; Penn 2008; Sambanis and Shayo 2013). Second, groups can take advantage of recognition to facilitate the use of ethnic appeals for (possibly violent) political mobilization, should they wish to do so. Lieberman and Singh (2012) find historically that institutionalizing ethnicity contributes to ethnic war. They theorize that, first, "institutionalization increases ethnic differentiation" and that, "second, ethnic differentiation, irrespective of power configurations, creates a competitive dynamic that increases the likelihood of spiraling aggression" (2012, 2). Notably, however, Lieberman and Singh focus on initial categorization. In this book, we are more interested in the choices after important mobilization and violence along ethnic lines has already occurred.

Overall, given the asymmetric strategic calculations for minority and plurality leaders, we expect both the adoption of recognition and the effects of recognition on peace to vary accordingly. For plurality group leaders wishing to address the mistrust of a minority, there are no conflicting pressures: they benefit from both effects. For a minority group leader, the possible losses due to the mobilization effects may outweigh the gains from the assuring effects.

The adoption question: the dilemma of recognition

Holding all other considerations fixed, our theory suggests that recognition should be a dominant strategy for plurality group leaders. Both the assuring and mobilization effects contribute to stability, which in turn provides a foundation for peace. For minority group leaders, the situation depends on the relative strength of the assuring versus the mobilization effects—a "dilemma of recognition." A dilemma of recognition arises when the assuring effects clash with the mobilization effects of ethnic recognition. As a result of these conflicting effects, we posit that, on average, governments led by a minority should adopt recognition much less often than regimes run by plurality leaders. The more vi-cious the dilemma, the less appealing is ethnic recognition and, when adopted, as we discuss in the next section, the more destabilizing it might be.

Our argument that recognition is more likely under plurality leadership is, to some, counterintuitive. One may reason that *minority* leaders would be most interested in recognition, in order to institutionalize respect for ethnic identities and minority groups, as noted by political theorists (Taylor 1992; Young 1990). Social psychologists have shown that people find value, pride, and self-esteem in group-based social identities (Tajfel 1981), and studies sug-gest that such identification is more important for minority groups (Gaertner and Dovidio 1986). Political scientists also stress that recognition allows for "group-differentiated rights" such as ethnic quotas or autonomy arrangements (Horowitz 2000; Kymlicka 1995; Kymlicka and Shapiro 1997) that address risks of "tyranny of the majority." Horowitz (2014) reasons that minorities would be more favorable to consociational arrangements that enshrine group rights than demographic majorities would be. Indeed, a preference for recogni-tion among minorities (and one for non-recognition among the majority), is a common finding in US- and European-based literature. In studies of the US context, for instance, black Americans more strongly endorse multiculturalism as compared to white Americans, who more strongly endorse colorblind, non-recognition approaches. The finding holds across other US-based minority groups (Ryan et al. 2007; Wolkso et al. 2006). Likewise, in a study of Dutch and Turkish participants in the Netherlands, minority Turkish residents were more likely to endorse multiculturalism than Dutch participants, who more strongly supported assimilation (Verkuyten 2005). More than a quarter century ago, Tajfel described a "world-wide push towards differentiation originating from minorities" (1981, 316). Yet such arguments about minority versus plurality group preferences overlook strategic considerations. As our theory clarifies, there is a difference between the strategic situation that minority group leaders face when they are in power as compared to minority group representatives who face a plurality leader in power. Our theory proposes that one needs to consider not just individuals' ethnic identities but also the ethnic power configurations in which they are embedded.

The effects question: implications and consequences for peace

In Chapter 1, we surveyed the "enduring debate" over the wisdom of recogni-tion versus non-recognition strategies as best contributing to peace. There are convincing arguments on both sides of the debate. We argue that, as is the case for adoption, the effects of recognition on peace are influenced by the weighting of the assuring effects against the mobilization effects and that this weighting works differently for minority versus plurality leadership. In other words, we propose that there is no single effect of recognition, but rather that effects depend on ethnic power configurations. This important ethno-structural condition may help to explain why those who argue that recognition promotes peace are sometimes right, and why those arguing the opposite are sometimes right.

Under plurality leadership, the assuring effects typically move in the same direction as the mobilization effects in terms of helping to shore up the leader's political standing. The assuring effects of recognition allow a leader to efficiently attend to opposition group demands, while the absence of a mobilization threat allows the leadership to use recognition without fear of being removed from power. We thus expect more progress toward peace with recognition than without. We examine this possibility in our case study on Burundi.

We deem cases where plurality group leaders avoid recognition to be, at least per the expectations of our theory, cases of "institutional mismatch." Recall that what we mean by mismatch is that the institutions in place are contrary to what our theory proposes to be the optimal strategy given the ethnic power configuration. In such cases, the consequences for peace are dependent on the relative success of the leader in finding some alternative way to overcome the fears and mistrust of opposition minority groups regarding the tyranny of the majority.

Minority leaders who adopt recognition openly expose themselves to a heightened possibility of ethnic mobilization by members of opposition groups. An incumbent leader intent on staying in power would have to take measures to contain this political threat. Such measures could include intensive policing of the opposition and other coercive and authoritarian moves. Presumably, then, these measures would undermine the otherwise assuring effects of recognition for opposition groups. If the mobilization threat can be contained through less coercive means, then minority group leaders could profit from the assuring effects that recognition offers. This characterizes the challenge in Ethiopia's ethnic federation, under minority leadership until early 2018, where leaders became increasingly authoritarian since the 2005 election, in which they faced the real risk of being displaced from power.

Under minority leadership, when leaders choose not to adopt recognition, they may mitigate the mobilization effects of recognition. They do not, however, reap the benefits from the assuring effects. In such cases, too, then, and for reasons similar to those operating when plurality leaders do not adopt recognition, the prospects for peace depend on whether the leader succeeds in finding some alternative way to overcome the fears and mistrust of the opposition majority. The exclusion of the majority may lead to continued mistrust. We explore these dynamics in the case of post-genocide Rwanda.

In sum, we expect the most progress toward peace in regimes under plurality leadership that adopt recognition. The forces that give rise to a dilemma with respect to adoption also create challenges for minority leaders in managing their survival and progress toward peace.

Scope conditions and limitations

The force of our logic depends on the starkness of the difference in the strategic positions of minority versus plurality groups, which is affected by the level of ethnic fractionalization. Ethnic fractionalization measures the probability that two randomly selected individuals from a country belong to different ethnic groups (Alesina et al. 2003) and offers, in effect, a measure of the degree of ethnic diversity. Ethnic fractionalization is low, for instance, in Burundi and Rwanda, with scores of 0.29 and 0.18 respectively, with populations comprising a large Hutu group, a relatively small Tutsi minority, and Twas representing fewer than 1 percent of the population. In contrast, ethnic fractionalization is much higher somewhere like Ethiopia, where the more than eighty different ethnic groups result in an ethnic fractionalization score of 0.76 or where more conservative estimates, focusing only on politically relevant groups, result in a score of 0.57, still on the upper end of the spectrum (Esteban et al. 2012; Posner 2004). We posit that minority status matters much more in situations of lower ethnic fractionalization. It is in cases of low ethnic fractionalization that the minority stands distinct relative to a clear majority or plurality group (Collier and Hoeffler 2004).

There are two ways in which ethnic fractionalization matters for our argument. First, minority leadership status may be less strategically meaningful under high ethnic fractionalization because no one group demographically dominates society. Minority leaders may be less worried about opposition mobilization in highly fractionalized states since it is well recognized that opposition groups cannot always agree on terms to act collectively. In contrast, when minority leaders confront fewer groups, under conditions of lower ethnic fractionalization, their minority status becomes more politically relevant. Second, plurality leaders may find recognition a less attractive strategy under high ethnic fractionalization. In such cases, recognizing other ethnic groups "risks surrendering the titular ethnicity's monopoly over the nation-state" because the plurality does not enjoy a large demographic advantage (Daly 2013, 8). We acknowledge the shortcomings of trying to collapse complex, constructed ethnic landscapes into a single ethnic fractionalization measure, practically in terms of demographic change and ethnic fluidity and methodologically in terms of getting the coding right (Posner 2004). In Chapter 4, we also consider alternative ways of defining the dominance of the plurality.

As with all theories, our theory of recognition is a simplification, relegating to the background many complicating factors. First, we believe that the relationship between assuring and mobilization effects is most relevant in contexts where there is some degree of political contestation, making the salience of the dilemma of recognition and the tension of the effects real. We also presume that the regime leader is not concerned with how recognition affects potential dissent from his/her own group. Our analysis also ignores the possibility that majority leaders may have an easier time enacting new provisions, for example because of the ability to command a legislative majority. We pass over the fact that different groups, within and across countries, exhibit different levels of cohesion and capacity for collective action, adding variation to the mobilization effect on the ground. We also skip over the idea of ethnic coalitions, acknowledging the added complexity they bring to the strategic calculations of leaders (Londregran et al. 1995). These are factors that we either control or disregard in our cross-national analysis but that we take up in the case studies.

As a result of these scope conditions and limitations, the relationship between minority/non-minority status and recognition or peace is unlikely to be perfect, but if the logic developed in this chapter plays a role in the adoption of recognition and its effects, we expect general patterns to conform to our predictions. Chapters 4 and 5 in Part II of the book test the logic of our dilemma of recognition using a new cross-national dataset. Our case studies then allow us to explore these nuances.

Conclusion

In this chapter, we have developed a theoretical framework to understand the conditions under which ethnic recognition may be adopted and to what effect on peace. Drawing on the theoretical and historical literature on ethnic conflict, we developed a theory that focuses on the dilemma that arises when the assuring effects clash with the mobilization effects of recognition. We point to a key structural condition that moderates the viciousness of this dilemma: whether the regime is under the control of a leader from a minority ethnic group or from a plurality ethnic group. Under either minority or plurality ethnic rule, the assuring effects of recognition enhance an incumbent leader's efforts to manage the mistrust of political opposition from other ethnic groups. However, under minority ethnic rule, these assuring benefits run up against the mobilization effects, through which political entrepreneurs from larger ethnic groups can use ethnic appeals to mobilize and challenge the minority incumbent. Plurality group leaders are less vulnerable to such mobilization effects.

These strategic considerations and ethnic power configurations have implications for the effects of recognition on peace. In cases with plurality leaders, we predict agreements that include recognition generally will result in improvements in terms of both positive and negative peace relative to those that do not. For minority leadership, the dilemma of recognition renders outcomes, on average, less stable.

In the chapters that follow, we use these theoretical insights to examine cross-national data on the adoption of ethnic recognition policies as well as the social, violence-related, political, and economic outcomes that follow. The cross-national analysis sets the stage for our country cases. These empirical analyses allow us to assess the predictive value of our theory and to discover qualifications to the theory.

PART II

CROSS-COUNTRY QUANTITATIVE ANALYSIS

In Part II, we examine fifty-seven countries that experienced organized political violence since 1990 and study their approaches to ethnic recognition. We also study the effects of these choices on high-level indicators of negative and positive peace. The cases stretch the alphabet, and the globe, from Afghanistan to the United Kingdom. They involve eighty-six "constitutional moments" that vary in whether they incorporate ethnic recognition or not.

In the first of the chapters in this section, Chapter 3, we focus on the concepts and definitions used to construct our cross-national dataset. With these definitions in place, we then present temporal and regional trends in the adoption or non-adoption of ethnic recognition.

Chapter 4 examines the factors that give rise to the adoption of recognition. It is here that we test a core prediction of our theory—namely, that regimes under plurality ethnic rule are more likely to choose recognition than regimes under minority rule. We account for potential confounding in estimating this predictive relationship, and we evaluate the strength of ethnic power configurations in predicting adoption relative to other factors.

The final chapter in this cross-national part of the book, Chapter 5, studies the effects of adopting recognition on peace. We first assess the extent to which the de jure adoption of recognition in a constitution or peace agreement translates into changes on the ground, measured in terms of ethnic inclusion in positions in power and in terms of the implementation of recognition policies in various governance domains. We then assess the effects of ethnic recognition on political violence, economic vitality, and democratic inclusiveness.

Our statistical analysis works at the macro level to establish high-level stylized facts. This allows us to assess the usefulness and generality of our theory for anticipating patterns across countries and over time. For the adoption of recognition, the cross-national results give us strong indication of the usefulness of our theoretical framework based on ethnic power configurations. Nonetheless, the analysis reveals a few empirical puzzles. This includes a non-trivial share of plurality-led regimes that do not adopt recognition as well as minority-led regimes that do. When it comes to effects, our analysis is predicated on certain assumptions—specifically, that trends in countries that do not adopt recognition provide an unbiased counterfactual for what would have happened in countries that did adopt recognition. Statistical analysis of observational cross-national data always leaves open questions about whether we are truly picking up on causal effects as opposed to the effects of other unmeasured confounding factors. Leveraging the power of mixed-methods research (Seawright 2016), we view our cross-national statistical results as motivation for the more detailed case studies in Part III of the book.

3

Trends in Ethnic Recognition

Our first task in the research for this book was to assess how often conflict-affected countries adopted recognition-based strategies like Burundi's ethnic quotas or Bosnia and Herzegovina's ethnic federation, places with which we were familiar from past work and research. Were countries that adopted recognition exceptions or the norm? Addressing this question required that we come up with a clear definition of ethnic recognition and then apply it to constitutional moments in conflict-affected countries. Chapter 2 provided details and justifications for our definition of ethnic recognition. In this chapter we explain how we make use of the concept for systematic empirical analysis.

We analyze trends in its adoption or non-adoption in conflict-affected countries since 1990. These trends describe the global landscape—to our knowledge, the first such mapping—and serve as a backdrop for the next chapters, where we explore the conditions under which recognition is adopted and its effects on peace. We use a dataset of eighty-six "constitutional moments"—the adoption of new constitutions, constitutional amendments, or comprehensive political settlements—that occurred in fifty-seven countries affected by conflict between 1990 and 2012. As the numbers suggest, many of the countries have had more than one constitutional moment since 1990. Figure 3.1 is a map showing the conflict-affected countries in our dataset, which span much of the globe. The map also shows which of these countries were operating under a recognition regime (dark gray) and which under non-recognition (light gray). It is visually apparent that incidence of recognition versus non-recognition varies considerably globally and by region, a point to which we return later.

In the rest of this chapter, we explain the operational definitions that we use for our cross-national analysis on the adoption and effects of recognition. We first explain our coding of ethnic recognition. Next, in exploring conceptual distinctions, we consider how our operational definition of recognition compares to concepts measured by social scientists studying related

Diversity, Violence, and Recognition. Elisabeth King and Cyrus Samii, Oxford University Press (2020). © Oxford University Press.
DOI: 10.1093/oso/9780197509456.003.0001

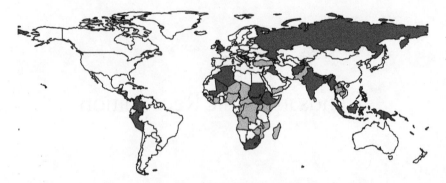

Figure 3.1 The set of countries considered in this book are shaded gray, with dark gray indicating that the country was under a recognition regime and light gray for a non-recognition regime by 2012. This set includes countries affected by violent conflict and that adopted new constitutions or political settlements ("constitutional moments") between 1990 and 2012. (Map source: http://naturalearthdata.com.)

phenomena, including formal versus informal recognition and factional power sharing. In anticipation of two key questions about the way we make use of the ethnic recognition concept, we then analyze the extent to which the recognition provisions captured in constitutions or settlements cover "politically relevant" ethnic groups. Finally, we display temporal and regional trends in the adoption of recognition. We show that recognition is adopted during 40 percent of constitutional moments and with little variation over time, although with important differences from region to region.

Coding ethnic recognition

As we explain in Chapter 1, we define ethnic recognition to mean public and explicit references to ethnic identities in state institutions. A clear expression of such recognition is when constitutions or agreements that define a political regime explicitly affirm that the body politic comprises multiple ethnic identities. The preamble to the 2005 Iraqi constitution, for example, references Shi'a, Sunni, Arab, Kurdish, and Turkmeni identities. The 1995 Dayton Accords for Bosnia and Herzegovina make repeated reference to Bosniak, Croat, and Serb identities. Such naming of ethnic groups in constitutions and political settlements serves as the operational definition that we use when conducting our statistical analysis of trends and cross-national patterns in the adoption and consequences of ethnic recognition. In rare cases, we consider not only the naming of a specific ethnic group but also the use of terms such as "indigenous" (in Guatemala) or "the communities" (in Northern Ireland) for which membership is defined strictly in ethnic terms.

There may be prerequisites for recognition, such as common understanding (if not consensus) about ethnic identity categories and how they apply. We posit that in the aftermath of a violent conflict in which ethnicity was a key demarcating line for opposing sides, targeting, or blame, such an understanding—however imperfect—often exists. Recognition is a state project that builds on such collective understanding. For recognition policies, such as group-differentiated rights, to be implemented, such knowledge needs to go further to also include relatively clear rules of interpretation to determine inclusion and exclusion (Chandra 2012). The impetus to categorize and render these classifications "legible" has long been considered a "central problem of statecraft" in the modern era (Scott 1995, 2; see also Anderson 2003 and Gellner 1983). Of course, we acknowledge a tension between institutionalizing ethnic categories on the one hand, and the constructed nature of ethnic identities on the other. This tension is central to our theoretical analysis of the dilemma of recognition: the categories may be relevant for redressing grievances (assuring effects) but have the simultaneous effect of increasing the salience and potentially entrenching ethnicity as a basis for mobilization (mobilization effects). We also acknowledge that our definition leaves open the question of whether the ethnic identities that constitutions or agreements affirm necessarily include all politically relevant ethnic groups, where such relevance is based on active political mobilization. We further address this question of political relevance later in this chapter and relate it to the issue of measuring ethnic power configurations in Chapter 4.

Based on King and Samii (2018), we analyze cross-national trends and patterns using a dataset that includes recognition decisions in conflict-affected countries between 1990 and 2012. We identified ninety-two conflict-affected countries using data from the Uppsala Conflict Data Program. This includes the Internal Armed Conflict Dataset (Gleditsch et al. 2002; Melander et al. 2016), Non-State Conflict Dataset (Sundberg et al. 2012; Melander et al. 2016), and the One-Side Violence Dataset (Eck and Hultman 2007; Melander et al. 2016). We define a country as "conflict-affected" if it experienced political violence leading to at least twenty-five deaths in a year. Note that twenty-five deaths is a fairly low threshold, meaning that our dataset includes countries affected by both lower-intensity violent conflicts as well as what scholars typically consider to be civil wars (Sambanis 2004). In our analysis, we consider differences between the two, finding that patterns of interest are starkest in ethnic civil wars. Constitutional moments occurred in fifty-seven of these countries. Our main analysis thus excludes the thirty-five conflict-affected countries within which no constitutional moments occurred. In Chapter 4, we describe methods used to ensure that our analyses are robust to potential complications from working with this selected set of countries. We can compare average fatality rates in countries that we study with rates in countries with no constitutional moments.

Fatalities include deaths in battle as well as instances of one-sided violence against civilians. For the fifty-seven countries that we study, fatality rates during years of violence range from 0.005 per 10,000 people in Bangladesh to 83.75 per 10,000 people in Rwanda. The mean fatality rate is 2.48 per 10,000, with a median of 0.23, if we include Rwanda, and a mean of 1.06 and median of 0.22 per 10,000 if we exclude Rwanda. This can be compared to a much narrower range of 0.001 to 4.32 and a much lower mean of 0.43 and median of 0.16 per 10,000 for the conflict-affected countries with no constitutional moments, which we exclude. As such, the cases with constitutional moments that we examine tend be cases of more intensely violent conflict.

In constructing our dataset, we did not screen cases on the basis of whether the conflicts are commonly labeled as "ethnic conflicts." The relevance of recognition may extend beyond such cases. First, nearly all fifty-seven of the countries in our dataset exhibit politically relevant ethnic diversity. Perhaps one exception is Haiti, which has the second-lowest level of ethnic fractionalization in our dataset after Yemen, although the coding for Yemen does not distinguish Sunni and Shi'a groups. As we explained in Chapter 2, a country's ethnic fractionalization measures the probability that two randomly sampled people from the country would be from different ethnic groups (Alesina et al. 2003). Countries with low ethnic fractionalization scores include, aside from Yemen and Haiti, the Philippines and Russia, both of which have hosted political mobilization on ethnic lines. Second, ethnic recognition can emerge as a demand even in conflicts conventionally understood as based on non-ethnic ideological or resource disputes. Consider the 1996–2006 civil war in Nepal, which is conventionally labeled as a non-ethnic, ideological conflict. However, such labeling masks the extent of mobilization based on ethnic grievances during the conflict, and there has been a vibrant discussion over institutionalizing ethnic rights in the new Nepalese constitution (Gellner 2007). We would rather not exclude such cases and therefore err on the side of over-inclusiveness. We do, however, examine whether results change when we consider only cases commonly regarded as ethnic conflicts.

We chose 1990 as the start date for our analysis because it defines a manageable time period that also keeps us within the post–Cold War era, thereby holding important international factors constant (Kalyvas and Balcells 2010). The 2012 end date is driven by two considerations. First, some other datasets, such as the Ethnic Power Relations dataset (Cederman et al. 2010), do not extend beyond this time period and rely on country-specific expert coding that would be infeasible for us to extend. Second, for tracking the effects of recognition, this timeframe defines a set of cases for which some minimum amount of time has elapsed since adoption or non-adoption of recognition, enabling us to examine the effects of this institutional choice. Figure 3.2, which displays the

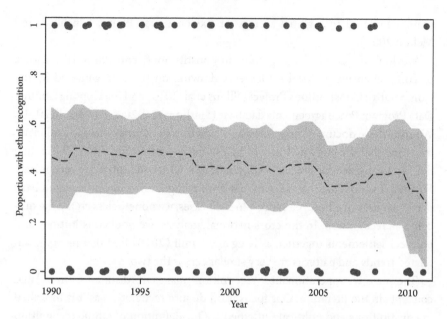

Figure 3.2 The graph shows the proportion over time of new constitutions and political settlements with ethnic recognition in conflict-affected countries, 1990–2012. The dashed line is a trend line produced using a kernel smoother with a 5-year bandwidth; the gray shaded area is a 95 percent confidence interval. The dots at the top and bottom of the graph show the timing of the actual recognition and non-recognition cases, respectively. From King, E., and C. Samii. 2018. "Minorities and Mistrust: On the Adoption of Ethnic Recognition to Manage Conflict." *Journal of Peace Research* 55(3): 289–304. Copyright © 2017 The Authors. DOI: 10.1177/0022343317707803.

rate of adoption of recognition from 1990 to 2012, also shows how our cases are distributed over time (the dots at the bottom and top of the graph). We see that the cases are nearly uniformly distributed through this period, suggesting that restricting our analysis up to 2012 does not hide any important temporal patterns in adoption. The figure also shows that the rate at which recognition was adopted held quite steady at around 40 percent.

We focus on constitutional moments in conflict-affected contexts, during which the foundations of political regimes are established (Lerner 2011, 210–11). These include the circumstances surrounding the adoption of comprehensive peace agreements, constitutions, or constitutional amendments amid or immediately following (that is, within a year of) violent conflict. Constitutions and peace agreements signal the priorities of the post-conflict government and have special standing as symbolic documents that outline post-conflict government commitments to both local populations and international actors (Cochrane 2008; Samuels 2006). While these events are relatively rare, ethnically fragmented states do replace their constitutions, on average, every eight years, compared to a global average of sixteen years (Elkins, Ginsburg, and Melton 2007).

We look for cases of recognition in constitutions, constitutional reforms, or comprehensive political settlements drawing on the data gathered by the Comparative Constitutions Project (Elkins et al. 2010) and the Uppsala Conflict Data Program Peace agreements database (Harbom et al. 2006; Hogbladh 2011). We code these documents on the basis of whether or not they include explicit affirmation that the body politic comprises multiple ethnic identities. The coding does not consider the precise configuration of which identities are recognized. Further, it is possible that a document both recognizes ethnic groups and bans particular uses of ethnic references. In such cases, we nonetheless coded the outcome as recognition. In the cross-national analysis, we pool constitutions and political settlements together, as King and Samii (2018) find that recognition-related trends and patterns are very similar across the two.

The way we operationalize recognition makes it distinct from related concepts in the literature. Our focus is on de jure recognition as it is inscribed in constitutions and political settlements. Our definition of ethnic recognition is thus distinguished from informal or, following political sociologist Frank De Zwart (2005), "indirect" forms of recognition. Formal recognition in a constitution or comprehensive settlement more clearly signals leaders' preferences for recognition than informal recognition does. We take the existence of indirect (that is, non-recognition-based) quotas or indirect autonomy arrangements not as cases of recognition but rather as an alternative strategy. As De Zwart (2005) discusses, Nigeria's early federal system (until 1976) was an obviously indirect approach to addressing equality between ethnic groups. The system used formulas to distribute state resources and public sector opportunities on the basis of region. Because of high levels of geographic clustering of ethnic groups, it helped to equalize resources and opportunities by ethnicity. However, the formulas did not make explicit references to ethnicity; indeed, the names of Nigeria's states were based on generic geographic criteria (Northeastern State, Northwestern State, Rivers State, and so on). Our analysis views these indirect cases differently than cases in which there is decentralization to territorial units that are defined explicitly in ethnic terms, such as the Kurdish autonomous region defined in Iraq's 2005 constitution or the Spanish system that is based on provinces defined in terms of locally dominant language and ethnicities (Brancati 2006). The difference is in whether explicit ethnic criteria are used.

We draw another distinction between ethnic recognition and factional power-sharing. Power-sharing, in its generic form, refers to the strategy of distributing power and domains of shared rule (versus self-rule) in a political regime between elites who represent the interests of different factions. When factions are strongly defined in terms of ethnic identities, explicit ethnic power-sharing is a possible recognition-based institutional configuration. This includes systems based on political scientist Arend Lijphart's (1977) consociational model. One also encounters factional power-sharing arrangements that operate indirectly as ethnic power-sharing arrangements (Roeder and Rothchild 2005, 8–15). We discuss the example of the 1993 Arusha Accords in Rwanda in Chapter 7. Drawing this definitional distinction helps to maintain an analytical separation between strategies that seek to balance power between factions, which could lead incidentally to balancing on the basis of ethnic criteria, and strategies explicitly based on ethnic group identity. In Chapter 6, we demonstrate how in Burundi the relationship between ethnic quotas and factional power-sharing in the 2005 constitution has become a central political controversy.

After coding for recognition, we conducted a number of validity checks. First, we consulted with country experts for each of the fifty-seven countries and eighty-six constitutional moments to ensure that their assessments were consistent with our own. Next, we assessed the degree of correspondence—which we ultimately find to be very strong—between our high-level coding of recognition and other datasets that attempt to measure related institutions. For example, political scientist Alan Kuperman (2015) codes current constitutions in sub-Saharan Africa in terms of whether they do or do not include "accommodation" provisions that protect the rights of ethnic groups or formally include those rights in the political system. Of the seventeen cases that overlap between our dataset and Kuperman's, we agree in the majority of instances—specifically, on the eleven cases of non-recognition/non-accommodation, as well as two cases of recognition/accommodation. The remaining four are split evenly in terms of the ways that our codings disagree, and these differences are attributable to the condition whereby we require that recognition entail explicit reference to ethnic group identities (as opposed to indirect provisions, as with the Nigerian federal system, for example).

Another comparable data project is the Peace Accords Matrix project (Joshi and Darby 2013), produced by the University of Notre Dame's Kroc Institute. The Peace Accords Matrix dataset codes comprehensive peace accords from 1989 to 2007 on whether or not they contain provisions in four relevant domains: interethnic councils, indigenous rights, minority rights, and self-determination. For the twenty-five cases that overlap in our respective datasets, our codings largely agree with the Peace Accords Matrix codings across these domains. Fifteen out of twenty-five agree for interethnic councils, and sixteen agree for indigenous rights, minority rights, and self-determination. Across all four domains, all but one of the cases of misalignment are cases that we have coded as recognition but that the Peace Accords Matrix does not code as having a provision. This speaks to the fact that not all of our recognition cases are ones in which either minorities or indigenous groups are those being recognized, and that the manner in which recognition is implemented does not regularly involve self-determination or interethnic councils. Overall, these exercises provided us with additional confidence in our recognition coding.

Recognition of politically relevant ethnic groups

In the earlier section on coding ethnic recognition, we explain that we interpret ethnic recognition to be public and explicit references to ethnic identities in state institutions at constitutional moments. But, one might ask, are the named groups really the groups that matter if the ostensible goal of recognition is building peace? Acknowledging both the importance of ethnic identities in politics and also their fluidity as social constructs, political scientists have endeavored to define "politically relevant" ethnic groups (Cederman et al. 2010; Chandra 2006; Fearon 2003; Fearon et al. 2007; Posner 2004, 2005). Political scientist Daniel Posner (2004) proposes that an ethnic identity is politically relevant in a given country and year if political mobilization occurs or appeals are frequently made on the basis of that identity. Such mobilization itself often depends on whether the identity's demographic share makes it useful for constructing a minimal winning political coalition (Posner 2005). For political scientist James Fearon (2003), whose body of work focuses on political violence, the political relevance of an identity depends on whether there is consensus in the population that the identity features in politics. Cederman, Wimmer, and Min (2010) provide perhaps the most up-to-date listing of politically relevant ethnic groups around the world. They conducted expert surveys for nearly all countries of the world and had experts on each country nominate groups as being politically relevant at different periods in the country's history.

To what extent do the recognition provisions in our dataset cover politically relevant ethnic groups? Table 3.1 attempts to address that question. It lists all thirty-six of the recognition-based constitutions and settlements in our dataset. We bring in data from the Ethnic Power Relations project (Cederman et al. 2010), which lists politically relevant ethnic groups and their population share by country and year. Then Table 3.1 lists the number of politically relevant ethnic groups in each country in the year of the agreement, the number of those groups recognized in the document, and the resulting percentage of the population that is covered by such recognition. For example, for Bosnia and Herzegovina in 1995, the Dayton Agreement recognized three out of four politically relevant ethnic groups—namely, Bosniaks (48 percent of the population), Croats (14 percent), and Serbs (33 percent)—but does not recognize Roma (1 percent) or any of the non–politically relevant groups (at least as coded) that make up the other 4 percent of the population. As a result, the Dayton Agreement explicitly recognizes group identities for 95 percent of the population. Contrast

Table 3.1 **Constitutions and political settlements with ethnic recognition in conflict-affected countries (1990–2012), with number of politically relevant ethnic groups, number recognized, and resulting percentage of population recognized**

Country	Year	Document	Number of politically relevant ethnic groups	Number of politically relevant ethnic groups recognized	Percent of population recognized
Afghanistan	2004	Constitution	14	12	91%
Algeria	1996	Constitution (amendment)	2	2	100%
Algeria	2008	Constitution (amendment)	2	2	100%
Bangladesh	1997	Chittagong Hill Tracks Accord	4	1	1%
Bosnia and Herzegovina	1995	Dayton Agreement	4	3	95%
Burundi	2000	Arusha Accords	3	3	100%
Burundi	2005	Constitution	3	3	100%
Colombia	1991	Constitution (amendment)	3	2	26%
Ethiopia	1991	Transitional Period Charter	11	11	100%
Ethiopia	1994	Constitution	9	9	100%
Georgia	2006	Constitution	6	2	4%
Guatemala	1996	Accord for a Firm and Lasting Peace	4	3	52%
India	1993	Bodoland Autonomous Council Act	20	2	26%
Indonesia	2005	MOU Between GOI and GAM (Aceh)	16	1	1%
Iraq	2005	Constitution	5	5	100%

(continued)

Table 3.1 **Continued**

Country	Year	Document	Number of politically relevant ethnic groups	Number of politically relevant ethnic groups recognized	Percent of population recognized
Macedonia	2001	Ohrid Agreement	5	4	96%
Mali	1992	Pacte Nationale and Constitution	3	1	7%
Moldova	1994	Constitution	4	2	25%
Myanmar	2008	Constitution	12	7	89%
Nepal	2007	Interim Constitution	7	4	62%
Nicaragua	1990	Constitution (amendment)	4	2	4%
Papua New Guinea	2001	Bougainville Peace Agreement	2	1	3%
Peru	1993	Constitution	4	2	37%
Philippines	1996	Mindanao Final Agreement	4	1	5%
Russia	1992	Constitution (amendment) and Constitutions of Republics	41	25	92%
Russia	1993	Constitution	41	25	92%
Russia	2000	Revisions to Constitutions of Republics	40	24	92%
Russia	2003	Chechen Constitution	40	1	1%
Serbia and Montenegro	1999	Rambouillet Agreement	7	3	80%
South Africa	1993	Interim Constitution	14	9	79%

Table 3.1 **Continued**

Country	Year	Document	Number of politically relevant ethnic groups	Number of politically relevant ethnic groups recognized	Percent of population recognized
South Africa	1996	Constitution	14	9	79%
South Sudan	2011	Transitional Constitution	10	1	40%
Sudan	2005	Sudan Comprehensive Peace Agreement	16	8	69%
Tajikistan	1999	Constitution (amendment)	5	2	81%
United Kingdom	1998	Good Friday Agreement	7	2	2%
Serbia and Montenegro	1992	Constitution	9	2	42%
		Averages:	**10.97**	**5.44**	**58%**

Note: Changes in the number of politically relevant ethnic groups in Ethiopia and Russia are due to the secession of Eritrea and former Soviet republics.

Sources: Sources include the Ethnic Power Relations project (Cederman et al. 2010) and authors' recognition data.

this to the 1997 Chittagong Hill Tracks Accord in Bangladesh, which recognizes the group identity of only the Chittagong Hill Tribes, who constitute 1 percent of Bangladesh's population. Across the dataset, the average population share covered by group-based recognition is 58 percent. The variation in the population share covered is due to the nature of the settlements or constitutions. Targeted autonomy arrangements such as the 1996 Mindanao Final Agreement in the Philippines, the 1997 Chittagong Hill Tracks Accord in Bangladesh, or the 2005 Memorandum of Understanding between the Government of Indonesia and the Free Aceh Movement (GAM) establish autonomy for the specific groups in the conflict, while ignoring the identities of other groups in the country. Recognition-based constitutions defining nationwide regimes tend to cover a much higher share of the country's politically relevant ethnic groups. There are exceptions, of course, such as the Georgian constitution of 2006, which grants special consideration to the Abkhazian autonomous area to the exclusion of explicit consideration of the Ossetian enclave or the Azeri or Armenian minorities. One can conclude that, typically, the recognition that we observe is either targeted in a manner that focuses on particular groups implicated in a conflict or covers the majority of politically relevant groups in society. That is to say, the recognition that we encode in our dataset is not trivial politically.

Trends in the adoption of ethnic recognition

Figure 3.2 and Table 3.2 show temporal and regional trends in the adoption of ethnic recognition in constitutions, amendments, and comprehensive political settlements in conflict-affected countries from 1990 to 2012. Recall that our dataset consists of a total of eighty-six constitutional moments in fifty-seven countries. Cases of recognition represent 43 percent (thirty-seven) of the cases. As of 2012, twenty-nine of the countries in our dataset were operating under recognition-based constitutions or political settlements. Between 1990 and 2012, eighteen countries had more than one constitutional moment. In only two cases did these involve constitutional moments that differed in terms of their adoption of recognition: Burundi had a non-recognition constitution in 1992 but adopted recognition under the 2000 Arusha Accords and 2005 constitution, and Sudan had a non-recognition constitution in 1998 but adopted recognition in its 2005 interim constitution. However, it is possible that other constitutional moments reflect changes in recognition status relative to constitutional provisions that precede 1990, which we see in all three case study chapters. For example, Rwanda moved from a pre-war recognition regime to a

Table 3.2 **Regional patterns in adopting ethnic recognition in constitutions and political settlements in conflict-affected countries (1990–2012)**

Region	Percent with recognition	N
Sub-Saharan Africa	17%	40
Americas	67%	6
East/Southeast Asia	60%	10
Europe	100%	11
Middle East/N. Africa	56%	9
South/Central Asia	40%	10
World	43%	86

Source: From King and Samii 2018.

non-recognition regime under the 1993 Arusha Accords and 2003 constitution, and Ethiopia moved from a pre-war non-recognition regime to a recognition regime under the 1991 Transitional Charter and 1994 constitution.

Of our eighty-six cases, 72 percent (sixty-two cases) are coded as taking place amid "ethnic conflict" by Cederman, Wimmer, and Min (2010) in their Ethnic Power Relations dataset. This is indicative of the 1990 to 2012 period as having been part of an "era of identity politics" (Eisenberg and Kymlicka 2011). Among such ethnic conflicts, recognition was adopted exactly half of the time (thirty-one cases), whereas it is in only a quarter (six cases) that recognition was adopted in a conflict typically considered non-ethnic.

Figure 3.2 shows that the rate of adoption held steady at about 40 percent over the years that we cover. We see neither important increases nor declines across time.

Different regions of the world exhibit substantial variation in the rates at which ethnic recognition is adopted, a fact that is apparent from the map in Figure 3.1 and even more clearly in Table 3.2. European cases include the Balkans, Northern Ireland, constitutional revisions in the Russian Federation, and the Caucasus. In all of these cases, the constitutions or political settlements include ethnic recognition. Chapter 2 noted how this commitment to recognition in Europe could be attributed to the interplay of regional norms and domestic ethnostructural considerations. The European pattern contrasts dramatically with sub-Saharan Africa, where only 17 percent (seven) of the forty constitutions, amendments, or political settlements we identified adopt recognition (Ethiopia in 1992 and 1994, Mali in 1992, South Africa in 1993 and 1996, and Burundi in 2000 and 2005). Chapter 2 also noted how non-recognition norms in Africa may play a role in explaining this low rate of adoption. Across the Middle East, North Africa, East and Southeast Asia, and the Americas, recognition occurs in a majority of cases, whereas in South and Central Asia recognition occurs in a minority.

Conclusion

This chapter has operationalized ethnic recognition as applied to political systems in conflict-affected countries. We focus on ethnic recognition adopted during constitutional moments, which we motivate by our interest in studying trends in leaders' decisions to make unequivocal public commitments to recognition and also in informing discussions of formal institutional design. Such ethnic recognition has been relatively common over the past two and half decades, occurring in about 40 percent of constitutions and comprehensive settlements. Having offered this conceptual clarification and assessment of basic trends, we turn next to a deeper empirical assessment of the political and structural conditions that give rise to ethnic recognition. We then turn to the consequences of adopting recognition for violence and political and economic progress.

4

Under What Conditions Is Recognition Adopted?

Chapter 3 illustrated that neither recognition nor non-recognition is a globally dominant strategy in the aftermath of violent conflicts. The two approaches that we witnessed in Burundi and Rwanda, and that we describe in the opening pages of the book, are roughly evenly split across the globe. We also discussed the ways in which regions of the world vary considerably in the rates at which countries adopt ethnic recognition at the constitutional level. In Europe, ethnic recognition was adopted in all conflict-affected contexts since 1990. We hypothesized that this could be due to regional norms of minority recognition promoted by European institutions. However, another condition that was common in all of these European cases is that a representative from each respective country's plurality ethnic group served as head of government at the time that recognition was adopted. In Africa, rates of adoption are much lower, perhaps reflective of regional non-recognition norms, although this leaves us to explain the seven cases that chose recognition. Under what conditions is recognition adopted?

In this chapter, we combine the ethnic recognition data introduced in Chapter 3 with other data on conditions in our set of conflict-affected countries. We use the resulting dataset to examine the conditions under which governments formally recognize different ethnic identities as a strategy to manage conflicts. Our empirical analysis draws upon the theory of recognition we developed in Chapter 2. The theory focuses on recognition's assuring effects on the one hand and mobilization effects on the other. When the effects work together, recognition should be an attractive strategy for leaders. In contrast, when these two effects clash, they give rise to a dilemma of recognition, making adopting recognition a less appealing strategy. A key condition that we explored in the theory is the ethnic power configuration—that is, whether a country is under minority ethnic rule or not. Dynamics associated with minority ethnic rule shape our empirical analysis in this chapter as well. Under minority ethnic rule, the mobilization effects of recognition threaten the position of the minority leadership

Diversity, Violence, and Recognition. Elisabeth King and Cyrus Samii, Oxford University Press (2020). © Oxford University Press.
DOI: 10.1093/oso/9780197509456.003.0001

because they generate a structural advantage for plurality groups. This phenomenon clashes with the assuring effects of recognition, which might otherwise allow a leader to quell mistrust from other ethnic groups. Thus we should expect minority leaders to be less likely to adopt recognition. In contrast, plurality ethnic rule should be conducive to the adoption of recognition.

As we show in this chapter, cross-national patterns since 1990 are largely consistent with our predictions. Plurality-led regimes are much more likely than minority-led regimes to adopt recognition. This relationship is strong and robust to accounting for numerous potential confounders. We also find that the importance of minority versus plurality rule depends on the starkness of the difference in population shares between the largest and the rest of the ethnic groups in the society. This further supports the importance of ethnic power configurations for the adoption of recognition. The sections that follow develop these findings in detail.

Ethnic power configurations

In this section, we provide a first-cut assessment of the conditions under which recognition is adopted. We focus first on the key factor that we detail in our theory of recognition in Chapter 2—namely, the ethnic power configuration and, in particular, whether minority ethnic rule prevails or not. In Chapter 3, we discussed how political scientists define "politically relevant" ethnic group identities. Even if one defines a set of politically relevant identities, complications can arise in applying such identities to determine the ethnic power configuration (Londregan et al. 1995, 6; Chandra 2009). For example, former South African president Nelson Mandela was a member both of the Xhosa minority, arguably a politically relevant ethnic group, as well as the more encompassing black (by apartheid definitions) majority. Assigning his tenure to be a case of minority as opposed to plurality ethnic rule is ultimately a judgment with which reasonable people may disagree.

Rather than inventing our own subjective way to measure ethnic power configurations, we rely on the expertise captured in projects devoted more specifically to this task. We work primarily with the country-level codings of political scientists James Fearon, Kimuli Kasara, and David Laitin (2007), who define minority ethnic rule to mean that the head of government comes from a minority ethnic group. Because their data only extend through 1999, we used their coding methodology to expand the data through 2012, which is the endpoint of our dataset. We checked the robustness of coding based on that rubric to what would be implied by the dataset of Cederman, Wimmer, and Min (2010), which does not code leaders but does provide a list of politically relevant ethnic groups and their demographic share, in which case we verified consistency in coding groups as minority or plurality. We find strong agreement across the two datasets in the ways they measure minority and plurality groups. Considering all conflict-affected countries between 1990 and 2012, including both the fifty-seven upon which we focus in our analysis of constitutional moments as well as the thirty-five conflict-affected countries in which there were no constitutional moments, Table 4.1 shows that 40 percent of the country-years in our broad set of conflict-affected countries were under ethnic minority rule. Note that the figures are in terms of country-years, so each country is counted on the basis of the number of years that appear for that country in the dataset. This allows us to account for countries that change from minority to plurality rule or vice versa. In the cases with constitutional moments, we see that 47 percent of country-years are under minority rule. There is no substantial trend over time in these proportions.

Using this coding of minority ethnic rule to test our theory relies on a presumption that heads of state will tend to be pivotal in deciding upon the adoption of ethnic recognition. There are exceptions to this, of course, such as in cases where insurgent forces are the dominant political actors in the negotiation of a political settlement. Nonetheless, such errors of measurement will manifest in terms of "attenuation biases" that will tend to dilute any statistical patterns. This would imply that the associations that we observe understate the true strength of the relationship. In addition, we pay careful attention to this presumption in our case study analyses.

Table 4.1 **Proportions of country-years experiencing minority ethnic rule in all 92 conflict-affected countries and for the subset of 57 countries with constitutions or political settlements (1990–2012)**

Region	All conflict-affected countries		Conflict-affected countries with constitutional moments	
	Proportion minority rule	Country-years	Proportion minority rule	Country-years
Africa	0.63	416	0.69	351
Americas	0.54	117	0.72	65
East/Southeast Asia	0.23	115	0.24	112
Europe	0.00	77	0.00	54
Middle East/N. Africa	0.22	188	0.21	95
South/Central Asia	0.20	123	0.27	91
Total	0.40	1037	0.47	769

In the top panel of Table 4.2, we present the basic relationship between minority ethnic rule and the adoption of recognition. As we hypothesize, we see a strong statistical relationship: for plurality-led regimes, 60 percent of settlements or constitutions in conflict-affected contexts from 1990 to 2012 incorporated ethnic recognition. For minority-led regimes, the share is much less, only 24 percent—a 36 percentage point difference. Of course, this bivariate analysis does not attend to various potential confounding factors. We return to those later, after next introducing variables that get at possible explanations beyond our theory.

Table 4.2 **Background conditions preceding adoption or non-adoption of ethnic recognition in 86 constitutions or political settlements or constitutions (1990–2012)**

Background variable	Value	Adoption of recognition in constitution or political settlement (Row percents)		
		No recognition	Recognition	N
Minority ethnic rule	No	40%	60%	45
	Yes	76%	24%	41
Other internal factors				
Freedom house rating	Free	0%	100%	6
	Partly Free	57%	43%	44
	Not Free	67%	33%	36
Military victory	No	58%	42%	74
	Yes	50%	50%	12
Other external factors				
International engagement	No	56%	44%	52
	Yes	59%	41%	34
Colonial history	United Kingdom	62%	38%	26
	France	84%	16%	19
	Spain	17%	83%	6
	Ottoman	25%	75%	8
	Other	52%	48%	27
Total		57%	43%	86

Other explanations

In Chapter 2, we reviewed a set of explanations that might account for the adoption or non-adoption of recognition. These included conditions internal to the leaders' domestic political system, and others that concentrated on international factors, external to the domestic political system. In the analysis informing Table 4.2, we operationalize these other internal and external factors. In the end, none present as striking a pattern as minority ethnic rule.

Such internal factors first include regime type—namely, the amount of democratic competition that a regime permits—under the premise that recognition is more compatible with democratic competition. We measure levels of democratic competition in terms of Freedom House's annual scoring of countries as being "free," "partly free," or "not free" (Freedom House 2016). Only six of our eighty-six constitutional moments occur in contexts of "free" democratic expression as per Freedom House's ratings. These six cases are Mali in 1992, the Philippines in 1996, South Africa in 1996, the United Kingdom in 1998, Papua New Guinea in 2001, and Indonesia in 2005. The rest of the constitutional moments are nearly evenly split between contexts of "partly free" and "not free" democratic expression.

Ethnic recognition was adopted in all six of the countries rated as "free," lending some support to the idea that recognition and democracy go hand-in-hand. Does this suggest an important qualification to our theory, along the lines of the argument that recognition is more compatible with democratic contexts, and that this relationship has nothing to do with minority versus plurality ethnic rule?

Consideration of the specific cases suggests, rather, that the apparent compatibility between recognition and democracy is precisely due to issues related to minority versus plurality ethnic rule. Indeed, in Mali, the Philippines, Indonesia, and the United Kingdom, we also have conditions of plurality rule. In South Africa, the 1996 constitution was adopted under President Nelson Mandela's tenure, which the Fearon, Kasara, and Laitin (2007) dataset codes as an instance of minority ethnic rule. This is on the basis of Mandela being a member of the minority Xhosa group, as discussed earlier. However, one might argue that the most salient cleavage managed by South African recognition policies (for example, quota provisions for the armed forces and quota requirements for businesses receiving government contracts) is the cleavage that divides what the apartheid regime designated as whites, on the one hand, from blacks and coloreds, on the other. One could very reasonably construe South Africa in 1996 as an instance of plurality rule with respect to the major recognition-related questions of the constitutional moment. In Papua New Guinea, we also find adoption of ethnic recognition under the rule of a minority government. It is worth noting, though, that Papua New Guinea exhibits the highest level of ethnic fractionalization in our dataset, thus the effect of minority rule may be less relevant in ways that we describe in Chapter 2.

Once we move down into the "partly free" and "not free" categories, we still see that recognition is more common in more democratic countries but, again, nothing nearly as pronounced as what we observe with respect to minority ethnic rule. All this is to say that the pattern associated with levels of democracy, while intriguing in its own right, hardly casts doubt on the first-order importance of minority versus plurality ethnic rule.

Table 4.2 also includes another internal factor related to regime type: namely, whether a political settlement or constitution followed from a military victory rather than a negotiated compromise. The coding is provided by the Uppsala Conflict Data Program. The vast majority of the constitutional moments in our dataset (seventy-four out of eighty-six) occur as the culminations of negotiated settlements rather than after military victories. Arguably, military victories are associated with a high degree of hegemony and are also more likely to permit authoritarian institution-building. This provides another take on the regime-type argument regarding the relative incompatibility of ethnic recognition with authoritarian regimes. Here we see no strong pattern; recognition is adopted at similar rates in cases of military victory as compared to negotiated settlement. For example, the cases of the Rwanda 2003 constitution and the Ethiopia 1991 transitional charter, which we detail later in this book, are both instances of military victory, but one is followed by non-recognition and the other by recognition.

We also consider external factors that might offer other explanations for recognition. In Chapter 3, we noted that regions differ considerably in their rates of adopting recognition. In Europe, the adoption rate was 100 percent, reflective perhaps of strong regional norms favoring recognition. Elsewhere, however, there remained variation to be explained. We consider another variable capturing the influence of international norms: namely, whether or not the settlement or constitution was negotiated with strong multilateral engagement. Multilateral institutions are primary channels for promoting international norms. They are also channels for powerful states to exercise influence and transmit normative preferences. We define multilateral engagement to mean the presence of an international peacekeeping operation, mediation by one of the five permanent members of the UN Security Council, or passage of resolutions by the UN Security Council in the years prior to the promulgation of the settlement or constitution. The coding is provided by the Uppsala Conflict Data Program peace agreements dataset, the Managing Intrastate Low-Intensity Conflict (MILC) dataset (Melander et al. 2009), and our own search of the UN Security Council online resolutions archive. Only thirty-four out of our eighty-six constitutional moments feature this type of multilateral engagement. Table 4.2 shows that no strong pattern is evident in the relationship between such engagement and the adoption of ethnic recognition. This challenges the idea that the spread of ethnic recognition is due primarily to the multilateral institutions or major powers imposing a normative preference for recognition.

Finally, we consider colonial history using the codings from the Issues Correlates of War Colonial History Data Set (Hensel 2018). We find that the colonial history is indeed predictive of subsequent recognition. For example, French republicanism, which dictates assimilation to a single national French identity, serves as an important model for non-recognition regimes (Weber 1976). This example is echoed in the states that were formerly part of the French empire: in our dataset, recognition is adopted only 16 percent of the time during constitutional moments in former French colonies. This is substantially lower than in states that had been subject to Ottoman rule, in which the millet system allowed religious groups to rule themselves under their own laws (Barkey 2008). In our dataset, eight of the constitutional moments occurred in former Ottoman territories (i.e., in the Balkans and Middle East), and in six out of the eight, recognition was adopted. In the six states that were former Spanish colonies, leaders adopted recognition in five out of the six constitutional moments. However, a reading of the histories for these states suggests that this had less to do with the political legacy of metropolitan Spanish institutions than with accumulated inequalities between descendants of Spanish settlers, who came to constitute significant and often majority shares of the population, and indigenous populations (De Ferranti et al. 2004, 112–22). In the states of the former British Empire, the rate at which recognition is adopted resembles the general global trend of close to 40 percent.

These patterns associated with colonial history are important, but they do not displace our interest in examining ethnic power configurations. This is for two reasons. First, whether a country was part of one or another empire is a variable that is fixed historically and therefore cannot explain changes over time. Yet we find that even in the twenty-two years that our dataset covers, we have numerous instances of shifts between non-recognition and recognition regimes. Second, in the multivariate analysis that we describe later in this chapter, we find that controlling for colonial history actually increases the magnitude of the measured association between plurality/minority rule and adoption of recognition. Thus, for countries that share the same colonial history, ethnic power configurations have substantial predictive power.

Addressing confounding factors

From Table 4.2 we have preliminary evidence that minority versus plurality ethnic rule is an important precursor to the adoption of recognition. This ethnostructural factor has a stronger bivariate relationship to the adoption of ethnic recognition than other candidate explanatory factors. Table 4.3 displays the cases that make up the basic relationship between minority ethnic rule and the adoption of recognition. The top right and bottom left quadrants display the cases that conform to our high-level theoretical prediction. Given this basic evidence, though, it is important to go beyond simple bivariate assessments to be sure that the pattern is not spurious in terms of a causal relationship. That is, we need to check whether the pattern is merely a reflection of other confounding factors correlated with both minority ethnic rule and recognition. An analysis presented by King and Samii (2018) does so using logistic regressions and statistical matching methods, controlling for a large number of potential confounding variables that frequently arise in the ethnic conflict and peace settlement literatures. The main analysis from the paper is reproduced in the Appendix at the end of this book, with some new additions. The control variables include various measures of ethnic relations in the country, including ethnic fractionalization, measures from Cederman, Wimmer, and Min (2010) of whether the conflict is an ethnic war and the share of the population excluded from power at the onset of conflict, and whether ethnic groups are regionally concentrated. The control variables also include structural conditions like income level and level of democracy, to see if recognition is confounded by level of development, and indicators for whether the country was a former British, French, Spanish, or Ottoman colony, to account for the colonial legacies discussed earlier. The control variables further include factors associated with conflict, such as terrain, conflict intensity, whether groups were making territorial or secessionist demands, and whether the conflict was terminated through a military victory. Finally, the control variables include aspects of the negotiation context, including whether the country had previously experienced power-sharing and whether there was international engagement in the form of UN Security Council resolutions or peacekeeping deployments. The negative relationship between minority ethnic rule and recognition remains strong even when accounting for all of these potential confounders (see Appendix for the full results).

Scope conditions

In the cross-national regression analysis, we also assess how the effects of minority leadership vary on the basis of contextual conditions that our theory suggests are important. First, our theory (and common sense) would suggest that the strength of the effect of minority leadership should be stronger in ethnic conflicts as a subset of a wider set of violent conflicts. Accordingly, our statistical analysis finds that the effects of minority leadership in conditions of ethnic

Table 4.3 Constitutions and political settlements with ethnic recognition and non-recognition, for cases with and without minority ethnic rule

Minority ethnic rule	No recognition	Recognition
No	Cambodia (1991)	Afghanistan (2004)
	Cambodia (1993)	Algeria (1996)
	Central African Republic (2004)	Algeria (2008)
	Djibouti (1994)	Bangladesh (1997)
	Djibouti (2001)	Bosnia and Herzegovina (1995)
	Eritrea (1997)	Burundi (2005)
	Kenya (2010)	Georgia (2006)
	Madagascar (2010)	Guatemala (1996)
	Niger (1995)	India (1993)
	Pakistan (1991)	Indonesia (2002)
	Pakistan (1997)	Indonesia (2005)
	Rwanda (1993)	Iraq (2005)
	Somalia (2004)	Macedonia (2001)
	Sudan (1998)	Mali (1992)
	Thailand (2007)	Moldova (1994)
	Turkey (2007)	Myanmar (2008)
	Turkey (2010)	Philippines (1996)
	Zimbabwe (2008)	Russia (1992)
		Russia (1993)
		Russia (2000)
		Russia (2003)
		Serbia and Montenegro (1999)
		Sudan (2005)
		Sudan (2011)
		Tajikistan (1999)
		United Kingdom (1998)
		Yugoslavia (1991)
Yes	Angola (1992)	Burundi (2000)
	Angola (1994)	Colombia (1991)
	Angola (2002)	Ethiopia (1991)
	Burundi (1992)	Ethiopia (1994)
	Chad (1996)	Nepal (2007)
	Chad (2005)	Nicaragua (1990)
	Congo (2001)	Papua New Guinea (2001)
	Congo, Democratic Republic (2005)	Peru (1993)
	Cote d'Ivoire (2003)	South Africa (1993)
	Cote d'Ivoire (2007)	South Africa (1996)
	El Salvador (1992)	
	Guinea (2001)	
	Guinea (2010)	
	Guinea-Bissau (1998)	
	Haiti (1993)	
	Laos (1991)	
	Liberia (2003)	
	Mozambique (1990)	
	Mozambique (1992)	
	Nigeria (1999)	
	Pakistan (1999)	
	Pakistan (2003)	
	Pakistan (2010)	
	Pakistan (2011)	
	Rwanda (2003)	
	Sierra Leone (1999)	
	Sierra Leone (2002)	
	Uganda (1995)	
	Uganda (2002)	
	Uganda (2005)	
	Yemen (1994)	

conflict are to reduce the probability of recognition by about 55 percentage points, as compared to the full set of cases, for which the estimated effect is between 31 and 36 percentage points, depending on the control variables included. Thus, the effect is much stronger for cases conventionally understood as ethnic conflicts.

Second, with respect to regional variation, we examine what happens when we omit Europe from the analysis. Recall that for our European cases, we had 100 percent adoption and 100 percent of cases with plurality rule. Omitting Europe, we find that minority-led regimes are still around 20 to 25 percentage points less likely to adopt recognition, which is to say that the pattern we observe related to ethnic power configurations is not a purely European phenomenon.

Third, we examine how the broader ethnic structure moderates the effect of minority rule. Our theory proposes that it is the potential for enabling a larger, rival ethnic group to mobilize that generates the dilemma of recognition for minority ethnic leaders. Likewise, the sense of security that plurality group leaders experience in pursuing recognition is a function of their demographic dominance. However, our theory is stylized insofar as it focuses attention on the leader's group and one potential opposition ethnic group. In countries where there are many ethnic groups, and in particular in countries where there are no groups that clearly dominate demographically, the leaders of plurality and minority groups may not differ much in the way they view the threat of mobilization by rival groups. In countries with comparatively high levels of ethnic fractionalization, the differences that our theory emphasizes may not be so salient. When there is high ethnic fractionalization, no particular ethnic group has a demographic advantage that could allow them to dominate elections or other political processes. Therefore, we would expect that the effect of minority versus plurality leadership would be weaker in countries with high ethnic fractionalization. Figure 4.1 uses the regression estimates (see Table A.2 in the Appendix) to demonstrate that this is indeed the case. In countries with very low ethnic fractionalization, such as Burundi and Yemen, plurality status implies demographic dominance. In such places, minority- and plurality-led regimes differ strongly in the rates at which they adopt recognition. But in places such as Ethiopia or Papua New Guinea, where high fractionalization means that the plurality group is not demographically dominant, we estimate no substantial difference in the adoption of recognition across minority- and plurality-led regimes.

Two additional and subtle patterns help us to understand the moderating effect of ethnic fractionalization. First, looking at Figure 4.1, we see that the moderating effect of fractionalization is driven primarily by a decrease in rates of adoption by plurality-led regimes. Second, another way to measure the demographic dominance of a plurality group is in the difference in the population share between the plurality and the second-largest group—what we call the

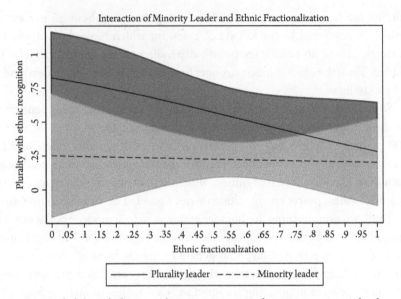

Figure 4.1 Probability of adopting ethnic recognition under minority versus plurality leadership, over levels of ethnic fractionalization. Shaded areas are 95 percent confidence intervals. Reproduced from King and Samii 2018.

"ethnic difference" measure. A larger ethnic difference should mean that there will be more pronounced differences in the ways that plurality and minority leaders view the mobilization effects of recognition, in which case the effect of minority rule will be stronger. Table A.2 in the Appendix shows results consistent with this prediction as well, although the estimates are noisier than for ethnic fractionalization. These patterns are suggestive as to the channel through which fractionalization's moderating effect operates. When fractionalization is high, plurality group leaders appear to see fewer advantages of adopting recognition. Their perception seems driven by the fact that there is at least one other group with whom they would have to contend politically.

As a final moderating effect, we consider how hegemonic authority interacts with the ethnic power configuration (Tables A.2 and A.3 in the Appendix). We measure this in terms of whether the constitutional moment occurred after a military victory and in terms of level of democracy, as measured by Freedom House. We have already noted how military victory was not associated with recognition in the aggregate and how autocracy also was not predictive of nonrecognition. When we go further and conduct regressions that include the other control variables described earlier, however, we find that rates of adoption are somewhat lower after military victories, conceptualized as a measure of hegemony, than in cases of negotiated settlement. However, the regression coefficient on military victory is less than half the magnitude of that for minority rule and, unlike the coefficient for minority rule, is not statistically significant in most specifications. Thus, the effect of minority rule remains strong even after accounting for military victories, although the number of cases of victories is small. We also examine the interaction of minority rule and military victory to the extent that our data allow us to explore it. In our data, we have five cases of minority rule following military victory: Ethiopia in 1991, Haiti in 1993, Yemen in 1994, Rwanda in 2003, and Chad in 2005. In one of these cases (Ethiopia in 1991), recognition was adopted, which yields a rate similar to that of negotiated settlement situations, for which nine out of thirty-seven cases of minority rule (25 percent) resulted in recognition. Using level of democracy as an alternative measure of hegemony, we recall that in all six of our cases in countries designated by Freedom House as "free," recognition was adopted. Then, excluding those cases from the analysis, we noted a general trend away from recognition as one descended to the "not free" category, although the effect of minority rule remained after accounting for this. As for the interaction effect, again we find that minority leaders are especially less likely to adopt recognition in "not free" cases, but there is no clear pattern for plurality-led regimes. Thus, we find that the appeal of recognition is much less for minority leaders in contexts where there is no political imperative to attend to opposition groups, as it is for minority leaders generally, per our theoretical considerations. For plurality leaders, we find no apparent moderating effect of degree of hegemony and democracy.

Conclusion

To summarize, then, we find strong evidence that in conflict-affected countries, minority-led regimes are substantially less likely to adopt ethnic recognition than plurality-led regimes. The relationship is stark: in the full sample of conflict-affected countries, minority-led regimes are 36 percentage points less likely to adopt recognition than plurality-led regimes. This effect is even more pronounced when we focus on ethnic conflicts, for which the difference is 55 percentage points. King and Samii (2018) and the Appendix to this book demonstrate that these findings are robust to adjustments for various types of potential selection bias and model misspecification.

We also estimate various moderating effects motivated by our theory. When ethnic fractionalization is high, plurality groups are not especially favored by the political mobilization effects of recognition. This dampens plurality group leaders' enthusiasm for recognition while also reducing the types of threats that give rise to the dilemma of recognition for minority groups. Accordingly, minority- and plurality-led regimes adopt recognition at about the same rate when ethnic fractionalization is high. We find a similar effect when we use the difference between the largest and second-largest ethnic groups in place of ethnic fractionalization. We also find that when hegemonic authority is high, as occurs after military victory or in relatively autocratic regimes, minority leaders are especially unlikely to adopt recognition, although this is not necessarily the case for plurality leaders.

These explanations for the adoption of recognition advance our theoretical and practical understanding of the origins of institutions and constitute a critical first step toward assessing the impact of recognition on peace. Chapter 5 examines these effects.

5

What Are the Effects of Ethnic Recognition on Peace?

When we have spoken with scholars of conflict management and policymakers, they are always interested in our analysis of the adoption and non-adoption of recognition in conflict-affected countries. However, inevitably they want to get to a more pressing question: which works better? This chapter studies the effects of ethnic recognition and non-recognition on peace. We estimate effects of recognition on the implementation of recognition-based policies, the political inclusion of ethnic groups, negative peace (captured by the reduction of violence), and indicators of positive peace (as seen in stronger economic vitality and more democratic politics).

As with Chapter 4, our analysis draws on the theory from Chapter 2. Our prediction is that the effects of recognition are most conducive to peace when its assuring effects and mobilization effects work together toward political stability. When the effects clash, a dilemma of recognition arises, and we predict that this will undermine stability. As with the adoption of recognition, the ethnic power configuration is again crucial for our analysis, as our theory proposes that it moderates the potential for recognition to promote peace. Under minority ethnic rule, the mobilization effects are expected to undermine the potential assuring effects of recognition, which makes recognition a less effective foundation for peace than under plurality leadership. Under plurality ethnic rule, recognition should have effects that offer assurance to both minority opposition members and the ruling plurality and, as a result, allow progress in terms of negative and positive peace.

The sections of this chapter examine these predictions working with data covering the period 1990 to 2012. First, we show that the adoption of recognition at the constitutional level tends to result in the implementation of meaningful recognition-based policies in various domains. There is good reason to be skeptical about pronouncements in constitutions and comprehensive settlements and whether they are genuine commitments to on-the-ground practice rather

Diversity, Violence, and Recognition. Elisabeth King and Cyrus Samii, Oxford University Press (2020). © Oxford University Press.
DOI: 10.1093/oso/9780197509456.003.0001

than cheap talk. These results clarify that constitutional pronouncements do in fact tend to translate into policies. Second, we demonstrate that recognition also leads to substantial reductions in the degree of ethnic exclusion, as measured by the population share of ethnic groups excluded from a country's power structure. Finally, we show that countries that adopt recognition tend, on average, to experience less violence, more economic vitality, and more democratic politics. When we look more closely, we find that countries under plurality rule drive this effect. For minority leaders, there are no clear peace-related gains to either recognition or non-recognition.

Implementation of recognition

We have focused on ethnic recognition in the sense that it captures public acknowledgment of ethnic differences in constitutions or political settlements. We argued that such recognition is important on its own because constitutions and political settlements define the structure of state institutions. At the same time, one may wonder whether such high-level recognition corresponds to policies or practices—such as quotas, other group-differentiated rights, or language policies—that affect people directly. This question arose frequently when we began presenting the project that would ultimately become this book. We address this question empirically in the current section.

Before doing so, we acknowledge that even thin forms of ethnic recognition, which do *not* couple recognition with more assertive policies, could have important effects. Our theoretical discussion in Chapter 2 detailed some of these effects. Thin recognition, without accompanying policies for redistribution or group-differentiated rights, can yield symbolic effects through the way that it signals inclusion. Micro-level studies have found that signaling inclusion can have important effects on perceived self-efficacy, perception of opportunity, and political and economic behavior among members of historically disadvantaged groups (Bobo and Gilliam 1990; Chauchard 2017; West 2016). Even in the absence of redistributive policies or group-specific rights, recognition can also have an effect by licensing ethnic categorization and the tracking of ethnic statistics, which improve visibility for assessing how ethnic group members are faring in their access to opportunities. This can promote trust, particularly among groups who have reason to fear being excluded. Finally, thin recognition can also yield political mobilization effects by licensing the use of ethnic identity in public discourse, which facilitates ethnic group mobilization.

That said, we show here that recognition during constitutional moments is typically coupled with policies and practices intended to directly affect public institutions and those who are served by them. Our analysis follows the suggestions of Borman and colleagues (2019) to examine the correspondence between pronouncements and concrete practices, based on their finding that concrete practices appear to mediate much of the effect of ethnic power-sharing provisions in political settlements. Thus, we relate our high-level measure of ethnic recognition to data that we collected on the implementation of recognition policies. Importantly, we did so for all of the fifty-seven conflict-affected countries experiencing constitutional moments, whether or not they had adopted ethnic recognition. This allows us to see whether the absence of ethnic recognition in a constitution may nonetheless mask ethnic recognition laws or norms. Given the enormous size of the endeavor, we did not seek to carry out this empirical assessment for all eighty-six of the constitutional moments in our dataset, but rather examined conditions that have prevailed in the fifty-seven countries since their most recent constitutional moment.

In constructing this "implementation dataset," we looked for evidence of the implementation of ethnic recognition strategies in seven domains. These are the executive, legislature and party system, security sector, justice sector, civil service, education sector, and language policy. We coded a sector as having a "yes" for recognition if we found what we refer to as de jure recognition. This includes indication of constitutional provisions. In this dataset, we also consider other legislation where recognition may appear. To earn a "yes," this presence must be combined with evidence that these terms were being applied, which we call de jure implementation. We coded a sector as having "partial" recognition if we found that de jure ethnic recognition was on the books but there was no indication of implementation. We also coded a sector as having "partial" recognition if we found that there was no de jure ethnic recognition but there were well-established ethnic recognition norms in practice—what we would call de facto recognition in the absence of de jure. These might be informal or indirect recognition strategies. Finally, we coded a domain as having "no" recognition if neither de jure nor de facto ethnic recognition was in effect. The coding strategy follows the example of the Multiculturalism Policy Index (2019) developed by scholars Keith Banting and Will Kymlicka, which assesses the depth and extent of multicultural policies across OECD countries. To provide just one example, Figure 5.1 illustrates the coding for the executive domain in Afghanistan. We code Afghanistan as having partial recognition in the executive domain. This is because there are no formal provisions for ethnic quotas or other recognition measures specifically for the executive in the most recent constitution. But, by consulting secondary accounts by country experts, we confirmed that there has been a consistently applied norm of ethnic balancing across cabinet positions. We conducted the same analysis for each of the seven domains. Indeed, for each of the fifty-seven cases, we code each of the seven domains in this manner, referencing the texts of constitutions, relevant legislation, media sources, and

Coding for the Executive Domain in Afghanistan

Evidence:

There are no formal provisions for ethnic recognition in the constitution; however, the cabinet of Hamid Karzai, the president of Afghanistan from 2001 to 2014, was ethnically diverse.

	Since 2004	
Overall	0.5	Partial
De jure	0	
De jure implementation	N/A	Partial
De facto	1	

De jure:

No formal provisions for ethnic recognition found in the constitution or other laws. The Afghan president and vice president must both be Muslim, but no specification with regards to Sunni or Shia sect. * Further, there are no ethnic or religious provisions to becoming a cabinet member.**

De jure implementation:

N/A

De facto:

Yes. Hamid Karzai (president of Afghanistan, 2001–2014) had cabinets that were ethnically balanced. For example, in 2005, the cabinet consisted of 10 Pashtuns, 8 Tajiks, 5 Hazaras, 2 Uzbeks, 1 Turkmen, and 1 Baloch, although ethnic Pashtuns were allocated the positions of ministers of defense, interior, and finance.***

---

* See Afghanistan constitution 2004, Art. LXII.
** See Afghanistan constitution 2004, Art. LXXII.
*** Adeney, K. 2008. "Constitutional Design and the Political Salience of 'Community' Identity in Afghanistan: Prospects of the Emergence of Ethnic Conflicts in the Post-Taliban Era." *Asian Survey* 48 (4): 535–557.

Figure 5.1 Implementation coding example for the executive domain in Afghanistan.

secondary accounts by country experts. We make this original dataset and the supporting coding materials available online (as discussed in the preface), and we include the codings for Burundi, Rwanda, and Ethiopia in the relevant case study chapters.

Using the implementation dataset, we examine the extent to which recognition in constitutional moments translates into policies and practices on the ground. Table 5.1 displays the results. The two columns at the top labeled "No recognition" and "Recognition" distinguish whether the conflict-affected countries in our dataset were under a recognition regime by 2012, as per our coding of constitutions and comprehensive settlements. By 2012, twenty-eight of the countries in our dataset were under non-recognition regimes, and twenty-nine were under recognition regimes. Then we present information on seven domains, listed under the "Domain" column. In the "Implementation" column, we list whether governments had actually enacted recognition policies in the given domain in the period between the most recent constitutional moment and the time of coding implementation in 2017. Recall the coding definitions from

Table 5.1 **Likelihood of implementing ethnic recognition policies in seven government and public sector domains, for non-recognition and recognition regimes, in percent**

Domain	Implementation	Adoption of recognition as per constitution or political settlement		
		No recognition (N = 28)	Recognition (N = 29)	Overall (N = 57)
Executive	No	79%	34%	56%
	Partial	18%	28%	23%
	Yes	4%	38%	21%
Legislature and Parties	No	61%	24%	42%
	Partial	32%	17%	25%
	Yes	7%	59%	33%
Security	No	75%	41%	58%
	Partial	21%	17%	19%
	Yes	4%	41%	23%
Justice	No	75%	31%	53%
	Partial	14%	28%	21%
	Yes	11%	41%	26%
Civil Service	No	79%	34%	56%
	Partial	14%	24%	19%
	Yes	7%	41%	25%
Education	No	54%	10%	32%
	Partial	32%	28%	30%
	Yes	14%	62%	39%
Language	No	57%	17%	37%
	Partial	21%	14%	18%
	Yes	21%	69%	46%

Notes: The designation of non-recognition or recognition is based on codings of constitutions and comprehensive political settlements. N = 57 country cases.

the preceding discussion: "yes" means that recognition policies were on the books and genuinely in effect, "partial" means either that policies were on the books but not in effect or that informal but otherwise commonly understood ethnic recognition norms were in effect despite the absence of written legislation, and "no" means that no formal or informal recognition was in effect.

The general pattern is that recognition policies are implemented with higher incidence in recognition regimes. This means that what we are coding as recognition is typically capturing what Chapter 2 calls thick recognition. Let us walk through the results for the executive domain in detail. For the executive, we see that for the twenty-eight countries that have not adopted recognition at the constitutional level, 79 percent of them have "no" implementation, while 18 percent of them have "partial" implementation. In only 4 percent of these twenty-eight non-recognition countries is there a full "yes" for implementation. In the twenty-nine countries that have adopted ethnic recognition at the level of constitutions or political settlements, the rate of "yes" implementation in the executive is about ten times higher—that is, 38 percent. Finally, 28 percent of these recognition countries have "partial" implementation, and the remaining 34 percent have "no" implementation.

We also see interesting variation across domains. As the table shows, the domains of legislatures and parties, education, and language have the greatest consistency between adoption of recognition in constitutional moments and on-the-ground implementation. For legislatures and parties, for instance, countries that adopted ethnic recognition at the level of constitutions or political settlements earned full "yes" scores, with implementation 59 percent of the time. We can contrast this to the non-recognition countries, for which 61 percent have "no" ratings for implementation. Similarly, in the education and language domains, recognition policies are consistently implemented on the basis of whether a country is under a recognition regime: when a country adopts recognition, implementation is common, with 62 percent and 69 percent with "yes" for implementation in education and language, respectively. In the majority of non-recognition regimes, no such implementation is in effect. For the justice and civil service domains, it is rare for a country with no recognition in the constitution or political settlement to implement recognition policies. However, implementation of recognition policies is somewhat inconsistent for countries that do adopt recognition in constitutions or political settlements. The patterns here resemble those of the executive domain.

We hypothesize that education and language are two areas in which governments tend to grant recognition more readily because they offer important symbolic effects but constitute part of a longer-term process of redistribution. People often continue to consider education, in particular, as neutral or apolitical, despite its inherently political nature (King 2014). Adoption and implementation in these domains are much more common than ethnic recognition in the executive, security sector, justice sector, and civil service, perhaps due to their more immediate effect on the distribution of power between groups.

For readers who see the high-level measure upon which we concentrate in previous chapters and want to know what happens on the ground, these findings offer important clarification. Generally speaking, across all of the domains, the correlation between adoption of recognition and implementation is very high. This implies that ethnic recognition in constitutions and political settlements typically comes with more aggressive policies intended to affect the functioning of public institutions. That is, recognition tends often to be thick, involving concrete efforts to ensure access to power and resources for different ethnic groups. This is especially apparent in the domains of legislature and parties, education, and language.

Ethnic power configurations and implementation of recognition

Given the strong link between ethnic power configurations and the adoption of recognition, we would expect to see that minority-led regimes are less likely to implement recognition-based policies as well. This is assessed in Table 5.2. The patterns in this table offer a deeper look into the choices that minority versus plurality leaders make in avoiding or pursuing implementation in different policy domains. This can shed light on these leaders' strategic considerations, since recognition in different domains likely comes with different types of risks and opportunities.

Relative to what occurs under plurality rule, we see that under minority rule it is very rare to implement recognition policies in the high-stakes domains of the executive and security sectors. For each of these sectors, 72 percent of minority-led regimes have "no" implementation, whereas in plurality-led regimes, these figures are 44 percent and 47 percent for the executive and security domains, respectively. Interestingly, we also see strong avoidance of recognition policies in the civil service for minority-led regimes, a sector that allows for substantial allocation of patronage benefits. Such "no" implementation outcomes arise in only 41 percent of plurality-led regimes. Differences between plurality- and minority-led regimes are less pronounced in the other domains, which appear to have lower stakes in terms of their potential to affect fundamental power relations, at least in the short run. These patterns are consistent with the premise of our theory that decisions on recognition strategies are fundamentally political and therefore require that one consider implications for the political standing of the incumbent leadership.

Table 5.2 **Implementation of ethnic recognition policies in seven government and public sector domains for countries under plurality versus minority rule**

Domain	Implementation	Ethnic power configuration		
		Plurality-led (N = 32)	Minority-led (N = 25)	Total (column %)
Executive	No	44%	72%	56%
	Partial	28%	16%	23%
	Yes	28%	12%	21%
Legislative	No	38%	48%	42%
	Partial	22%	28%	25%
	Yes	41%	24%	33%
Security	No	47%	72%	58%
	Partial	25%	12%	19%
	Yes	28%	16%	23%
Justice	No	50%	56%	53%
	Partial	22%	20%	21%
	Yes	28%	24%	26%
Civil Service	No	41%	76%	56%
	Partial	28%	8%	19%
	Yes	31%	16%	25%
Education	No	25%	40%	32%
	Partial	28%	32%	30%
	Yes	47%	28%	39%
Language	No	31%	44%	37%
	Partial	16%	20%	18%
	Yes	53%	36%	46%

Note: N = 57 country cases.

Ethnic exclusion and inclusion after recognition

We now turn to the effects of recognition on ethnic inclusion and exclusion captured in a state's power structure, as measured in the Ethnic Power Relations dataset (Cederman et al. 2010). The expectation is that recognition-based regimes would tend to exhibit lower levels of ethnic exclusion. Cederman,

Wimmer, and Min (2010) measure the level of ethnic exclusion in a given country and year by taking the total population share of ethnic groups that country-specific experts deem to be excluded from power. Figure 5.2 displays trends for countries that adopted recognition (shown as a solid line) and those that did not (shown as a dashed line). Countries that went on to adopt recognition tended to start at higher levels of ethnic exclusion prior to the agreement on a new constitution or comprehensive settlement. The trend was decreasing prior to such agreement. These two aspects of the trend line suggest that recognition tends to be adopted in places where, historically, exclusion was a somewhat bigger problem, but that the actual processes of negotiating recognition involved steps toward inclusion. For cases that went on to institute non-recognition, the trend prior to agreeing on a new constitution or comprehensive settlement is flat, and we see an increase in average levels of exclusion after the agreements. The result is a substantial gap—on the order of 30 percentage points—in the population share of excluded groups in non-recognition regimes as compared to recognition regimes. This large difference implies that our operationalization of recognition captures important institutional variation. That is, recognition as we define it leads to what experts judge as concrete ethnic inclusion in a state's power structure.

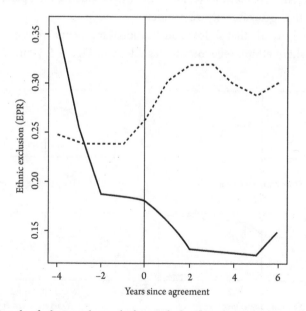

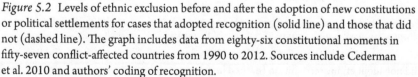

Figure 5.2 Levels of ethnic exclusion before and after the adoption of new constitutions or political settlements for cases that adopted recognition (solid line) and those that did not (dashed line). The graph includes data from eighty-six constitutional moments in fifty-seven conflict-affected countries from 1990 to 2012. Sources include Cederman et al. 2010 and authors' coding of recognition.

Average effects on peace

Having established that the adoption of recognition is associated with on-the-ground implementation as well as increased political inclusion, we now turn to estimating the effect of recognition on peace. We examine both negative peace, measured in terms of levels of political violence, and positive peace, measured in terms of economic vitality and democratic governance. The political violence data are from the Uppsala Conflict Data Program. The measures that we use include the number of conflict-related fatalities in a given year (which we work with on the logarithmic scale, to address the strong skew in the variable) and a binary indicator of conflict-related violence, which indicates whether or not there were at least twenty-five conflict-related fatalities in a given year. We measure economic vitality in terms of the gross domestic product per capita, measured in purchasing power parity terms, as reported by the UN Statistics Division. The democratic governance outcome measure is from the Varieties of Democracy (VDEM) project (Coppedge et al. 2017). We use their summary "polyarchy" index, which aggregates various features of democratic competition, rule of law, and freedom of expression. We conducted analyses using the component measures from the VDEM project, such as indices measuring civil liberty or freedom to contest elections, and each yielded similar patterns to what we find for the aggregate polyarchy index.

In general, trends that follow constitutional moments are more positive in the cases where ethnic recognition was adopted. Figure 5.3 offers a first-pass

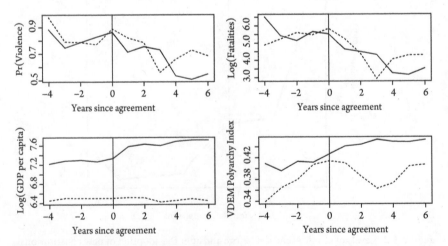

Figure 5.3 Pre-agreement and post-agreement trends in the probability of violence, conflict-related fatalities, GDP per capita, and VDEM polyarchy index for countries that were affected by ethnic conflict and that either adopted ethnic recognition (solid lines) or did not adopt ethnic recognition (dashed lines).

assessment of such trends. As one might expect, patterns turn out to be more pronounced for ethnic conflict cases than for the full set of conflicted-affected countries, and it is for this reason that we focus our attention on them. Figure 5.3 thus displays average levels of violence, gross domestic product (GDP) per capita, and polyarchy index scores in years prior to and following the agreements or constitutions in cases commonly deemed ethnic conflicts.

With respect to violence, both the binary violence indicator and the measure of fatalities per year (displayed on the log scale to attend to the skew in their distribution) show similar trends. Lower values signify improvements with respect to peace. In early years post-agreement, both recognition and non-recognition regimes perform similarly, with drops in the level of violence. However, as the years pass, we see a trend after about three or four years toward increases in violence in non-recognition regimes. Such trends are not apparent in recognition regimes.

For economic vitality, GDP per capita in recognition versus non-recognition regimes differs markedly, even prior to political settlements or constitutions being promulgated. Countries adopting recognition tend to be richer than those that do not by about USD 700 per capita (note that the graph in Figure 5.3 is on the logarithmic scale). Regardless of starting point, in the period following the constitutional moments, countries with recognition tend to register a slight uptick, reflective of somewhat stronger growth. We see no such uptick in non-recognition regimes.

A similar pattern holds for our measure of democratic vitality as measured by the VDEM polyarchy index. In the years just prior to an agreement, trends are roughly similar and upward-trending in countries both with and without recognition. But in countries without recognition, the trend reverses sharply, while it remains positive for countries with recognition.

While these trends are suggestive, they omit consideration of an important factor: the ethnic power configuration. Both our theoretical framework and the empirical analysis in the previous section point to minority versus plurality ethnic rule as an important structural condition for understanding dynamics associated with recognition. This is true both for the adoption of recognition, as demonstrated in Chapter 4, and for its potential effects on peace. We turn now to a more refined analysis that takes this moderating factor into account.

The effects of recognition under minority and plurality rule

To test our theory of recognition rooted in ethnic power configurations, we analyze results separately for the two types of political systems. Our theory-informed expectation is that recognition should be effective in promoting peace under the rule of plurality groups, but potentially destabilizing under minority rule.

Moreover, the trends in Figure 5.3 are imprecise in that they do not adjust for potential confounding variables in estimating the effects of recognition versus non-recognition. It may be that the trends are merely picking up on heterogeneity across regions or countries that are also correlated with the likelihood of adopting recognition. For example, violence trends may depend on pre-war levels of democracy, and this could also affect whether recognition is adopted.

To produce more robust estimates, we employ a "difference-in-differences" regression approach (Angrist and Pischke 2009). To estimate the effect of adopting recognition during a constitutional moment, this approach effectively starts by computing the differences between measures of peace before the constitutional moments versus after the constitutional moments for each country. It then compares the before-after differences for countries that adopted recognition to the before-after differences for countries that did not.

To implement this difference-in-differences approach, we use panel data on conflict-affected countries from 1990 to 2012. This extends our dataset beyond the 57 countries we have considered up until now to also include conflict-affected countries that had no constitutional changes or political settlements during this period. A country enters the dataset when it becomes conflict-affected: when the annual number of conflict-related fatalities reaches at least twenty-five, per Uppsala Conflict Data Program estimates. For example, while Afghanistan appears in the data for all thirteen years, Bahrain enters the data in 2011. We regress our outcomes of interest on an indicator variable that takes the value of 1 if a political settlement was reached and enacted, and 0 otherwise. We use a similar indicator variable for whether the settlement incorporated ethnic recognition, and additional indicator variables for the year and country. In econometrics, this is known as a two-way (year- and country-level) fixed effects model. The political settlement indicator variable accounts for the effect of simply reaching an agreement. This allows us to isolate the effect of recognition above and beyond what is achieved by virtue of coming to an agreement. One could think of this as isolating the "added value" of recognition to a political settlement. The country indicator variables allow us to control for differences between countries that might confound a simple cross-sectional analysis. The year indicator variables allow us to account for trends and time shocks that might confound a simple before-after analysis.

The difference-in-differences analysis assumes that the average yearly trend in countries where recognition was *not* adopted provides an unbiased counterfactual for what would have been the average no-recognition trend in countries where recognition *was* adopted. We have already seen from the basic analysis of trends in Figure 5.3 that pre-agreement trends sometimes line up well across countries that ultimately did or did not adopt recognition. This is the case with the violence measures, GDP per capita, and VDEM scores just prior to the agreements. We can use the nature of these trends to speculate about the potential for bias from the difference-in-differences estimates. For the VDEM polyarchy measure, we are likely underestimating the positive gains from recognition, given that pre-trends for cases that adopt recognition are flatter than the more upward-sloping pre-trends for cases that do not adopt recognition. These qualifications are part of the reason we use case studies later in the book.

Nonetheless, taking advantage of the data that we have at our disposal, Figures 5.4 and 5.5 illustrate the results from the difference-in-differences analysis for negative and positive peace outcomes. Tables presenting the results of this statistical analysis are presented in the Appendix. We focus on these figures because they offer a clearer interpretation of the results. The figures plot trends that we estimated for regimes that were under minority and plurality rule at the time that a constitution or comprehensive settlement was agreed. (The estimated trends use a second-order polynomial specification and are meant to estimate how average trajectories would look in the absence of recognition.) On the *x*-axis, we trace out five years prior and five years following such agreement. For the five years prior to agreement (marked as –5 to 0 on the graph), the

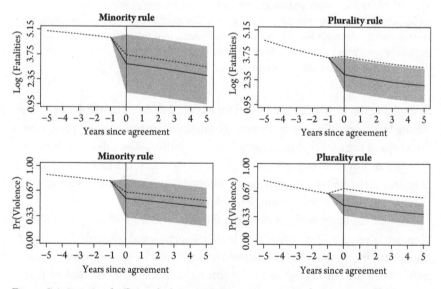

Figure 5.4 Estimated effects of ethnic recognition on violence (negative peace) in countries affected by ethnic conflict and depending on whether the regime is led by a member of a minority or plurality ethnic group. The dashed lines are estimated trend lines (using a second-order polynomial) for a typical country that does not adopt recognition. The solid line shows how recognition is estimated to affect this trend based on the difference-in-differences regression that includes country and year fixed effects. The gray area is the 95 percent confidence interval for this estimate of the effect of recognition on the trend.

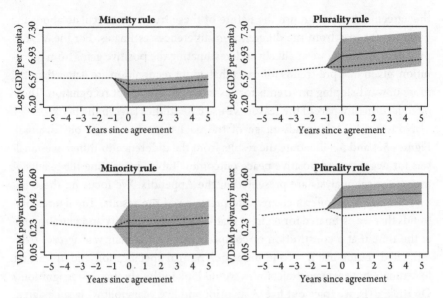

Figure 5.5 Estimated effects of ethnic recognition on GDP per capita and the VDEM polyarchy index (positive peace) in countries affected by ethnic conflict and depending on whether the regime is led by a member of a minority or plurality ethnic group. The dashed lines are estimated trend lines (using a second-order polynomial) for a typical country that does not adopt recognition. The solid line shows how recognition is estimated to affect this trend based on the difference-in-differences regression that includes country and year fixed effects. The gray area is the 95 percent confidence interval for this estimate of the effect of recognition on the trend.

dashed line traces an estimated trend for a typical country in our dataset. Then, for the five years following agreement, the dashed line traces an estimated trend for a typical country that does not adopt recognition. The solid line shows our estimate of how this trend would differ if recognition had been adopted. The gray area is the 95 percent confidence interval for this estimate of the effect of recognition on the post-agreement trend.

We find similar results for both the fatality measure and the probability of violence. Pre-agreement trends in both minority- and plurality-led regimes are downward-sloping. In minority-led regimes, reaching an agreement results in a downward kink in violence (evident from the kink in the dashed line at zero). However, recognition does not affect this trend in a substantial or statistically significant way. In plurality-led regimes, the story is different. The typical plurality-led regime experiences a slight uptick in violence when a non-recognition-based agreement is struck. However, recognition changes things dramatically, reducing levels of violence in a manner that is both substantial and statistically significant. Moreover, in both cases, the difference in the estimated effects across minority- and plurality-led regimes is itself statistically significant.

As for positive peace, we find mixed results. For economic vitality, we do not estimate statistically significant estimates for the effect of recognition in either minority- or plurality-led regimes. Nonetheless, focusing just on the points estimates (the solid trend lines, as compared to the dashed ones), we have suggestive evidence of a negative effect of recognition in minority-led regimes but a positive one in plurality-led regimes. For democratic vitality, as measured by the VDEM polyarchy index, the results are more clearly in favor of recognition for plurality-led regimes. We find that recognition has a substantial and statistically significant positive effect on democracy trends in plurality-led regimes, but not so in minority-led regimes. Again, this difference across minority- and plurality-led regimes is itself statistically significant.

To summarize, on average, recognition is associated with more progress toward negative and positive peace. Such progress is driven by recognition's positive effects in plurality-led regimes. In minority-led regimes, we have no indication that recognition tends to contribute to negative or positive peace, nor to clearly worse outcomes.

Conclusion

The cross-national quantitative analysis in this chapter offers general insight into the effects of recognition on peace, a pressing question for scholars and policymakers. We find that in countries marked by ethnic violence, recognition-based constitutional moments lead to the implementation of meaningful recognition-based policies in various domains. The implementation of such policies has a strategic logic: minority-led regimes are less likely than plurality-led regimes to adopt recognition and also less likely to implement recognition-based policies in the high-stakes executive, security, and civil service domains, as compared to domains such as the legislature, education policies, and language policies. We also find that recognition is followed by substantially lower levels of ethnic exclusion in state power structures, as measured by expert assessments. Finally, recognition precedes lower levels of political violence, higher economic vitality, and more democratic governance. After accounting for temporal and country-level sources of confounding, we find that the positive effects of recognition are driven by the experience of plurality led-regimes, as anticipated by our theory. For minority-led regimes, we find no clear indication that recognition tends, on average, to make things better or worse.

Our statistical analysis works at the macro level to assess the logic of our theory. It identifies the causal effect of recognition under certain assumptions— namely, that trends in countries that do not adopt recognition provide an unbiased counterfactual for what would have happened in countries that did adopt recognition. We now turn to Part III of the book, our case studies, which allow us to assess whether our theory provides a reasonable interpretation of more detailed accounts of the adoption or non-adoption of recognition and its effects on peace.

PART III

QUALITATIVE CASE STUDIES

Here in Part III, we build further on our global cross-national analysis to delve deeper into the experiences of three countries: Burundi, Rwanda, and Ethiopia. We dedicate a chapter to each in order to illuminate the processes by which political outcomes are realized.

As we discuss in Chapter 1, we selected Burundi and Rwanda as an excellent controlled set of comparisons. These two countries share many likenesses in structural conditions and histories of conflict. Yet each embraced a different recognition strategy—and, furthermore, each changed its recognition strategy over time—in a manner that conforms to our theoretical expectations on adoption. Historically, both recognition and non-recognition preceded large-scale violence, and the questions this prompted for us, given our on-the-ground work in the region, were an important part of the genesis of this book. We also include the case of Ethiopia, which diverges from our theoretical expectations, at least in terms of adoption. Until 2018, Ethiopia was always led by a minority regime, yet post-conflict leaders embraced recognition-based ethnic federalism starting in 1991. This case further allows us to examine the effects of recognition when adopted by a minority regime.

Our case selection also assists us in limiting the extent to which some of the other explanations for the adoption of recognition, which we reviewed in Chapter 2 and tested in Chapter 4, might confound our interpretation. In considering conditions internal to the leaders' domestic political system, for example, we see important variations that limit the relevance of arguments that authoritarians with consolidated authority avoid recognition. The cases of Burundi and Ethiopia show that even authoritarian leaders had to attend to opposition grievances and negotiation. In Rwanda we see different, equally authoritarian leaders adopting recognition and non-recognition before and after the genocide, respectively.

In considering factors external to the domestic political system, the general norm in post-colonial sub-Saharan Africa has been the avoidance of ethnic recognition. This fact was apparent when we considered rates of adoption in Africa as compared to other regions. Nonetheless, Rwanda broke with regional norms with its recognition regime, which lasted from independence in 1962 until the 1990–93 civil war; Burundi strayed from the norm with its recognition regime, beginning with the constitution of 2005; and Ethiopia adopted an ethnic federal regime beginning in the early 1990s. To the extent that a norm of non-recognition in Africa has been a constant, it also does not explain variation over time in each of our three cases.

The impact of colonialism on recognition decision-making is also limited by our case selection. Rwanda and Burundi both experienced the same Belgian colonial influence and yet adopted different strategies post-independence. Ethiopia was not colonized.

Finally, the more recent influence of international actors, who might promote recognition, has also varied in ways that limit the explanatory power of this factor. Both post-war Burundi and Ethiopia adopted recognition, but only Burundi experienced important international involvement in negotiations, and even there we assess the process as largely a product of domestic factors. Moreover, the military victories in Ethiopia and Rwanda granted leaders significant autonomy in decision-making, and each adopted a different approach to ethnic recognition. Overall, such internal and external factors are surely relevant to some degree, as we explore in the earlier parts of this book, but our case selection goes a good way toward controlling for their influence.

We thought carefully about the types of evidence we would need to support, extend, or negate our theory. In each of the next three chapters, we follow a similar investigation and chapter structure. If our theoretical explanation is valid, we should first find evidence of the relevant contextual conditions for the theory that we lay out in Chapter 2: a credible regime leader, a basis of ethnic rivalry and mistrust, and the potential for remobilization. We then trace if and how the mechanisms of our theory capture the on-the-ground dynamics of the questions of the adoption of ethnic recognition and the effects on peace.

On the question of adoption, our theory is agent-centered, insofar as it focuses on leaders' choices. The most compelling evidence would thus reflect leaders' thinking (Lieberman 2005). To assess whether leaders are reacting to interethnic mistrust, we draw upon the histories of the violent conflicts in question as well as analyses of fears and concerns among leaders' constituencies. To assess the interests and decisiveness of leaders, we examine the political landscape and behaviors of leaders during the periods that lead up to the adoption or non-adoption of recognition. To assess whether incumbent and opposition ethnic group leaders were cognizant of the potential assuring effects of recognition and to assess whether leaders were sensitive to mobilization effects, we look to actions, statements, and writing from leaders and others close to the institutional and peace-building processes, and to expert analyses. We acknowledge the perpetual problem of inadequate information in regard to what leaders are thinking and the accuracy of their perceptions (Jervis 1976). We try to overcome this problem through triangulation of multiple sources and the selection of cases with sufficiently elapsed time since the recognition and non-recognition decisions to have produced robust secondary literature. If our interpretation of the cross-national results is faulty, we would expect the case studies to diverge from these patterns and, moreover, that we would find other, more convincing, explanations (Van Evera 1997).

On questions of effects, we review evidence of subnational distribution of positions across multiple domains such as the civil service and security sector. We also assess qualitative perceptions and secondary analyses of the successes and limitations of recognition and non-recognition strategies. We further draw on primary fieldwork that King conducted in Rwanda and that Samii conducted in Burundi between 2006 and 2009.

While the three cases we selected for qualitative inquiry are all in sub-Saharan Africa, ours is not just a story about Africa. We draw on insights from Burundi, Rwanda, and Ethiopia not only to help us learn about these countries but also to inform our understanding in ways that could be relevant in other places that have similar structural circumstances, of which we think there are many. In the conclusion, Chapter 9, we consider a broader set of challenges of diversity, violence, and recognition facing the world today.

6

Recognition Under Plurality Rule and the Paradox of Recognition in Burundi

This book opened with incumbent Burundian president Pierre Nkurunziza's triumphant reflection on the course that his country had taken since the onset of civil war in 1993, proposing that "before there was exclusion . . . but today, all Burundians are together in the army, police, administration, education, everywhere." Bonaventure Niyoyankana, a Tutsi leader in the *Union pour le Progrès National* (UPRONA), offers additional details about the strategic logic of Burundi's current constitution, adopted in 2005 and based on peace accords negotiated in Arusha in 2000. Niyoyankana notes:

> We had a politico-ethnic problem, where the minority ethnicity occupied the most important place, especially in the armed forces and police. So we had to give power to the majority via democracy. . . . We also had artificially to ensure that the armed forces were half and half, to calm the minority. And we had to give the minority the chance to participate in politics. . . . So no one is scared of the others. Because if Hutus won everything, Tutsis would be scared. That was the spirit of Arusha. And it is working. (Mthembu-Salter 2016, 72)

This chapter recounts the history that led to the adoption of Burundi's recognition-based regime and analyzes political dynamics through the lens of our theory. This story is a remarkable case for scholars of conflict management. What was agreed through the 2000 Arusha Accords and 2005 constitution went far beyond a factional division of spoils. Rather, it represented an attempt by political elites at societal transformation in the context of extreme ethnic polarization and violence.

Diversity, Violence, and Recognition. Elisabeth King and Cyrus Samii, Oxford University Press (2020). © Oxford University Press.
DOI: 10.1093/oso/9780197509456.003.0001

On the question of adoption versus non-adoption of recognition, Burundi's recent history largely corresponds to the expectations of our theory. With respect to the question of institutional choice, the 1992 constitution adopted under minority Tutsi ethnic rule did not include ethnic recognition, while the 2005 constitution adopted under the rule of a leader from the majority Hutu ethnic group did include recognition. Throughout the chapter, we argue that our theory helps explain why each of these leaderships chose these respective approaches to recognition. However, the 2000 comprehensive Arusha Accords were adopted under minority Tutsi rule and include recognition, which runs counter to our basic expectations. We argue that our theory remains useful and that the circumstances, including an ascendant Hutu majority, draw attention to the importance of thinking in terms of power transitions and expectations about who will be ruling, rather than in terms of who is the head of state at a given moment in time.

With respect to the question of effects, we find that outcomes are generally consistent with our proposition that recognition can operate smoothly in conditions of plurality group rule. The case study also demonstrates the problems that can arise when institutional choices are misaligned (according to our theory) with the ethnic power configuration. Based on these results, we elaborate our theory to incorporate insights into what we call "institutional mismatch" and the "paradox of recognition." The adoption of the 1992 non-recognition constitution set off a democratizing process that resulted in the 1993 electoral victory of a majority-Hutu dominant party. In this respect, the 1992 constitution failed to promote the political survival of the incumbent Tutsi-dominated leadership. By the logic of our theory, this was an institutional mismatch in which a majority Hutu-dominated leadership took power in a constitutional system that offered no group-specific guarantees to members of the Tutsi minority. A spiral of mistrust following these elections led to the outbreak of civil war in 1993. The 2000 accords and 2005 agreement helped to reduce violence and bring about a period of positive peace and democratic flourishing, although that period itself was followed by a slide toward more authoritarian rule under the country's Hutu-dominated leadership. We also argue that, despite that slide toward authoritarianism, political lines of contestation no longer cleanly coincide with ethnic lines, indicative of a "depoliticization" of ethnicity (Raffoul 2018). Such depoliticization reflects what we call the paradox of recognition. The paradox refers to ways that the political salience of ethnicity may be reduced with recognition, contrary to conflict management literature predictions about entrenching ethnic identities. The paradox also highlights how recognition is compatible with constructivist theories of ethnicity.

This chapter follows a structure that, first, provides context on Burundi and the conflict. It then tracks ethnic power configurations and recognition over time through two constitutional moments since 1990. The first constitutional moment is the period surrounding the adoption of the 1992 constitution. The second is the period surrounding the 2000 Arusha Accords and the 2005 constitution, which we consider together, given that they were part of a common negotiation process. For both of these constitutional moments, we first assess leaders' choices in adopting or not adopting ethnic recognition and relate them to our theory. Then, for each period, we examine consequences of these institutional choices for negative and positive peace. The chapter concludes by examining prospects for peace under Burundi's recognition regime.

Context and nature of the conflict

Like neighboring Rwanda, the focus of Chapter 7, Burundi is a country with a land size of about 26,000 square kilometers, comparable to the size of Haiti or Macedonia, with one of the highest population densities in sub-Saharan Africa (with a population of approximately 10 million in 2017). Burundi gained independence in 1962, and since then it has consistently ranked toward the bottom of indices of human development in terms of income per capita, health metrics, and educational attainment. However, these indices mask features that distinguish Burundi, like Rwanda, from many other low-income countries. This includes a long history of early state consolidation under a kingdom that ruled over the territory prior to becoming part of a joint European colony with Rwanda, first as part of German East Africa and then under half a century of Belgian colonial rule. In this sense, the borders of Burundi and Rwanda are less arbitrary than many of those crafted in the "scramble for Africa." It also includes intensive post-independence investments in infrastructure in the 1970s and 1980s. Indeed, Burundi and Rwanda enjoy a degree of institutional and infrastructural consolidation that distinguishes them from their neighbors; to travel across the border from Burundi or Rwanda to the Democratic Republic of the Congo is to experience a dramatic change in institutional conditions. This point is important to note, because it helps us to understand the stakes associated with control over public institutions in these countries.

The Hutu-Tutsi issue is a defining feature of politics in the Great Lakes region of Africa, and Burundi's own—at times tragic—history has contributed significantly to the narrative. Those less familiar with the history of the region have a tendency to draw on notions of "tribe," as applied elsewhere in sub-Saharan Africa, to describe these two largest groups in Burundi and Rwanda. Notwithstanding the historical debate around the possibly extraregional origins of the Tutsi lineage going back many centuries (Chrétien 2003), such notions fail to capture the essence of the ethnic distinction that exists despite the absence of linguistic or regional differentiation between those who are associated with the two identities. In origin, the Hutu-Tutsi cleavage more closely resembles a caste cleavage rather than a tribal one. Conventionally, the identities connote descent from lineages in an occupational stratification of the pre-colonial social and political system—loosely, a system of herder Tutsi patrons and land-working Hutu clients operating under the authority of a small royal caste. Even this stratification is rife with exceptions in terms of occupation, status, and inter-marriage (Chrétien 2003; Lemarchand 1970). Despite the origins, and the fact that the meaning of the terms "Hutu" and "Tutsi" have changed over time, Hutu and Tutsi identities have taken on important political significance, constituting a key cleavage since before colonization and intensifying with the arrival of colonial rule.

Ethnic demographics have long been an important political factor. A census of dubious methodological quality in 1933–34, during the period of Belgian colonial rule, established the commonly referenced demographic breakdown of 14 percent Tutsis, 85 percent Hutus, and 1 percent Twas (the smallest and most marginalized ethnic group) in Burundi and Rwanda, at the time a joint colony. Through decades of conflict, displacement, and differential birth patterns, the true population shares may differ somewhat from these figures (Ngaruko and Nkurunziza 2000). Nonetheless, this demographic breakdown continues to serve as the basis for common understanding. In their engagement with the population and their personnel decisions, colonial authorities in Burundi and Rwanda subscribed to the view of an elite Tutsi stratum and Hutu commoners. In Rwanda, this was applied with an arguably higher level of intensity, contributing to dynamics that led to the social revolution of Hutus in Rwanda, which sent hundreds of thousands of Tutsis into exile as the country was freed of its colonial yoke in 1962 (Mamdani 2001; Newbury 1988). Keen on maintaining their minority group's hold on power, the example of the Hutu-led revolution next door inspired the Tutsi elite in Burundi to take preemptive action over the ensuing decades to prevent something similar from happening at home. At independence and subsequently, Burundian society, economy, and politics were defined by what Horowitz (1991) describes as a "ranked ethnic system" of a minority Tutsi-dominated elite and a largely excluded Hutu majority.

A cycle of intense interethnic violence following independence has generated legacies that continue to sustain the salience of Hutu and Tutsi identities and interethnic mistrust. The decade following independence in 1962 featured violent jockeying for power among Hutu and Tutsi leaders. This culminated in 1966, when Michel Micombero took control of the UPRONA party, led a series of coups d'état that deposed the monarchy, and forcefully concentrated political authority into the hands of a clique of Tutsi military officers from Bururi province in the south of the country. The result was nearly three decades of single-party UPRONA rule led by this minority Tutsi military clique.

The events of 1972 were crucial in intensifying interethnic mistrust and constitute what experts characterize as the first genocidal violence in the region (Chrétien and Dupaquier 2007; Lemarchand 1996, 2009). An insurrection of Hutu soldiers in the south led to a broader Hutu uprising that involved a massacre of Tutsis by Hutus, with the suspected complicity of Hutu officers (Lemarchand 1996, 91–93). The Tutsi-dominated military regime, led by Micombero, responded with a brutal crackdown on the Hutu population. Described by scholar René Lemarchand (2009), who specializes in ethnic conflict in Burundi and Rwanda, as a "selective genocide," the Micombero regime sought to "decapitate" the Hutu population by targeting Hutus who exhibited any potential to take positions of leadership—elites, teachers, students, clerks, and even those who merely wore glasses. The military regime killed an estimated 100,000 to 300,000 Hutus, with scores more fleeing to neighboring countries (Chrétien and Dupaquier 2007). As former US Ambassador Howard Wolpe states, the events of 1972 "transformed the elite driven conflict between the dominant Tutsi and the excluded Hutu into a mass phenomenon" (2011, 8).

The 1972 violence brought about fifteen years of further consolidation of power into the hands of the southern Tutsi clique, extreme barriers to social mobility for Hutus, and, through the forceful dominance of a single-party military regime, relative calm in the country. Micombero was ousted in a 1976 coup by Jean-Baptiste Bagaza, a Tutsi from the south, who had been a military logistics officer during the 1972 crackdown. Bagaza presided over a period of investment in national infrastructure and some modest attempts at interethnic reconciliation, but he generally kept in place the UPRONA-dominated regime that relegated Hutus to second-class status. Political calm began to unravel by the late 1980s, and Pierre Buyoya, a member of the same clique of southern Tutsi officers as Micombero, took power from Bagaza in a coup in 1987.

By the late 1980s, Hutu agitation at their suppression increased. In the north of the country, land disputes were managed by the government in a biased manner against Hutus. This led to a 1988 Hutu uprising and another brutal repression by the Tutsi-dominated army and police. Militant mobilization among Burundian Hutu refugees in Tanzania and Rwanda (where the majority Hutu held power) had begun earlier in the 1980s and was becoming more visible. The Burundian Hutu intellectual class, with leading members operating from exile, became more vocal in demanding rights. This internal ferment occurred alongside pressure from European powers, first in condemnation of the 1988 crackdown, then as part of more general pressure for countries of sub-Saharan Africa to liberalize (Manirakiza 2002; Lemarchand 1996).

Through a constitutional moment we describe later in this chapter, the first competitive multiparty presidential elections in Burundi's history took place in 1993, and they are generally regarded as having been free and fair (Reyntjens 1993). As a reflection of both demographic and historical realities, Melchior Ndadaye, leader of the overwhelmingly Hutu party Front pour la Démocratie au Burundi (FRODEBU), was elected president, defeating Buyoya in a landslide, 65 percent to 32 percent. FRODEBU also took a supermajority of legislative seats. Ndadaye's election represented a stark break in Burundi's political leadership. Ndadaye was Hutu, civilian, and from the center-north of the country. The electoral result was indicative of the "ethnic census" character of elections in settings affected by ethnic conflict—and of the degree of polarization that had built up after years of exclusionary rule (Reyntjens 1993). The results of these elections represent the beginning of a gradual transition in the ethnic power configuration from long-standing minority Tutsi rule to the consolidation of rule by a party dominated by majority Hutus.

This democratic experiment, with its peaceful transfer of power from Tutsi to Hutu hands, would come to a tragic conclusion in less than five months. In a bungled coup attempt in October 1993, Ndadaye was assassinated by a renegade faction within the Tutsi-dominated military. The shock wave after the announcement of Ndadaye's death triggered mass upheaval across the country, resulting in the death of some 30,000 to 100,000 civilians, including massacres of Tutsis by angered and politically stirred Hutus, brutal reprisal killings of Hutus by the Tutsi-dominated army, and, again, a massive outflow of refugees. Ndadaye's successor as president, Cyprien Ntaryamira, another Hutu member of FRODEBU, was himself killed along with Rwandan president Juvénal Habyarimana in the historic April 6, 1994, airplane crash that preceded the beginning of the Rwandan genocide. The 1993 assassination and subsequent violence in Burundi is understood by experts as a precursor event to the Rwandan genocide. Hutus would ask whether Tutsis could ever accept "Hutu liberation"; Tutsis would ask whether Hutu leadership would inevitably imply Tutsi subjugation as a despised minority. Political dynamics in the two countries have long been, and continue to be, highly interconnected.

These events in 1993 also marked the beginning of the Burundian civil war. After Ntaryamira's death, another Hutu FRODEBU leader and former foreign minister, Sylvestre Ntibantunganya, took office. His tenure was almost immediately subject to attempts to undermine his authority by members of the Tutsi-dominated military, Tutsi elites, and the Buyoya-led UPRONA faction. In response to Ndadaye's assassination, a militant insurgent faction of FRODEBU members organized themselves in 1994 under the banner of the Conseil national pour la défense de la démocratie (CNDD) and its military wing, the Forces pour la défense de la démocratie (FDD). The CNDD and FDD conducted an insurgency with the stated goal of winning power so as to restore the 1992 constitution and assure Hutu leaders renewed access to power.

Fallout from the war and genocide in Rwanda, insurgent violence, and factional politics in Burundi's capital culminated in a 1996 "soft coup," displacing Ntibantunganya from office. Buyoya used the coup to reclaim the presidency with the Tutsi-dominated military's backing. The main axis of fighting was between the majority Hutu-led CNDD-FDD and the Tutsi Buyoya-led regime. Other militant factions also escalated their fight against the government—most notably the Front pour la libération nationale (FROLINA) and Forces Nationales de Libération (FNL), which was the armed wing of the Parti pour la Libération du Peuple Hutu (PALIPEHUTU), a radical Hutu faction. Indeed, the very name of the party, Liberation of Hutu People, reflects the salience of ethnicity as an axis of contention, as well as the sense of mistrust and inequality that had built up along ethnic lines. Likewise, explicit in the CNDD-FDD's strategy was the defeat and dismantling of the so-called *armée monoethnique*, labeled as such because the officer corps was nearly exclusively southern Tutsi (Samii 2014). Most of the country was directly affected by the fighting, resulting in an estimated 300,000 deaths out of a total population of 6 million to 8 million (Gilligan et al. 2013). The war severely stalled development for over a decade, resulting in an estimated 20 percent decline in real GDP from 1993 to 2002 (World Bank 2004, 6).

A peace process—described in more detail later in this chapter—had begun in 1996, although it did not achieve any major breakthroughs until the Arusha Accords, signed by certain of the warring factions in 2000, followed by a global cease-fire signed in Pretoria in 2003. The Hutu-led CNDD-FDD forces were largely successful on the battlefield, although the national army, still comprising mostly Tutsi members, was not defeated outright. The rebel successes are nonetheless reflected in the agreements, as well as in the 2005 constitution that marked the onset of the post-war era. The provisions of these agreements and constitution reflect a near reversal in the country's ethnic distribution of power.

The civil war can be viewed as a three-phase transition in the ethnic power configuration. This transition started with the 1996 coup that restored dominance of the minority Tutsi faction led by Buyoya. The second phase was the period of political and military stalemate between the Tutsi-dominated regime and the Hutu-dominated CNDD-FDD. The third phase was the period of ascendancy for the Hutu-dominated CNDD-FDD after the 2003 global cease-fire. In de jure terms, Buyoya was head of state at the time of the 2000 Accords, and FRODEBU leader and Hutu politician Domitien Ndayizeye at the time of the 2005 constitution. However, de facto political authority over large segments of the population was contested and, in some places, under the consolidated authority of insurgent movements, with the CNDD-FDD strongest. Our cross-national statistical analysis characterized conditions of minority versus plurality group rule in terms of strict binaries. In reality, Burundian power configurations were more nuanced in trending from concentration in the hands of Tutsi leadership to Hutu leadership.

These decades of conflict have generated legacies that have sustained the salience of Hutu and Tutsi identities, broadly held "blood-feud resentments" (Harden 1988), and among politicians a zero-sum "politics of mistrust" (Cheeseman 2015). Many Burundians suffer enduring psychological effects caused by collective targeting on the basis of ethnicity (Samii 2013a). This includes enduring sorrow and anger among Hutus from the remembrance of those who were targeted and killed on the basis of their ethnic identity, fears among Tutsis who themselves were collectively targeted, as well as the guilt and anxiety from being either directly implicated in violence or having loved ones who were (Ingelaere 2009). The salience of ethnic rivalry and mistrust is also found in the legacy of material losses and resulting inequalities. These material legacies include a generation of lost opportunities for education or mobility among Hutus, an issue that featured in the mobilization of insurgency starting in 1993 (Samii and West 2019). Lands that were abandoned by Hutus fleeing as refugees in 1972 and allocated by the regime to Tutsi loyalists, and subsequently sold or rented again (Schwartz 2017), have prompted collective bitterness among the displaced as well as collective implication of those who benefited materially from the genocide, each defined in ethnic terms.

Recognition over time

Toward non-recognition in the 1992 constitution (1966–1992)

As discussed earlier in this chapter, the period between 1966 and 1993 was characterized by single-party (UPRONA) dictatorships. Throughout this period, regime leaders were drawn from a clique of southern Tutsi military officers, so the ethnic power configuration from 1966 to 1993 was minority Tutsi rule. Throughout the period as well, de jure institutions were based on non-recognition, despite de facto practices that institutionalized Tutsi privilege. The dual nature of the regime was apparent, for example, in the indirect systems of ethnic identification used to screen Hutus out from advancement into secondary and post-secondary education as well as extreme regional biases in the education system (Jackson 2000; Samii and West 2019). As Chapter 7 details, a similar dynamic prevails in Rwanda today.

The first constitutional moment we consider for Burundi involves the events surrounding the 1992 constitution, which, consistent with Burundi's post-independence history, avoided ethnic recognition. But the path toward a non-recognition regime was a sinuous one. By the late 1980s, it was clear to all, and most certainly to Buyoya, that there was a pervasive sense of mistrust among Hutus toward the Tutsi-dominated leadership. In 1988, a historic open letter from twenty-seven Hutu intellectuals to Buyoya pointedly called for Hutu exclusion to be addressed (Lemarchand 1996). Buyoya initiated reforms in 1988, including organizing a National Commission to Study the Question of National Unity. Buyoya took the ethnically conscious step of appointing twelve Hutus and twelve Tutsis to the commission. Other reforms included the appointment of a Hutu prime minister as well as allocation of other government posts in a manner that balanced Hutu and Tutsi representation. The commission report, released in 1989 and endorsed by Buyoya, discussed the Hutu-Tutsi issue in explicit terms, albeit in terms that obscured successive post-colonial governments' repression and policies of exclusion. Sections of the report appeared intent to minimize references to ethnic cleavages as they pertained to circumstances at the time, denying that ethnicity offered a reasonable way to view inequities in society or public institutions. For example, the Charter of National Unity, which was promulgated on the basis of the national unity commission report and adopted through referendum in 1991, declared, "The truth is that there is no discrimination within the army" (Lemarchand 1996, 139). With respect to ethnic recognition, there were important differences between the inclusive and ethnically based reform process and the institutionalized results of the reform that enshrined non-recognition (Vandeginste 2009). The explicit recognition of ethnic difference in the reform process brings into sharp relief the conscious avoidance of formal ethnic recognition in the 1992 constitution resulting from this reform process.

Our theoretical framework has us anticipate that Buyoya and his ruling coterie of Tutsi elites would avoid ethnic recognition in the constitution, and the 1992 constitution is consistent with this expectation. It advances, above all else, a superordinate national identity, expressed through the concept of "national unity." This concept had been developed in the Charter of National Unity. The 1992 constitution's preamble reaffirms "faith in the ideal of national unity," Article 42 declares that "every Burundian has a duty to preserve and strengthen national unity," political parties are to contribute to "a project of a democratic society based on national unity" (Article 54), the president is to "embody national unity" (Article 70), and nominations for parliamentary candidates are to reflect a "spirit of national unity" (Article 101). Articles 160–63 specify terms for a presidentially appointed Council of National Unity. Hutu and Tutsi identities are not referenced explicitly. In discussing composition of political parties and procedures for nominating candidates, only oblique reference is made to "taking into account the diversity of the Burundian population" (Vandeginste 2009).

This ubiquitous emphasis on "unity" is remarkably similar to what one sees in Rwanda today under the leadership of Paul Kagame, a minority Tutsi—a point we develop in Chapter 7.

Toward recognition in the 2000 Accords and 2005 constitution (1993–present)

The 1992 constitution stands in contrast to the recognition provisions that feature in the 2000 Arusha Accords and the 2005 constitution. The evolution toward a recognition regime followed the transition from minority to plurality ethnic rule, described earlier in this chapter as a gradual three-phase process. A 1998 interim constitution continued to avoid ethnic recognition, but the 2000 Arusha Accords introduced extensive quota-based ethnic recognition. The 2003 Global Ceasefire and Army Reform Agreement applied ethnic quotas for restructuring the armed forces, and ultimately the 2005 constitution further elaborated the ethnic quota formula of Arusha. It is in this gradual way that the Burundi case can be read as consistent with our theory: the transition from minority- to majority-ethnic dominance runs along with a transition from a non-recognition regime to a recognition regime. We see gradualism in the changes from recognition to non-recognition, or vice versa, in the case studies in Chapters 7 and 8 as well.

Turning to the terms of the different agreements in this process, the 1998 transitional constitution served merely to institutionalize minority Tutsi leader Buyoya's restored authority. As a conflict management document, the 1998 transitional constitution continued the 1992 constitution's emphasis on national unity and avoidance of explicit ethnic recognition. Such similarities between the 1992 and 1998 constitutions reflect the similarities in the ethnic power configuration in place at the promulgation of each: the incumbency of Buyoya as a leader from the minority Tutsi.

The 2000 Arusha Accords, by contrast, established a formal ethnic recognition regime, stipulating that the president must appoint two vice presidents, each from a different ethnic group; that ministers must be capped at a maximum of 60 percent Hutus and 40 percent Tutsis; that the membership of parliament must be 60 percent Hutus and 40 percent Tutsis; that the senate must include a representative of each ethnicity from each province; and that the passage of legislation requires a qualified majority that includes members of both ethnic groups (and different parties). Quotas are also applied in other domains of the public sector, including a 60–40 Hutu-Tutsi allocation over leadership positions for state-owned enterprises and, crucially, progressive recruitment and promotion to achieve 50–50 ethnic parity within the military. A transition process had Buyoya serve as transitional leader from 2001 to 2003, with power then transitioning to Hutu leader Ndayizeye, from FRODEBU.

The next major step in the peace process was the 2003 Global Ceasefire signed in Pretoria. This cease-fire served as a bridge between the 2000 Arusha Accords and the 2005 constitution. The key element of the 2003 accord was the Forces Technical Agreement, which spelled out the precise manner in which CNDD-FDD forces would be incorporated into a reformed military based on the principle of ethnic parity from the Arusha Accords (Samii 2014). These terms were institutionalized in the 2005 constitution.

The peace process culminated under Ndayizeye's tenure with the promulgation of the 2005 constitution, approved by referendum in February 2005. The 2005 constitution fully institutionalized the quota-based ethnic recognition regime defined by the Arusha Accords, combining quota-based ethnic recognition with factional power-sharing. It is important to note the distinction between recognition and power-sharing in Burundi, a conceptual distinction that we drew in Chapter 3. Consider the army, for example. Articles 255, 257, and 258 of the 2005 constitution call for ethnic-balancing based on Arusha principles. The 2003 Forces Technical Agreement had worked within this ethnic quota framework to establish a power-sharing formula for integrating the CNDD-FDD and other *Partis et mouvements politiques armés* (PMPA) into a new military, alongside the army old guard. Power-sharing agreements reference *factional* affiliation—that is, they are based on power considerations at the time of the agreement. In the context of the 2005 constitution, a common interpretation was that the ethnic quotas were implicit power-sharing arrangements. But this is not formally inscribed into the terms of the constitution, *except* in certain explicit cases. These explicit cases include, for example, Article 124, which requires that vice presidents be from different ethnicities *and* different parties, or Article 180(3), which guarantees former heads of state a senate seat for life. In other places, these explicit power-sharing conditions are absent, such as in the requirements for ethnic diversity in cabinet positions, meaning a minister could be from the same political party but a different ethnic group.

Table 6.1 shows that these constitutional provisions have led to implementation of recognition policies in nearly all government and public sector domains. In the executive domain, Burundi's constitution provides for a president elected by majority vote, and additional provisions in the constitution provide for two vice presidents, one from each ethnicity; this policy has been implemented consistently since 2005. Similarly, in the legislative domain, the parties and governments have complied with the requisite ethnic quotas for the assembly, government appointments, and senate. In the security sector, the government has tended to comply with the ethnic parity quota and maintained that the Minister for Police and the Minister for National Defense must differ in their ethnicity. In the judiciary, both the judicial corps and the Superior Council of Magistrates must be ethnically balanced; however, implementation in this sector

Table 6.1 **Implementation of ethnic recognition policies in seven government and public sector domains in Burundi**

Implementation following 2005 constitution	
Executive	Yes
Legislative	Yes
Security	Yes
Justice	Partial
Civil Service	Yes
Education	Partial
Language	N/A

Note: Ethnic groups speak the same language (Kirundi).

Source: Authors' implementation dataset, described in Chapter 5.

was apparently slower than in other sectors (Peace Accord Matrix 2017). In the civil service, the constitution stipulates that appointments take into account the need to maintain ethnic balance, and this was put into effect through government mandates. For example, a mandate was promulgated shortly after 2005 that required commune administrations to have no more than 67 percent of their members from one ethnic group (Vandeginste 2014). The education domain was not covered by the constitution and thus does not have the same de jure institutionalization of recognition as other domains. Nevertheless, policies within the education system have explicitly called for ensuring ethnic balance in access and admissions. Finally, Burundi has no recognition policies in the language domain because Kirundi is the common language of all Burundians, Hutus, Tutsis, and Twas alike.

The adoption question: assessing the theory

Leaders' interests and ethnic power configurations

We show that pivotal leaders were well aware of ethnic power configurations in choosing how to address ethnic identity at each of these constitutional moments. Our analysis of the 1992 constitutional moment focuses on the leadership role of Buyoya in the establishment of institutions to manage a vicious interethnic conflict. Buyoya faced the demands of Hutu elites who sought to remove the barriers they faced under Tutsi domination of the military and UPRONA's one-party state. In negotiating these demands, there is no doubt that all parties were keenly sensitive to ethnic demographics. Radical Hutu elites made references—sometimes vague, sometimes explicit—to the need for Hutu leaders to take total control of the country given the demographic predominance of Hutus. Tutsi elites called for sustained dominance of their ethnic group so as to defend against the threat of genocide given their minority position (e.g., Perlez 1988). Hutu elites tended to phrase their demands not so much in terms of recognition but rather in terms of "democracy" and an even playing field, presumably in appreciation of their demographic advantage. Adrien Sibomana, the Hutu prime minister appointed by Buyoya in 1988, proposed that "the problem in Burundi is a problem which in my opinion is linked with social justice, with fairness and democracy" (BBC 1989). Buyoya and other Tutsi leaders resisted such calls for democratic opening—for example, in rejecting multipartyism as posing a "risk [of] lapsing back" to the violent factionalism of the period just after independence (BBC 1990).

During the 2000 and 2005 constitutional moments, actions and statements by leaders on all sides also reflected sensitivity to ethnic demographics. For example, the CNDD-FDD's insistence that their primary interest was to restore the free electoral regime of the 1992 constitution was presumably because they knew their ethnic demographic advantage would translate into an electoral advantage. For Tutsi leaders engaged in the negotiations prior to the 2000 accords, mere reversion to the 1992 constitution was a non-starter for precisely the same reasons. Their reading of the 1993 elections was a revolutionary transfer of authority that robbed minority Tutsi elites of their access to power and resources. The violence that followed the election, the Rwandan genocide, and events during the insurgency made all too clear the potential for victimization of minority Tutsis.

The assuring effects

The actions of Buyoya, a minority Tutsi leader, also reveal an appreciation for the potential assuring effects of recognition, even if he ultimately avoided formal recognition in the constitution. The reform process between 1988 and 1992 involved explicit actions by Buyoya to increase Hutu representation in government posts and the reform commission. Such inclusiveness was in line with the 1988 open letter from Hutu intellectuals to Buyoya, which explicitly requested a "multiethnic national commission" (Lemarchand 1996, 133). These actions in themselves give strong indication of general awareness among both Tutsi and Hutu elites of the role that recognition *could* play in addressing sources of grievance and mistrust among Hutus.

Both minority Tutsi faction leaders and certain majority Hutu faction leaders demonstrated their appreciation of the assuring effects of recognition through the negotiations of the 2000 Arusha Accords and the 2005 constitution. It was during the negotiations in Arusha that the idea of special quotas to guarantee the security of the Tutsi minority population was first raised by Tutsi leaders. Initially, Hutu leaders were strongly opposed to this idea, seeing it as part of Buyoya's and other Tutsi elites' attempts to retain power non-democratically. What brought Hutu faction leaders around was ultimately an appreciation of the assuring effects of the quotas, which thereby offered a mechanism to manage an electoral transition away from Tutsi to Hutu leadership. Such an electoral transition was commonly taken to be inevitable given the continued political salience of ethnic identity and Hutu demographic superiority. The lessons from 1993 were clear: given the degree of ethnic polarization, a winner-take-all electoral transition would present an existential threat to the Tutsi minority, who still retained the military means to use violent repression to block political change. Hence the assessment quoted at the start of this chapter by Bonaventure Niyoyankana, the Tutsi UPRONA leader, was that quotas were crucial to ensure that "no one is scared of the others . . . [t]hat was the spirit of Arusha" (Mthembu-Salter 2016, 72).

Parties to the negotiations, and Tutsi faction leaders in particular, recognized that the political arrangement had to be rooted in explicit ethnic group assurances and that non-discrimination clauses would be insufficient. As South African lawyer Nicholas Haysom, who was part of the South African mediation team, indicated:

> [For] Tutsi parties, legal institutions did not have the strength to guarantee rights. They didn't think a bill of rights could stop a genocide. So checks and balances weren't going to work here. We needed explicit minority guarantees. (Mthembu-Salter 2016, 77)

On the basis of these explicit institutional guarantees, Nelson Mandela, who steered South Africa's mediation effort at Arusha, extracted a pledge from UPRONA leader Buyoya that he would not lead throughout the transition back to democracy (International Crisis Group 2000). For the Hutu leadership at Arusha, and in particular the FRODEBU heads Domitien Ndayizeye and Jean Minani, quotas could be viewed from a position of relative certainty that eventually a Hutu leadership would assume executive authority in the country, given the majority status of Hutus demographically.

While Hutu leaders eventually came to agreement that assuring the minority would be a worthwhile step forward, the quotas decided upon at Arusha and implemented in the 2005 constitution overrepresent Tutsis relative to their demographic share. Hutu faction leaders differed in their views about such overrepresentation. FRODEBU leaders Minani and Ndayizeye pushed for an overrepresentation formula during the Arusha negotiations as a transparent gesture of interethnic cooperation. The political calculation was that this might help FRODEBU to draw in political support from constituencies, including influential Tutsis, who were interested in seeing an end to war and rewarding pro-peace statesmen (ICG 2000; Mthembu-Salter 2016). Overrepresentation helped to offset the imbalance in the ethnic mobilization potential of Hutu faction leaders relative to Tutsis. The CNDD-FDD, by contrast, was concerned mostly with obstacles to expanding their power. During the Arusha negotiations, the CNDD-FDD leadership rejected the overrepresentation formula. The CNDD-FDD military leader at the time, Jean Bosco Ndayikengurukiye, described them as "very dangerous" and an "overprotection of the Tutsi minority." Bentley and Southall (2005, 80) noted that the CNDD-FDD rejected the Arusha Accords in September 2000, stating that "institutionalised ethnicity" served only to maintain a "putschist military-civilian oligarchy." Reyntjens (2006, n. 43) reads the CNDD-FDD's "rejection of ethnic quota [as meaning] in effect the refusal of Tutsi over-representation in the institutions." CNDD-FDD leader Pierre Nkurunziza railed against the proposal to govern "on the basis of ethnic clichés" (BBC Monitoring International Reports 2001), and CNDD-FDD political leader Hassan Radjabu stated that his party "is not interested by ethnic calculations" (BBC Monitoring International Reports 2004). The CNDD-FDD's initially uncompromising stance reflected their dominance on the battlefield, widespread grassroots support, and their position as outsiders to the Arusha process. The FRODEBU, on the other hand, presided over a relatively weak political network that was limited primarily to the capital, Bujumbura, and that had no military might.

The different views of the two parties reflects Vandeginste's assessments that "elites representing the large Hutu majority are likely to oppose consociational power-sharing and to prefer bare majority rule, while elites representing the Tutsi minority are likely to want a consociation," and so preference for quotas and other ethnic protections would only occur for majority groups that "are momentarily weak" (2017, 175). However, CNDD-FDD opposition eventually ceded. CNDD-FDD leader Evariste Ndayishimeye explains that his party came to "accept the principle of sharing power," adding that "one day, we might have to change it, but for now we have decided to accept it" (Mthembu-Salter 2016, 71).

Vandeginste (2009) also points to the external influence of South Africa and Belgian mediators in helping the Burundian factions to recognize the appeal of quotas. Indeed, the use of quotas resembles the transition settlements and institutions established in South Africa, and also resembles the consociational recognition regime in Belgium. Nevertheless, as we have already described, from the manner in which demands were submitted and developed during the negotiation process, it appears that the main forces behind the quotas came from within. It was the minority Tutsi elites, recognizing their vulnerability in the future, as well as Hutu elites from the declining FRODEBU party and thus seeking to expand their constituency, who were pressing for the quotas. Burundian elites engaged in the negotiations exercised agency, while at the same time drawing on the experience of their mediation partners from South Africa and Belgium to elaborate the quota-based institutional reforms.

The mobilization effects

While the value of assuring the other group was well appreciated, leaders also clearly understood the threat to minority Tutsis and the possible benefits for majority Hutus of mobilization along ethnic lines. Minority Tutsi leader Buyoya's actions and statements surrounding the 1992 constitution suggest a goal of trying to neutralize mobilization along ethnic lines. The Buyoya regime's sensitivity to ethnic mobilization was made evident by the preemptive arrests of Hutu leaders in 1988 (including seven of the authors of the letter calling for more Hutu inclusion), as well as the heavy military hand in quelling the 1988 uprising (Lemarchand 1996). It was also evident in Buyoya's regular dismissal of any attempt to apply an ethnic lens to interpreting conflict or political events. For example, in the aftermath of the 1988 violence, when asked how many Hutus had died compared to the number of Tutsis, Buyoya responded, "When you have bodies, you don't go around identifying which tribe they come from. We weep for all those who died" (quoted in Perlez 1988). The sensitivities to ethnic mobilization colored Buyoya's views of multiparty competition. Buyoya confided in 1988 that his hope was "to co-opt as many Hutu intellectuals as he could, [and] keep the Hutu peasants happy" so as to sustain a one-party system, and that "all Burundians should rather gather within the [ruling] UPRONA party" (quoted in Perlez 1988). In 1990 remarks criticizing multipartyism, Buyoya proposed that such party competition was inappropriate for African countries, because they are "divided not by ideologies but by ethnic divisions" and that party competition would imply "one party for each tribe," thereby posing a threat to stability (BBC 1990). Buyoya justified the preemptive arrests of Hutu activists in 1991 by saying that they posed a threat to national unity insofar as they were promoting "a democracy which in their view would be based on political parties of an ethnic nature" (BBC 1992a). He even repeated such sentiments as late as 1992, when reforms toward multipartyism were in full swing, claiming that the democratic process in Africa is difficult because it produces "instability, insecurity, ethnic conflicts and divisionism" (BBC 1992b). The remarks reflect Buyoya's sense that his political survival, and the sustainment of privilege among

the clique of Tutsi elites, would be best served by continued UPRONA dominance in a single-party state.

That Buyoya would be concerned about how formal recognition of ethnic
differences would undermine his political standing is apparent. That said, to the
extent that Buyoya sought to neutralize the threat of Hutu opposition mobilization, a core puzzle is why he ultimately ushered in multipartyism. By all accounts
and by his own words, Buyoya was moved to do so essentially against his will,
by international pressure and the conditioning of foreign aid on progress toward multiparty democracy (Lemarchand 1996; Manirakiza 2002). Moreover,
Reyntjens (1993) and Manirakiza (2002) provide insider accounts suggesting
that the dramatic 1993 election result was not only what the UPRONA leadership sought to avoid but also something that they heavily discounted as a real
possibility. The accounts suggest that Buyoya believed that his "statesmanlike"
efforts to win over Hutus would secure his political survival. Of course, history
judged these beliefs to be mistaken.

For the 2000 accords and the 2005 constitution, mobilization effects were
not a key point of tension, given that power transitioned to majority Hutu-
dominated factions. Hutu factional elites were presumably indifferent toward
the potential effects of quotas on ethnic mobilization since ethnicity was already
so salient, and of course, any mobilization along ethnic lines redounded to their
benefit, as we described in the section on the ethnic power configuration earlier
in this chapter.

The effects question: implications
and consequences

The 1992 constitution and consequences
of institutional mismatch

The 1992 constitution was inadequate to the task that Buyoya and his associates
intended—namely, a return to calm and their continued hold on power. In
this way, the strategy that the document embodied also failed to secure peace.
Recall that the 1993 election, the first in which Burundians directly elected a
president, swept Buyoya's predominantly minority Tutsi UPRONA party from
power. The elections brought to power the Hutu-dominated FRODEBU party
under the leadership of Melchior Ndadaye. After the election, the country's
institutional configuration combined a government led by majority-group
leaders with a non-recognition constitution. With the ethnic power configuration turned around in this manner (as seen through the lens of our theory),
we have a case where institutions are misaligned relative to the ethnic power

configuration, or what we deem an institutional mismatch. Note that in *informal* terms, Ndadaye had made efforts to ensure Tutsi representation: even though FRODEBU held 80 percent of assembly seats, seven of twenty-two ministers (32 percent) were Tutsis, predominantly from UPRONA. Ndadaye also named a Tutsi prime minister (Curtis 2012). Absent were *formal* recognition-based guarantees for the Tutsi minority against the tyranny of leaders from the Hutu majority, the consequence of which was a backlash by mistrusting Tutsi leaders. The 1993 coup attempt and assassination were reflections of this mistrust, motivated by fears among Tutsi elites of the "replacement of the established Tutsi elite in public sectors and in the military, and the return of an enormous number of Hutu refugees (and their land claims)" (Curtis 2012, 80). The tragic irony is that, as our theory also suggests, this might have been avoided: had cooler heads prevailed on all sides, such that the displaced Tutsi elites lobbied the newly incumbent Hutu leadership for constitutional reforms to incorporate recognition and attendant minority protections, the structural advantage that the Hutu incumbents enjoyed should have disposed them toward accepting such protections. But, in the revolutionary fervor, surprise, and fears that surrounded the electoral outcome, such a renegotiation of constitutional terms stood no chance. The subsequent violence in Burundi and in Rwanda pushed this even further from the realm of possibility.

The paradox of recognition after the 2000 accords and 2005 constitution

The Arusha Accords and the 2005 constitution were the product of negotiation and compromise between elite factions who then competed against each other in the electoral arena structured by these agreements. This distinguishes the post-conflict period in Burundi from ones where settlements are imposed after military victory, such as in post-genocide Rwanda and post-Derg Ethiopia. Nonetheless, the CNDD-FDD dominated in the 2005 elections, winning 59 percent of the vote for the national assembly. The other 41 percent of the vote was mostly distributed among the Hutu-dominated FRODEBU and the Tutsi-dominated UPRONA parties. These results gave the CNDD-FDD a strong majority of seats in the assembly and allowed them to appoint to the presidency their political head, Pierre Nkurunziza.

The immediate post-war period was one of progress in terms of both negative and positive peace. Onlookers in donor capitals in Europe and the United States, as well as in international organizations such as the United Nations and World Bank, viewed the 2005 elections and the attendant peaceful transfer of power in a very positive light. The elections had taken place with security assistance provided by a United Nations peacekeeping mission deployed in 2004. The World

Bank assisted in the management of a large-scale and generally well-functioning program to demobilize and reintegrate tens of thousands of rebel combatants into civilian life (Gilligan et al. 2013). The United Nations Peacebuilding Commission, established in 2005, selected Burundi, along with Sierra Leone, as an inaugural country for receiving combined political, economic, and security assistance. A U.S. diplomatic cable revealed through WikiLeaks indicates that the attention to Burundi, particularly among European partners such as Belgium, France, and the Netherlands, was based on the desire to promote Burundi as a model for democratic peace-building in an ethnically polarized country, serving as a contrast to neighboring Rwanda and the Democratic Republic of the Congo (WikiLeaks 2016).

Implementation of the quotas produced genuine change in key institutions. De Roeck and colleagues (2017) document the effects of the quotas across the spectrum of government institutions. They analyze data on the ethnicity of Burundian elites and show how the Arusha Accords and then the implementation of the 2005 constitution brought about dramatic changes in the ethnic composition of the military officer corps, judiciary posts, and provincial governors. Less dramatic were the changes in the executive, owing to the fact that Tutsi leader Buyoya already operated according to a norm of ethnic parity within the cabinet. Samii (2013b; 2014) details the ethnic integration of the formerly Tutsi-dominated army, perhaps the most sensitive issue during the peace negotiations. Recent history established a potential coup d'état by a Tutsi-dominated army as the key threat to be mitigated if Burundi was to move beyond the crisis triggered after the 1993 election, hence the emphasis of army reform (Vandeginste 2016, 8). Quota-based integration resulted in a dramatic transformation of the ethnic composition at the officer level as well as the creation of mixed-ethnicity units. The ethnically integrated army operated both domestically—in prosecuting campaigns against the FNL—and internationally in 2007, as it deployed as part of the African Union peacekeeping mission in Somalia.

Apparent successes of the recognition regime are evident when we consider the macro-level economic and political indicators for negative and positive peace. Figure 6.1 shows Burundi's trends for the various outcome variables considered in the cross-national analyses in Chapter 5. The first graph shows how the Ethnic Power Relations project (Cederman et al. 2010) codes the shares of the population politically excluded over time. We see no political exclusion under the 1992 constitutional regime that led to the 1993 elections. This comes to an end in the aftermath of Ndadaye's assassination, when we see exclusion of Hutus (and thus around 85 percent of the population) being imposed. This exclusion ends following the Arusha Accords and the moves toward negotiating the Global Ceasefire in 2003 that preceded the 2005 constitution. Levels of violence peak just after the 1993 elections, stay high through the war, and then fall precipitously

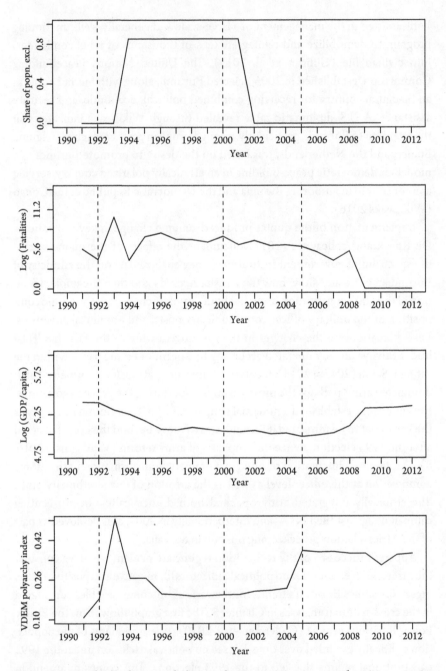

Figure 6.1 Trends in indicators of ethnic exclusion, negative peace, and positive peace in Burundi.

as the post-2005 regime consolidates. Economic income returns to a positive trajectory alongside this decline in violence after years of high volatility and negative growth. The VDEM polyarchy measure of democratic vitality, which we introduced in Chapter 5, marks the hopes and subsequent disappointment that surrounded the 1993 election, given the aborted transition from Tutsi- to Hutu-dominated government. For at least the first few years after the 2005 elections, we see a period of democratic flourishing, although the graph does not extend through to the 2015 elections and beyond, when the ruling CNDD-FDD party began a steep authoritarian slide. We discuss these developments later in this chapter.

In broad economic and political terms, the two years following the 2005 election suggested a much more positive trajectory than the years immediately following the 1993 election. To what extent can we attribute the differences to the changes in the recognition regime per se? There are a number of confounding factors, including, among other things, differences in the operating style of the CNDD-FDD compared to that of the FRODEBU, lessons political actors took from the war, the weariness the war created among the population, and the intensive international engagement. Moreover, the military outcome of the war, and the manner in which it was reflected in the reformed army, limited the potential for another coup attempt. That said, two post-2005 trends suggest that the recognition regime was crucial in establishing conditions conducive to peace. The first was the trend for political elites to regularly reference the Arusha Accords and its strategies for ethnic balancing. In particular, Tutsi parties have regularly sounded alarm bells regarding deviations from Arusha's principles. This demonstrates the visibility mechanism of the assuring effect of recognition operating as expected by our theory. In defending their performance, the CNDD-FDD also regularly seeks to make the case that they are living up to the principles of Arusha. Thus, at least in the terms that political elites have used themselves, the ethnic recognition of the Arusha Accords and 2005 constitution is central.

Another trend was the emergence of political contestation that cut across the ethnic divide, illustrative of a "paradox of recognition"—whereby recognition may, ironically, reduce the salience of ethnic cleavages as a line of political contestation. As it happens, the lines of political demarcation have never fallen purely along ethnic lines. For example, Tutsis had served as high-ranking members of the CNDD-FDD prior to the end of the war, and we have the remarkable case of Charles Mukasi, a Hutu by ethnic origin who nonetheless leads a radical faction of the Tutsi-dominated UPRONA party. That said, as discussed in detail earlier, interethnic mistrust is a core theme in Burundi's history. The Arusha Accords and the 2005 constitution helped to damp the pull of ethnic affiliations more systematically. Early in the Arusha process, Filip Reyntjens (2006, 132), a close observer of Burundian politics for decades, commented on the ethnic quota policy, noting that "at first sight, this would seem to rigidify the ethnic divide, but the opposite appears to be happening." The accession of the last, most radical faction of the PALIPEHUTU-FNL to the peace process in 2008 was testament to the reduction in ethnic polarization, insofar as that faction was willing to accede to terms that fell far short of their more radical pro-Hutu ideals.

The manner in which the 2010 election played out was also indicative of the new, non-ethnic axis of politics. Accusations of malfeasance by the CNDD-FDD in the early communal electoral round resulted in the opposition candidates boycotting the presidential polls. These included five Hutu candidates (from the FNL, FRODEBU, MSD, UPD, and a splinter CNDD faction) and one Tutsi candidate, Alexis Sinduhije. All but the Tutsi-dominated UPRONA party candidate had joined together to withdraw simultaneously. The UPRONA candidate had previously served as a vice president, appointed by Nkurunziza—as per the constitutional requirement to have at least one non-co-ethnic, non-co-partisan vice president—and presumably hoped to be reappointed. Nonetheless, following the other opposition candidates' withdrawal, the UPRONA candidate eventually withdrew. The primary axis of politics was between the incumbent CNDD-FDD party and a multiethnic opposition.

Raffoul (2018) describes this as the "depoliticization" of ethnicity in post-war Burundi, proposing that the ethnic quotas offered protections that removed the strategic necessity of mobilizing on the basis of ethnicity. Rather than interethnic polarization, intraethnic jockeying and cross-ethnic alliances in opposition to the ruling CNDD-FDD became much more important. The salience of ethnicity has not disappeared, and fears regarding ethnic targeting and incitement on the basis of ethnicity have continued to be an issue at times. But, as a basis for active political mobilization, the recognition regime has ushered in a period in which ethnic cleavages and factional cleavages do not overlap completely, as they did in the past. Micro-level studies also support the idea that recognition strategies such as quotas can in themselves increase interethnic cooperation. For Burundi, Samii (2013b) provides evidence that serving in ethnically integrated units caused soldiers, and in particular Tutsi soldiers, to exhibit less distrust toward their non-co-ethnic counterparts.

Burundi's quota-based system helps to ensure that institutions are not monopolized by one or another ethnic group, but the system does not provide robust brakes on single-party dominance. The opening of intraethnic and cross-ethnic lines of contestation resulted in a worrying political gridlock. This gridlock can be linked to two important points of controversy regarding the ethnic quotas of Arusha and the 2005 constitution. These points of controversy concern, first, whether the quotas were intended as a form of factional power-sharing, as distinct from a mechanism to specifically address ethnic underrepresentation, and, second, whether the quota formulas were fair with regard to their overrepresentation of the Tutsi minority. Tutsi factional leaders argued for an interpretation of the quotas as a means of factional power-sharing. In an interview with researcher Gregory Mthembu-Salter (2016, 48), former president Buyoya indicated that, on the one hand, "Burundians fought for power utilizing ethnicity, so the solution was to share it so that all groups had access to power," but, on the other hand, "during negotiations, we all came to see that the real question was not ethnicity but the management of power." Buyoya's suggestion is that ethnic polarization was a product of factional conflict, and so factional power-sharing would be the solution to ethnic polarization. Hutu leaders presented a more structural analysis of mass exclusion not only from the highest reaches of power but also from opportunities for mobility more generally. In a public forum that we observed in 2009, a CNDD-FDD party leader proclaimed that "up until now the priority has been peace, but the real goal is redistribution." This analysis resonated with mediators Nyerere and Mandela, who saw the root cause of the conflict being jealously guarded Tutsi domination across political and economic domains. Mandela noted a strong resemblance to South African apartheid (Wolpe 2011; ICG 2000a; Mthembu-Salter 2016, 58).

In moving from the Arusha Accords, through the Pretoria global cease-fire, and to the 2005 constitution, Reyntjens (2005, 119) notes that Tutsi party leaders became uncomfortable with the diminished emphasis on factional power-sharing, fearing that "Tutsi aligned with 'Hutu' parties would take up most or all functions in government and parliament allotted to Tutsi." Mthembu-Salter (2016, 72) notes that in the 2004 negotiations for constitutional quotas in the national assembly, Tutsi parties objected to the use of ethnic criteria alone and argued that "ethnic proportions should be allocated on a party, not individual, basis." The CNDD-FDD's political approach was to make appeals to Tutsi elites, recruiting many into leadership positions and thereby satisfying the quota provisions while also helping to chip away at the authority of the traditionally Tutsi parties such as UPRONA. Witnessing the political ascendance of the CNDD-FDD after the 2005 elections, UPRONA leader Jean-Bosco Manwangari remarked that the "constitution does not respect the spirit of Arusha . . . because the quota is just ethnic and not political. If you say it is just about ethnicity, you can have just one party dominating, as we do today" (Mthembu-Salter 2016, 73).

Prospects

The post-electoral honeymoon for the Burundian political system did not last long. Some commentators have attributed the decline in democratic vitality to the authoritarian character of Nkurunziza and his inner circle (Brabant and

Vircoulon 2015), but we argue that attention should go to the structural context defined by ethnic demographics and the power configuration. Related to this is the question of whether Tutsi overrepresentation in the constitutional quotas contributes to peace or not, and whether the ethnic quotas, as implemented, actually clash with factional power-sharing. In this section, we develop these ideas in discussing the prospects for the recognition regime and peace in Burundi.

By late 2007, the CNDD-FDD itself was caught up in a bitter internal factional dispute. Most worrying was an apparent slide toward authoritarianism on the part of the CNDD-FDD. Indicators of this slide included clampdowns on the press and civil society, appointments of loyalists to key positions such as in the army, unilateral suspension of the transitional justice processes, and the reckless pursuit of a third presidential term for Nkurunziza amid controversy over its legality. This authoritarian slide reflected broader regional dynamics, such as in nearby Rwanda and Democratic Republic of the Congo, where presidents also sought previously outlawed third terms, as well as in nearby Uganda and Zimbabwe, whose leaders had established themselves as would-be presidents for life. At the same time, opposition parties, far from making moves to restore consensus, seemed more intent on playing on the CNDD-FDD's vulnerabilities to amplify the crisis. Politically, one sensed that the choices were between an "electoral authoritarianism" dominated by the CNDD-FDD and the pursuit of crisis to provoke an extraconstitutional settlement that would override electoral outcomes to establish a power-sharing government (Vandeginste 2015).

What role, if any, has the recognition regime played in this downward political spiral and what might it foretell? While the CNDD-FDD's respect for the terms of the recognition regime has held to date, continued consolidation of power into the hands of the Hutu-dominated ruling party may erode the sustainability of Arusha's "overprotection" formula for Tutsis. This prognosis is informed, in part, by our analysis of the 1993 Arusha Accords in Rwanda, which provided for similar overprotection, albeit in factional rather than ethnic terms, and as such was judged as unacceptable by the Rwandan Hutu elite at that time. Chapter 7 develops this idea. In Burundi, Hutu and Tutsi leaders agreed on the overprotection formula in a moment of Hutu-Tutsi military balance that overrode demographic imbalance. However, such a balance of de facto power no longer exists. Crucial indications of such change came with the 2015 electoral crisis and 2018 constitutional referendum (International Crisis Group 2019).

In 2015, Nkurunziza decided to stand for a third term as president, claiming that the constitution's two-term limit did not apply because his first term had been a transitional appointment by the national assembly rather than a proper term by direct election. Nkurunziza's candidacy led to a deep division within the CNDD-FDD, which, when combined with the brewing mistrust among opposition factions, brought Burundi the closest it has come to a resumption of civil war in over a decade. The climax of the crisis was a May 2015 coup attempt, led by a breakaway faction of soldiers from the CNDD-FDD. The coup attempt featured a pitched battle in the capital, Bujumbura, but was ultimately contained by the segment of the army loyal to Nkurunziza. In the aftermath of the coup attempt, Nkurunziza appointed a new defense minister, who, while being a Tutsi and therefore respecting the principle of ethnic balancing within the cabinet, was nonetheless a member of the CNDD-FDD rather than the pre-2005 Burundian army. This represented a dramatic change from past conventions and emphasized the diminished position of the old-guard southern Tutsi elite (International Crisis Group 2017).

The May 2018 constitutional referendum introduced terms that strengthened the presidency while introducing some ambiguity as to the state of the ethnic quotas (Vandeginste 2018). The terms strengthening the presidency include lengthened term limits, from five to seven years, and the authority to appoint the prime minister. With respect to the quotas, however, the implications are not straightforward. On the one hand, the constitutional formulas were maintained in a number of key institutions, such as the assembly, senate, and army, and were newly extended to the judiciary. On the other hand, the intelligence services were exempted from the ethnic parity requirement, and the senate was charged with evaluating the continuation of quotas in five years. The amendments remove both the qualified (two-thirds) majority provision in the assembly and the guarantee of ministerial positions for all parties obtaining at least 5 percent of the vote, thus removing factional power-sharing provisions.

Critics of the ruling CNDD-FDD often point to the party's authoritarian moves as a violation of the Arusha Accords' spirit of ethnic cooperation, with worrying implications for the Tutsi minority. This is part of a broader rhetorical game that both the CNDD-FDD and its political opponents play with the terms of the accords. On the one hand, ruling party elites propose that the Arusha Accords and 2005 constitution are extremely generous to members of the Tutsi minority, yet Tutsi opposition leaders "still complain." This is a tactic through which the recognition regime can be employed to silence dissent, labeling dissenters on the basis of ethnic lines. If the ruling party maintains tight control over those who are able to occupy the quota-provided posts, then recognition can very much serve authoritarian interests, as the posts can be stacked with loyalists who are then used as examples to accuse dissenters of fostering divisions. This possibility reinforces the need for safeguards, such as clear democratic processes for selection to posts, to help ensure that recognition is not used as a tool for authoritarians. For the intent authoritarian, institutions can offer tools just as much as they constrain. One reading of Burundi's recent history suggests such Machiavellian repurposing of ethnic recognition by the ruling party, as in the case of the 2015 defense minister appointment.

On the other hand, members of the traditional Tutsi leadership class could be accused of playing a game that willingly confuses protection of their personal privilege with protection of the broader Tutsi population. The episode with the defense minister is instructive in this regard as well. It highlights the differences between quota-based ethnic recognition and political power-sharing: the minister who was appointed fulfilled the specific ethnic requirements. The defense minister's apparent violation of the "spirit" of Arusha was that he did so without simultaneously pursuing balance between new elites from the CNDD-FDD and traditional elites from UPRONA and the pre-transition army dominated by southern Tutsis.

Ultimately, there are two issues that will determine the potential for a return to democratic flourishing. The first is whether the CNDD-FDD itself can return to a commitment to democratic principles. Nkurunziza's announcement in 2018 that he would step down after his third term was encouraging in this regard, although time will tell whether this pronouncement was made in good faith, and many commentators doubt its sincerity. The second is whether respect for ethnic balancing can be done in a manner that is disentangled from political power-sharing with old-guard Tutsi elites. This would reduce tensions associated with the "overprotection" of the Tutsi minority. It may also allow for a more open, pluralistic politics that allows for further reduction of ethnic identity's role as an axis of political competition.

This account offers a contrast to the challenges in neighboring Rwanda, which has moved from a recognition to a non-recognition regime under the authority of minority Tutsi president Paul Kagame. Chapter 7 discusses the origins and consequences of these dynamics in Rwanda through the lens of our theory, highlighting both the dilemma of recognition and the paradox of non-recognition.

7

Non-Recognition Under Minority Rule and the Paradox of Non-Recognition in Rwanda

In 2006, Rwanda's Senate published a report entitled *Rwanda: Genocide Ideology and Strategies for Its Eradication*. The document states that "the quest for an assimilating and an all-inclusive national identity means the regression, even better, the disappearance of divisive identitarism" (Republic of Rwanda 2006, 268). In Rwanda today, non-recognition is a central strategy. As we detail in Chapter 1, Kagame explained that "we are trying to reconcile our society and talk people out of this nonsense of division." He continued, referencing common physiological stereotypes of ethnic groups in Rwanda, "Some are short, others are tall, others are thin, others are stocky. But we are all human beings. Can we not live together and happily within one border?" (quoted in Pilling and Barber 2017).

Current non-recognition contrasts with Rwanda's historic approach to ethnic identity. Between independence and the 1993 Arusha Accords, Rwanda's two Hutu majority leaders implemented recognition throughout state institutions. Under increasingly contested Hutu leadership facing a powerful Tutsi minority insurgency, the 1993 Arusha Accords did not explicitly recognize ethnic groups, but did so informally through party-based power-sharing. In the aftermath of the 1990–93 civil war and the 1994 genocide and mass killings, a Tutsi minority government instituted a far-reaching non-recognition regime that endures to this day. Through the lenses of the theory we have put forth, and like its southern neighbor, Burundi, Rwanda's past and present approaches to the adoption and non-adoption of recognition conform to our theoretical expectations. This chapter examines the motivations behind Rwanda's historical and current approach to recognition questions and also the implications for peace.

We argue that our theory on the adoption and effects of recognition usefully sheds light on the Rwandan case. In terms of adoption, we focus on two

Diversity, Violence, and Recognition. Elisabeth King and Cyrus Samii, Oxford University Press (2020). © Oxford University Press.
DOI: 10.1093/oso/9780197509456.003.0001

constitutional moments—the 1993 Arusha Accords and especially the 2003 constitution—while also surveying recognition historically. We show that the pivotal leaders had a keen understanding of minority-majority dynamics within the country and that these dynamics informed their strategic decision-making. We show that weighing the assuring effects against the mobilization effects is a useful lens with which to understand and interpret leaders' thinking and decision-making. We also find the case of Rwanda helps us refine our theory in a couple of important ways, especially as it relates to the effects of recognition and non-recognition. In terms of consequences and implications, we find that leaders' intentions behind their choices of recognition or non-recognition are crucial to its effects. We also introduce a new concept, the "paradox of non-recognition," wherein efforts to negate ethnicity may result, rather, in sustaining its salience. This runs contrary to conflict management theories proposing that non-recognition allows societies to transcend ethnic identity.

First, this chapter considers the Rwandan context today and historically, the nature of the conflicts in Rwanda, and the backdrop of ethnic rivalry and mistrust. Second, it presents the dynamics of recognition over time. The third section addresses the adoption question, examining leaders' sensitivity to ethnic demographics, and explores whether and how plurality and minority leaders weighed the assuring effects of recognition against its mobilization effects in the way our theory proposes. The fourth section examines the consequences and implications of the varied approaches to ethnicity over time with an emphasis on the post-genocide period. The conclusion looks forward to prospects for peace.

Context and nature of the conflict

Rwanda, one of the smallest, most densely populated, and historically poorest countries in the world, is unfortunately best-known as the site of a 1994 genocide that left an estimated 800,000 dead. Like Burundi, Rwanda is composed of Tutsis, Hutus, and Twas. Although population figures are no longer collected, in line with the current government's non-recognition policies, historical estimates—discussed in Chapter 6—suggest the populations of each group are about 14 percent, 85 percent, and 1 percent, respectively.

Ethnic rivalry and mistrust have been persistent features of Rwanda's landscape. Nonetheless, the meaning of Hutu, Tutsi, and Twa identities have changed with time. While the current government talks of a pre-colonial golden age when Rwanda's three ethnic groups lived in harmony, scholarship suggests that, far before the arrival of Europeans, labor practices and a patron-client system set up an antagonistic and hierarchical Tutsi-Hutu relationship. After Rwanda became a Belgian protectorate in 1918, the Belgian colonial administration favored Tutsis through a divisive and indirect rule strategy that fostered negative intergroup relations and further entrenched an ethnic divide onto what had historically been more fluid identities (Newbury 1988).

Violence along ethnic lines has also been long-standing. In 1959, the "social revolution" switched power from Tutsi to Hutu hands. At Rwandan independence in 1962, a Hutu government came to power under the leadership of Grégoire Kayibanda, from the country's south-center, creating the first Hutu republic. Kayibanda claimed to be overcoming four hundred years of economic and political injustice and incorporated the logic of *rubanda nyamwinshi*—the right to power of the indigenous majority—throughout government policy. In the period from 1959 through 1963, there was widespread violence in Rwanda, which had class and regional dynamics but played out principally along ethnic lines. Estimates suggest thousands of homes were burned and pillaged, between 10,000 and 20,000 Rwandans were killed, more than 20,000 people were internally displaced, and between 100,000 and 300,000 people—mostly Tutsis— were forced to flee the country. Important international figures deemed it "the most terrible and systematic genocide since the genocide of Jews by Hitler" (quoted in Lemarchand 1970, 224). In the ensuing years, some of the Tutsis who had gone into exile in Uganda engaged in armed raids into Rwanda, with increasing targeting of Hutu officials and government reprisals against the Tutsi population within Rwanda. In 1973, Juvénal Habyarimana, an army chief from northern Rwanda, overthrew the Kayibanda government in a coup d'état. Habyarimana built a developmental state that was often praised by the international community and continued the policy of *rubanda nyamwinshi* throughout his time in power.

Rwanda's civil war began in October 1990 when the Rwandan Patriotic Front (RPF), composed mostly of Tutsi exiles who had been in Uganda since the late 1950s, set out to return to Rwanda militarily, launching multiple incursions and successfully claiming territory. The war lasted through 1993, when key players negotiated the Arusha Accords, the first of two constitutional moments in Rwanda that enter our cross-national dataset. Estimates suggest that, over the course of the war, more than ten thousand Rwandans were killed. The war resumed when the plane carrying President Habyarimana, a Hutu (as well as Burundian president Cyprien Ntaryamira, also a Hutu), was shot down, setting the 1994 genocide in motion.

In a context where neighbors were regularly of different ethnic groups and interethnic marriage was not uncommon, the genocide tore apart neighborhoods, or *collines*, along victim-perpetrator lines. It is estimated that in about one hundred days, from April through July 1994, 75 percent of Rwanda's resident Tutsi population was killed. Estimates suggest that 14 percent to 17 percent of the male adult Hutu population participated. At the same time, and often overlooked, likely hundreds of thousands of Hutus were killed, including so-called moderates who opposed "Hutu Power" as well as victims of the RPF's violence against Hutus (Straus 2006, 2015, 2019).

The genocide ended in July 1994 after the RPF, led by then-general Paul Kagame, seized control of Rwanda through military force. After ending the genocide, the RPF installed a broad-based transitional government. Pasteur Bizimungu, a comparatively rare Hutu member of the RPF, became president, and Paul Kagame served as vice president and defense minister. Kagame, however, was already the decisive leader far before he took over as president in 2000. In the immediate post-genocide period, many Hutu Rwandans viewed the RPF as occupiers rather than liberators, and RPF leaders were, in turn, suspicious of large proportions of the population. An RPF text likely written in early 1994 warns: "Let us not be fooled, many of them have not detached themselves from Habyarimana because they see him as their 'chief'" (quoted in Reyntjens 2013, 82). Reyntjens recounts monthly reports on "enemy internal activity" (2013, 5). He finds that even Hutus within the post-genocide government were suspected of trying to "find a way of fighting for the rights of the (Hutu) majority" (Reyntjens 2013, 5–6). The approach and statements of the current regime suggest both disdain and distrust of the population in general (Ansoms 2009; Reyntjens 2013; Thomson 2013).

In the streamlined theory we have advanced in this book, we focus on leaders' decisions about how to deal with ethnicity in situations characterized by ethnic rivalry and mistrust. One should not overlook factions within ethnic groups or the existence of moments at which cross-ethnic appeals achieved relative salience. Neither should one blame primordial ethnic hatred as the root cause of violence—politics and power underlay key strategic decisions. Yet ethnic rivalry and mistrust are common in Rwanda, and especially so at the key moments of decision we discuss next.

Recognition over time

Recognition in the Hutu republics (1962–1993)

Today's non-recognition regime represents a dramatic shift from the recognition strategies that predominated under majority Hutu leadership until the 1993 Arusha Accords. The 1957 Hutu Manifesto, upon which Rwanda's first president, Kayibanda, based government policy, argued that ethnic identification needed to remain on identity cards as it had in the colonial period, to "monitor" the "race monopoly" of Tutsis, who were strongly favored under colonial rule (our translation of Niyonzima et al. 1957, 29). Through this policy, Kayibanda was not trying to offer protection to the Tutsi minority but rather to expand

Hutu control. Kayibanda's party, the Parti du Mouvement de l'Emancipation Hutu (Party of the Hutu Emancipation Movement), or PARMEHUTU, decreed that all national education reports needed to indicate the "racial" proportion of Hutus, Tutsis, and Twas in schools, and introduced ethnic quotas for promotion past primary school. There were also quotas for public employment. These policies were called *iringaniza*, which roughly translates as "social justice." The ideology of *rubanda nyamwinshi*, equating demography with democracy, justified the political marginalization of Tutsis.

In 1973, when Juvénal Habyarimana launched a coup and took control of the country, he claimed that Kayibanda had insufficiently addressed "tribal and regional conflicts" (Sullivan 1994). According to historian Jean-Pierre Chrétien, Habyarimana sought "equilibrium"; the idea was that, as an authoritarian leader, he did not need to improve democracy since power was already with the majority, whose interests would be ensured through quotas to avoid the over-representation of Tutsis (2003, 309). Indeed, with his party, the *Mouvement républicain national pour la démocratie et le développement* (National Republican Movement for Democracy and Development, MRND), Habyarimana aimed to concretize the gains of the revolution by formalizing Kayibanda's quotas for education and civil service jobs. As Tutsis represented between 9 and 15 percent of the Rwandan population, they were to be granted 9 to 15 percent of positions in schools and the civil service (different sources put the quotas at different numbers between these extremes). In contrast to Burundi, where post–Arusha Accords recognition included overrepresentation for Tutsis to bolster assurances, quota allocations in Rwanda matched ostensible representations of each group in the population. Scholar Gérard Prunier calls Rwanda under the Hutu republics a "quota democracy," whereby a de facto ethnic census replaced the need for elections and broader democratization (1997, 46).

Informal recognition in the Arusha Accords (1993)

The Habyarimana regime came to an end through civil war between the Hutu-dominated government and the Tutsi-led Rwandan Patriotic Front, which began when the latter invaded Rwanda in October 1990. From June 1992 until August 1993, these actors negotiated with each other and with domestic opposition parties that had emerged in the early 1990s in the pressure on sub-Saharan African countries to liberalize. The negotiations resulted in the 1993 Arusha Accords, the first constitutional moment that enters our dataset, and began the shift away from ethnic recognition. The accords laid out a broad-based transitional government that was to include the RPF and five main Rwandan political parties. It set out provisions for general elections, respect of the rule of law, a framework for the repatriation of refugees, and a consolidated army made up of government and rebel forces. Reflecting the distinction we drew in Chapter 3, the parties included in the power-sharing agreement generally aligned with ethnic factions, and key players appear to have understood the accords through ethnic lenses (Prunier 1995). A panel established by the Organization of African Unity (OAU) to investigate the 1994 genocide in Rwanda also emphasized demographic power dynamics, in this case writing critically of the way the Arusha Accords handled them (International Panel of Eminent Personalities 2000). They also clearly understood the informal power-sharing agreement as an ethnic one. The Arusha Accords, however, included no explicit ethnic recognition. Indeed, it provided that "the Broad-Based Transitional Government shall, from the date of its assumption of office, delete from all official documents to be issued any reference to ethnic origin" (1993, art. 16). We explore later in this chapter why this plurality leadership did not adopt recognition, as our theory would have predicted.

At least part of the answer lies in the fact that identifying the pivotal leader is more complex than in the previous periods or the period that comes after the genocide, as is the case in Burundi around that country's Arusha Accords. While Habyarimana remained the president of Rwanda, and the accords were thus ultimately adopted under Hutu majority leadership, the Rwandan government was represented by at least three different political parties—including three opposition parties, the Mouvement Démocratique Républicain (MDR), the Parti Libéral (PL), and the Hutu hard-line party Coalition pour la Défense de la République—and power was thus diffuse (Jones 2001). Habyarimana faced intense external pressure from the international community as well as internal pressure on economic, political, and military fronts. In the end, while the signing of the accords allowed him to retain the presidency, most powers were slated to devolve to a cabinet led by a prime minister. Moreover, the RPF was ascendant in power with the ongoing armed conflict and is described as "extremely disciplined and effective," sending a cohesive, high-powered team to negotiate (Jones 2001, 72). Like the Burundi Arusha Accords in 2000, which were arguably a product of a complex negotiation in which the ascendance of the CNDD-FDD was factored in, the complexity of the power configurations in Rwanda at this time make it harder to situate the 1993 Arusha Accords clearly on one or another end of our theoretical spectrum of plurality adoption and minority non-adoption.

It is well documented that the accords prompted significant fears on all sides and that none of the parties to the accords expected them to be implemented (Guichaoua 2015; Prunier 1997). Rather, all sides continued to prepare for renewed conflict (Dallaire and Beardsley 2004), and, in fact, the 1994 genocide began less than a year after the Arusha Accords were signed. Commentators often say that, instead of genuinely addressing underlying tensions, the Arusha

Accords were rather a "proximate cause" of the 1994 genocide that followed (Jones 1999, 54).

Non-recognition after the genocide (1994–present)

After three months of violence, the advancing RPF seized Kigali, putting a military end to the 1994 genocide as well as more than forty years of Hutu-dominated rule. Under the leadership of President Paul Kagame, from the minority Tutsi group, the government is following a strict non-recognition strategy and promoting an all-encompassing Rwandanness: "One Rwanda for all Rwandans." Rwanda's 2003 constitution sets out to "eradicate . . . ethnic, regional and other divisions and promot[e] national unity" (Article 9). Rwanda's new national anthem, written by former *génocidaires* (those found guilty in perpetration of the genocide), includes a line as to how "our common culture identifies us, our single language unifies us" (quoted in Pilling and Barber 2017). While formalized in the 2003 constitution, the non-recognition approach was already a well-enshrined RPF policy. As early as its 1990 eight-point political program, the RPF formally committed to "the abolition of all forms of sectarianism [in this case taken to mean ethnic identity] and the creation of one unified people" (point 1). Kagame continues to be president to this day, and in 2015, the country voted to amend the constitution so that he could remain in power, contingent upon reelection, until 2034.

The argument follows, as Rwanda's National Unity and Reconciliation Commission puts it, that "the ideas of Hutu and Tutsi are not compatible with those of citizenship" (Republic of Rwanda 2004). The government has since passed two vague laws rendering classification of the population as Hutus, Tutsis, and Twas illegal. Article 3 of Law 41/2001 first banned "sectarianism," later called "divisionism," punishable by up to thirty years in prison and a fine of up to 5 million Rwandan francs (nearly USD 6,000; see Thomson 2009, 314). Interestingly, highlighting ongoing parallels with neighboring Burundi, Burundi's minority-led non-recognition government had also earlier used the language of "divisionism" (Lemarchand 1994). Rwanda's law stated that "sectarianism is a crime committed through the use of any speech, written statement, or action that causes an uprising that may degenerate into strife among people" (Republic of Rwanda 2001). The "genocide ideology" Law 18/2008 made it an offense, punishable by up to twenty-five years of imprisonment, to have "an aggregate of thoughts characterized by conduct, speeches, documents and other acts aiming at exterminating or inciting others to exterminate people bas[ed] on ethnic group, origin, nationality, region, colour, physical appearance, sex, language, religion or political opinion" (cited in Reyntjens 2013, 74–75) (An amendment to the law adds intent and specifies additional acts such as "incitement to commit genocide; negation of the genocide against the Tutsis, trivializing the genocide or justifying it; and hiding or destroying of evidence of genocide or of other crimes against humanity" [Kayitare, quoted in Gashugi 2013, 1]). Twas, members of the smallest and most marginalized ethnic group in Rwanda, are also not allowed to self-identify as Twa or to claim associated minority or indigenous rights (Thomson 2009).

Rwanda's current non-recognition strategy stretches beyond discourse into all state institutions. Table 7.1 illustrates the government's approach to recognition across key domains of the state. The government removed ethnicity from identity cards, a designation that was first introduced by the Belgians and maintained by Presidents Kayibanda and Habyarimana, and outlawed identification by ethnic group in official documents. Government positions, previously allocated according to ethnically and regionally based quotas, became ostensibly meritocratic and blind to ethnic identity. The RPF also later added a ninth point to the 1994 eight-point RPF plan that stipulated that "no leadership posts are acquired through segregation in any form." The military arm of the RPF became Rwanda's national army without power-sharing of the type that had been laid out in the 1993 Arusha Accords. Quotas and all ethnic identification were also eliminated in schools. By the fall of 1994, the RPF placed a moratorium on teaching history in Rwanda's schools and has since, in reintroducing civics and social studies, changed the discourse about identity in Rwanda such that ethnicity is rarely mentioned, ethnic identification itself is presented as a problem (largely of the past), and discussion of ethnicity is allowed only in certain state-sanctioned ways, such as in the *gacaca* courts (community courts) and in the commemoration of "the genocide of the Tutsis" (King 2014; King 2017).

Table 7.1 **Implementation of ethnic recognition policies in seven government and public sector domains in Rwanda**

Implementation following 2003 constitution	
Executive	No
Legislative	No
Security	No
Justice	No
Civil Service	No
Education	No
Language	N/A

Note: Ethnic groups speak the same language (Kinyarwanda)

Source: Authors' implementation dataset, described in Chapter 5.

In 1998, the government established the National Unity and Reconciliation Commission (NURC), reminiscent of the similarly titled commission that President Buyoya, from the minority Tutsis, established in Burundi in the late 1980s. Rebuilding the unity of Rwandans and "monitor[ing] the adherence of the population to policies of national unity" were central parts of the NURC's mandate (Republic of Rwanda 2004, 19–20). In 2007, the government added the National Commission for the Fight Against Genocide, an "independent and permanent" institution with a mission to "to prevent and fight against genocide, its ideology and overcoming its consequences" (Republic of Rwanda 2017). The government also implemented *ingandos*, informal mandatory civic education programs, to reeducate certain segments of the Rwandan population. The "ethnicity question" is said to "dominate" their program of "political indoctrination" for students, including "erasing myths of ethnic difference" (Mgbako 2005). The focus on non-recognition is also targeted at the international community. Participants of a 1995 government policy and planning meeting for the education sector, for instance, asked the international community, in a statement representative of many, to "never again make reference . . . to the ethnicization of Rwandans" (Republic of Rwanda 1995, 51). After first exploring the adoption question, this chapter turns to assess the consequences and implications for peace of today's non-recognition regime.

The adoption question: assessing the theory

Leaders' interests and ethnic power configurations

We argue that leaders' interests and awareness of ethnic power configurations are important parts of the explanation at each of the key moments detailed earlier in this chapter. It is clear that Rwandan leaders have long had a keen awareness of ethnic demographics and that this awareness has informed strategic decision-making. We have described the common argument in the post-independence period that Hutus should hold power as the demographic majority. This was the narrative underlying the 1959 "social revolution" that aimed to transfer power from minority Tutsis, favored by the colonial power, to the majority, and *rubanda nyamwinshi* discourse and associated policies were thereafter invoked by Hutu elites during the first and second republics.

It is also well documented that a clear understanding of ethnic power configurations influenced strategic decisions during the negotiations for the Arusha Accords. Scholar André Guichaou, who specializes in the African Great Lakes region, explains that Habyarimana emphasized the democratization clauses of the Arusha Accords over the power-sharing clauses, counting on the fact that the votes he would have come ballot time would more than compensate for short-term losses. The Arusha Accords set elections to take place within twenty-two months. In contrast, the RPF's knowledge that the reverse would be true in their case—that they could garner only a minority of votes—led them to oppose post-transition elections and focus on military victory as their route to power. As an RPF ideologue generalized in 1996, "The Hutu elites as a whole entirely subscribe to the fundamental thesis of the ethnist ideology, namely that power belongs to the Hutu because they are the majority" (quoted in Reyntjens 2013, 19). The elections in Burundi in mid-1993, bringing the Hutu Ndadaye to power and removing Tutsi leaders, reinforced their concern about elections as ethnic census. Reyntjens calls the RPF's concern with ethnic voting an "understandable . . . obsession" (2013, 7). In the RPF Declaration of July 17, 1994, Concerning the Establishment of Institutions, the transitional period was extended to five years, and there is no mention of elections (Schabas and Imbleau 1997).

Scholars have also often understood key political decisions and challenges in Rwanda as being informed by majority-minority dynamics. According to Lemarchand and others, "ethnic amnesia" is a rational strategy to detract attention from Tutsi dominance and to prevent the delegitimization that would likely ensue (Lemarchand 1994, 31–32; see also Bradol and Guibert 1997; King 2014; Pottier 2002). Political scientist and anthropologist Mahmood Mamdani writes that in the post-genocide period, "Rwanda's key dilemma is how to build a democracy that can incorporate a guilty majority alongside an aggrieved and fearful minority into a political community" (2001, 266). Anthropologist Johan Pottier analyzes the current government's mastery and promotion of a simple, easy-to-grasp, historical narrative of a pre-colonial golden age as "vital to the justification of minority rule" (2002, 9). We argue that it is also this understanding of one's position as a leader from a minority group or a plurality group that provides a useful lens through which to consider the choice of recognition or non-recognition policies.

Writing in 2005, the authors of the African Peer Review Mechanism's country report (a voluntary self-monitoring process for African Union member states) on Rwanda well summarized the dilemma of recognition:

> Undoubtedly, the unity of Rwandans and their reconciliation are the political priority of Rwanda's government. Foremost among its concerns is the eradication of ethnic discrimination. Thus, the Constitution outlaws any form of discrimination based on colour, creed and gender. This is understandable and desirable—after all, ethnic discrimination is what in the past caused the country to disintegrate and collapse into carnage. It is important to remember, however, that failure to grapple

with the problem of diversity sparked the genocide, which continues to inform most of what is going on in the country. The Government faces an uncomfortable dilemma—how to promote political pluralism in a country where political parties [and we would add political and violent mobilization] have, in the past, been organised along two main ethnic lines. (African Peer Review Mechanism 2005, 140)

We next examine if and how Rwandan leaders' understanding of ethnic power dynamics and their respective status as leaders from minority or majority groups were important to informing their choice about recognition and, in particular, to how they viewed the assuring effects of recognition and the mobilization effects.

The assuring effects

In this book, we make the argument that, regardless of a leader's minority or plurality status, recognizing groups may be politically useful in activating assuring effects and thereby alleviating possible concerns about exclusion on the part of members of the opposition group. In Rwanda, the country's first president, Kayibanda (a Hutu), argued that ethnic identification could help "monitor" the "race monopoly" of Tutsis, fearing that not conveying information about ethnicity "would create a risk of preventing the statistical law from establishing the reality of facts" (quoted in Prunier 1997, 46). This points to the importance of the visibility mechanism we discussed in Chapter 2 as part of the assuring effects. Here, though, the goal was to address the mistrust of the historically marginalized incumbent *majority*, rather than overcoming minority mistrust. Rwandan Rev. Dr. André Karamaga called "ethnic equilibrium" a "bizarre manner of protecting the majority against the minority" (quoted in Longman 2010, 95).

More consistent with the mechanisms underlying our theory, once there had been some redistribution in favor of Hutus, some observers positively noted Habyarimana's maintenance of ethnic quotas in the sense of guaranteeing minimum representation and rights for Tutsis and enabling them to monitor their status. International consultants who visited Rwanda at this time "noted with approval that access to schooling appears unusually equitable" (Hoben 1989, 104). Likewise, as late as 1990, Rwanda's Catholic bishops also praised Habyarimana's policy of ethnic quotas, suggesting that Rwanda's conflicts would be solved if the population were to embrace these distributive policies (Longman 2010). However, others argued that the maintenance of ethnic identity cards in particular was problematic and could facilitate violence. This is the case, for example, for genocide studies and prevention scholar Gregory Stanton, who served as a foreign service officer in the U.S. State Department and drafted the UN Security Council resolutions that created the International Criminal Tribunal for Rwanda. He recalls that during a 1998 visit to Rwanda he told the president of the country's supreme court that identity cards needed to be abolished, as "someday they will be used for genocide" (Stanton 2009, 8). International donor governments also discussed the importance of abolishing ethnic identity cards, which they understood as a tool of discrimination, but they never made this a condition of aid (Des Forges 1999).

While the Arusha Accords are coded as non-recognition, we wondered whether the assuring effects were contemplated from the perspective of the plurality Hutu government and parties. As we have noted, the Arusha Accords were a party-based power-sharing agreement but clearly understood in ethnic terms. It does not seem, though, that the assuring effects were seriously weighed by any of the parties. The crux of the negotiations had to do with ethnically based distribution of power, and mobilization concerns—which we discuss later—predominated. While Hutu leaders did ultimately agree to a greater share of power for the RPF than equitable Tutsi representation in the population would suggest, we have already reported that none of the parties really believed the Arusha Accords would hold.

In the post-genocide period, despite an overarching non-recognition approach, Kagame appears to have appreciated the assuring effects of recognition and took some key public steps, at least in the first years after the genocide, to put Hutus into symbolic positions of power—albeit in a way we term "informal" in Chapter 3, given that the appointments were not in a *publicly* "Hutu" capacity. This suggests that Kagame was not ignorant of the possible symbolic benefits of recognition, nor was he acting in a manner that suggested complete confidence in his ability to rule without broad legitimacy, as proponents of a hegemony explanation for non-recognition might suggest.

The RPF, for instance, placed prominent Hutu defectors in visible and important positions. This was partly in line with the power-sharing orientation of the Arusha Accords. For example, as previously noted, Pasteur Bizimungu, a self-identified Hutu of mixed ethnic parentage and the former general manager of the state-owned electric company, was appointed president, and Faustin Twagiramungu, a former civil servant and a Hutu, was appointed as prime minister. Additional examples include Alexis Kanyarengwe, a former army officer who helped President Habyarimana seize power in 1973 and later served as chairman of the RPF, and businessman Seth Sendashonga, who was appointed minister of the interior. Most cabinet ministers were also Hutu (Kinzer 2008). Reyntjens deems their appointment "a symbolic expression of national unity" (2013, 19). Joseph Karemera, who served as the post-genocide minister of health, and later as minister of education and as Rwandan ambassador to South Africa, explained the logic of putting Hutus in prominent positions:

> [It] was very necessary after all the tension and the genocide. . . . We knew we were unpopular. They thought we were going to kill them. So we said, "Let's do the reverse to win their confidence." Some of us had difficulty believing this. Paul [Kagame] was saying "Bring them in." We'd say that these were very bad people. He said "Bring them in and teach them to be good." Some of us were annoyed. All of us had relatives killed. It was difficult to think that way at the time. (Quoted in Kinzer 2008, 186)

Similar efforts extended to the security sector. Researcher Colin Waugh writes that "one important step taken by Vice President Kagame was the reintegration of 4,000 former Hutu soldiers and officers into the Rwandan army, to boost confidence among the ethnic majority and dispel the sentiment that the country was somehow 'under occupation' by a foreign army" (Waugh 2004, 120). Deploying many to northern Rwanda, a historic Hutu stronghold and a region where the RPF had been especially viewed as an occupier, was reported to have "helped calm Hutu fears" (Kinzer 2008, 216). Reyntjens assesses that "token Hutu" were routinely co-opted into politics and the army and that this practice became sufficiently widespread that Tutsi survivors complained about the possible inclusion of *génocidaires* (2013, 18).

These actions and the interpretations of them—"win[ning] their confidence," "calm[ing] fears"—suggest that Kagame was aware of the importance of building legitimacy and not blind to the value of assuring the majority. These early distributive compensations were not, however, coupled with formal recognition of the type we might see in Burundi today, or in Rwanda under the first and second republics, in that individuals were not appointed on the basis of a public commitment to recognize or endeavor to balance ethnic groups. As such, they lack the degree of assurances that formal recognition would offer. Moreover, these early efforts at informal recognition did not last long or inform the overall strategy.

In short, Kagame did pursue distributive strategies and may even have endeavored to reap assuring benefits. Some of his early actions could plausibly be interpreted as seeking to attend to the potential grievances of the Hutu majority. Nonetheless, he avoided enhancing these efforts by coupling them with recognition. We will argue that Kagame's government avoided continuing or enhancing these efforts by coupling them with recognition because of the predominance of mobilization fears.

The mobilization effects

Throughout Rwanda's history, leaders have recognized that "playing the ethnic card" has been fruitful when mobilization is needed for political or violent purposes. For example, as Rwanda expert Catharine Newbury argues, at the time of independence, "an appeal to Hutu solidarity became, for Hutu leaders, the most effective rallying point for revolutionary activity" (Newbury 1998, 213). It has also been a particularly attractive strategy at times of intra-Hutu fractionalization in order to shift blame to Tutsis and to build intra-Hutu cohesion. For example, in a 1973 effort to resuscitate a government in trouble, Kayibanda tried to unite Hutus by organizing "public committees" to search secondary schools, universities, the civil service, and businesses for Tutsis. The ostensible purpose of these raids was to ensure that Tutsis had not bypassed the ethnic quota regulations put in place to rectify colonial inequalities that favored Tutsis over Hutus (Prunier 1997). Decades later, Habyarimana employed a similar "ethnic card" tactic to promote Hutu mobilization when he faced the RPF threat from Uganda, pressure from the international community to embrace multiparty democracy, and internal threats to his leadership. In a statement characteristic of many by the ruling elite at that time, Rwanda's foreign minister appealed to Hutus to mobilize, claiming that the RPF aimed "to restore a *minority* and feudal regime which was abolished in 1959 under the guise of liberation and democracy" (quoted in Khadiagala 2002, 466; emphasis added). These actions suggest that the plurality leadership was well aware of the latent power of mobilization in the recognition approach it had embraced.

At the Arusha Accords, leaders also clearly took into account the idea that recognition can facilitate mobilization. Recall that the accords were based on factional power-sharing and recognized ethnicity only indirectly. We can, nonetheless, observe general trends in key parties preferring recognition and non-recognition in the ways our theory would predict. "Especially in relation to the rule of law, the [minority] RPF argued for the creation of a pluralistic Rwandan society that guaranteed individual rights and was not based on ethnicity" (Stettenheim 2000, 225). In contrast, the most radically Hutu MRND-CDR had advocated for ethnic and regional power-sharing during the negotiations (Guichaoua 2015). This appears to be more driven by the possibilities (for Hutus) and fears (for Tutsis) of ethnic mobilization than endeavoring to offer assuring effects to the other side. As Guichaoua argues, there were concerns among the RPF in Uganda that "even in the best of circumstances, the refugees' *minority status* could hardly assure them a significant voice in the context of a *majoritarian* democracy, let alone defend their interests" (2015, 26; emphasis added).

Fear of mobilization along ethnic lines is an important consideration in strategic decision-making in Rwanda and a driver of today's non-recognition strategy. In the words of a journalist who interviewed him, and reminiscent of Burundi's Buyoya's comments about the perils of elections, President Kagame critiques Westerners "who fail to understand that pluralist prescriptions could be fatal in a country where the majority recently attempted to expunge the minority" (quoted in Pilling and Barber 2017).

The Rwandan government clearly articulates that recognition of ethnicity could facilitate a return to war. Indeed, the mere existence of ethnicity is often equated with genocide ideology. The government blames the genocide on "bad government of previous regimes" and pervasive "genocide ideology" (Republic of Rwanda 2006, iii). In a government-approved school text, ethnic identities are equated with ethnic division (King 2017). Students educated in post-genocide schools tied ethnicity with war. As one told us, in a statement representative of many, "If we keep teaching and talking about [ethnicity], there will be another genocide, another war can be born." The government claims that genocide ideology is still pervasive and could lead to renewed war, if not properly contained. For example, in 2007, a Parliamentary Commission testified to extensive genocide ideology in Rwanda's schools, with some schools "scoring as high as 97 percent" (Buyinza 2007; see also BBC 2008), although without clarity as to what such a rating means.

Alongside justifying the non-recognition strategy, the government also rationalizes Rwanda's related restrictions on freedom of speech and authoritarianism with the idea that ethnic recognition could facilitate ethnic mobilization. Summarizing this logic, one author describes "fear amongst Tutsis that press freedom would regress into another spell of ethnic conflict" (Berman 2016). Likewise, Rwanda's broadly authoritarian approach to governance is often justified through fear that, without it, a "genocidal mindset" would prevail (Bekken 2011). The narrative surrounding Kagame's successful 2017 run for a third presidential term—the constitution was changed to allow it and he won with 98.7 percent of the vote—stressed that the current leadership and approach is all that prevents Rwandans from, in Kagame's words, "bringing down what we have built" (quoted in Pilling and Barber 2017).

The government's simultaneous emphasis on the stability it provides and on the risk that a return to war is barely contained applies not only within its borders but also to the Democratic Republic of Congo (hereafter Congo). The government of Rwanda explained its intervention in Congo in 1996 as preventive of another war, chasing down *génocidaires* who had become refugees and launched—and may have continued to launch—attacks against Tutsis in Rwanda (Prunier 2008). The second Congo war, starting in 1998, was also justified on security grounds, this time that Hutus were organizing a genocide within eastern

Congo against Banyamulenge, considered to be ethnic Tutsi (Autesserre 2010). The continued presence of the Democratic Forces for the Liberation of Rwanda (FDLR), a Congo-based group of largely Hutu rebels opposed to Tutsi influence in the region, provides further credence to the fears of remobilization along ethnic lines. As Kigali's special envoy for the Great Lakes, Richard Sezibera, put it, his government was "not willing to sit back and watch these people come back and complete the genocide" (quoted in Prunier 2008, 197). As Kagame himself explained, "We went into the Congo because of what the Congo constituted in terms of a huge security threat to our existence" (quoted in Kinzer 2008, 219). Of course, a deeper assessment of the politics of the region speaks to a range of political and economic interests that drove Rwandan participation in violence in the Congo.

It is hard to disentangle whether concern over the mobilization effect has to do with renewed war—the Rwandan government's public messaging is that ethnic naming would lead to ethnic mobilization and renewed war—or with loss of power. Both are consistent with the mobilization mechanism of our theory. "Keeping alive the fear of Hutu revenge," writes Reyntjens, for example, "became a powerful ideological weapon that allowed the RPF to acquire and maintain victim status and to enjoy impunity for its own crimes" (2013, 192).

In Rwanda, at the time of independence, the Union Nationale Rwandaise (UNAR), a pro-monarchy Tutsi party, called on the "children of Rwanda" to "unite our strengths." They went on, "There are no Tutsi, Hutu, Twa. We are all brothers!" (Lemarchand 1970, 161). The historical pattern of non-recognition advocated by Tutsi leadership, and likewise in post-independence Burundi (Chapter 6), provides further support for our interpretation of the importance of strategic considerations grounded in ethnic power configurations. Moreover, the manner in which the non-recognition strategy has been implemented, discussed later in this chapter, further supports this interpretation.

The effects question: implications and consequences

Historical non-recognition and informal recognition at the Arusha Accords

It is difficult to assess the effects of the recognition strategy that prevailed through the Hutu republics in light of the war, genocide, and mass killings. It is also difficult to isolate the impact of one set of policy decisions that occurred alongside a host of others. Some assessed the ethnic quotas as ensuring a minimum representation for Tutsis and guarding against tyranny of the majority (Hoben 1989).

Under a majority government, our theory would have predicted that this type of recognition would help contribute to peace. However, it is important to consider that leaders focused their justifications for the strategy not on assuring the mistrustful minority but rather on ensuring the rights of the majority. For instance, at the time of the 1973 raids of education institutions, PARMEHUTU leaders are reported to have been unhappy seeing Tutsis occupying more spots than their representation in the population would have warranted. In the context of education-based quotas, *both* Hutus and Tutsis reported that the ethnic quotas were unfair to them (King 2014). Moreover, there is much controversy surrounding the identity cards, that listed ethnicity, as a potential example of a perverted recognition system of the type we discussed in Chapter 2. Habyarimana had even announced his intention to eliminate the ethnic notation on the identity cards on November 13, 1990, not long after the beginning of the civil war, at the same time that he announced a new multiparty system (Gourevitch 1998).

What these experiences illustrate is that seeing positive effects of ethnic recognition, even under plurality contexts, appears to be conditioned on the goals of the regime. The assuring effects do not appear to have widely materialized in that Tutsis still felt persecuted. This might be a case then, alongside those we described in Chapter 2, where recognition served to exclude rather than include, reassure, and protect.

At the Arusha Accords, since the factions were widely understood to parallel ethnic groups but there was no explicit recognition that would invoke the symbolic or informational mechanisms we discuss, assessments of the accords were often through the lenses of distribution. "It is hard to think of any agreement," wrote the OAU panel, "more perfectly calculated to enrage virtually everyone in Rwanda with whom the RPF would need to work. It was one thing to say that an 85 percent Hutu population did not mean that Hutu rule equaled democracy. It was another to say that the Tutsi, with less than 15 per cent of the population, should be entitled to almost half the army. Even moderate Hutu, caught in an impossible tug of war between the two sides, found that objectionable" (International Panel of Eminent Personalities 2000, 51).

In the end, Hutu-dominated parties claimed that the RPF "won at the conference table what it had yet to win on the battle field" (Mamdani 2001, 210). For example, while the government of Rwanda suggested that 15 percent of the national army be composed of predominantly Tutsi RPF, the RPF lobbied for a 50–50 split in the national army, and the accords ultimately mandated that 40 percent of the national army and 50 percent of military leadership and strategic military positions be composed of RPF (Jones 2001; Scorgie 2004). Habyarimana and his MRND party, as well as other Hutu parties, appealed to the "majority people" (Guichaoua 2015, 76), as Hutu elites feared a loss of power. While there had been some alliance between moderate Hutu opposition parties and the RPF, when the RPF broke the cease-fire in February 1993 the MRND effectively portrayed the RPF as a Tutsi party in pursuit of power (Khadiagala 2002), a characterization supported by a good deal of later scholarship. We now know that the Arusha Accords fell apart and the war continued, escalating into the genocide and mass killings of 1994.

Non-recognition today

In the post-genocide period, the implications and consequences of the non-recognition strategy present a complex story. On one hand, Rwanda has seen quite dramatic economic revitalization, as illustrated in Figure 7.1. Rwanda averaged impressive 7 percent growth rates in the years immediately after the genocide (1994–1997) and grew an average of 8 percent per year between 2001 and 2014 (Hutt 2016). It has also made significant gains in terms of infrastructure and attracting private investment. Since the genocide, Rwanda's human development index (HDI) rating has risen twenty-eight places, to twenty-ninth from the bottom, although at least some of this is accounted for by other countries' declines. Yet growth has been concentrated in the capital, and the rural majority who continue to eke out a living on subsistence agriculture has not seen the fruits of this growth (Thomson 2018). Moreover, on questions of democracy, Rwanda remains "not free" (Freedom House International 2018), and Figure 7.1 shows some improvement but also overall low scores on political indicators. Rwandans have been asked to trade loyalty to an authoritarian regime for economic growth (Thomson 2018). These trends prompt questions about if and how a peace-building model focused principally on economic development, without some of the other dimensions often considered crucial to positive peace, such as democratic political institutions, might be successful.

The complexities multiply when we draw on a more nuanced picture that considers both the official non-recognition policy and the everyday lived reality. We find that ethnicity remains an important line of cleavage and distrust, as do horizontal inequalities, many along ethnic lines, that have long been the object of intergroup conflict in Rwanda. There are potentially destructive contradictions between the non-recognition policy (or perhaps the way in which it is being implemented) and the everyday experience of Rwandans that are leading to what we call a "paradox of non-recognition."

Of course, there are challenges in trying to assess the non-recognition strategy in Rwanda and its success, or lack thereof, in contributing to peace. Rwanda is an exceptionally difficult place to conduct research and to ask participants to share their genuine opinions. For example, Afrobarometer, Africa's largest public opinion survey, successfully gathers data in thirty-six countries but has decided

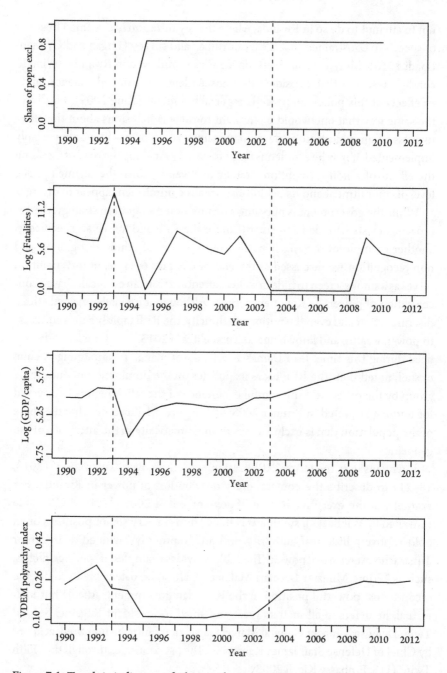

Figure 7.1 Trends in indicators of ethnic exclusion, negative peace, and positive peace in Rwanda.

not to attempt to do so in Rwanda, where the organization has deemed freedom of speech so constrained that it cannot run a valid survey (Logan and Gyimah-Boadi 2016). Moreover, since ethnic identity is outlawed in Rwanda, trying to conduct research that considers its transcendence, continued salience, and/or effects of this policy on peace is especially difficult (King 2009). Finally, in the same way that one would be hesitant to draw conclusions about the effectiveness of an education or development intervention that was only partially implemented, it may be erroneous for us to go very far along the road of assessing the effects of a non-recognition strategy in Rwanda, since the regime's public level of commitment and its behind-the-scenes commitment appear to diverge.

While the government is pursuing a de jure non-recognition strategy, the approach coexists with de facto favoritism for the RPF and for Tutsis specifically, another example of the Machiavellian repurposing of ethnic recognition and non-recognition we discussed at the end of Chapter 6. Here, non-recognition serves as a smokescreen to hide or deflect attention from an ethnically based concentration of power. As Reyntjens writes, "Although it officially rejected ethnic discrimination and even the notion of ethnicity, the RPF rapidly reserved access to power, wealth, and knowledge to Tutsi elites" (2013, 19). One Rwandan official during this time, Jean-Damascène Ntakirutimana, Twagiramungu's chief of staff, noted that "the RPF bases its policies on the domination of one ethnic group by the other, as if the painful experience of the fallen regime had served for nothing" (quoted in Prunier 2008, 44). Figure 7.1 illustrates that the share of the population that is excluded has risen dramatically in the aftermath of the genocide.

Reyntjens uses the terms "RPF-ization" and, moreover "Tutsization" (2013, 18–21) to describe the contemporary distribution of power in Rwanda. For example, in the executive branch of government, a 2008 classified U.S. cable (unveiled by Wikileaks), summarizes that "Hutus in very senior positions often hold relatively little real authority, and are commonly 'twinned' with senior Tutsis who exercise real power." The cable provides examples of specific officials, such as "Prime Minister Bernard Makuza: A Hutu, he ostensibly occupies the second-most powerful position in the Rwandan government. Affable but ineffectual, he defers in all matters great and small to President Kagame. Second Twin: Defense Minister General Marcel Gatsinzi. A Hutu, he is entirely eclipsed by Chief of Defense Staff James Kabarebe." The list continues through the "Fifth Twin" (U.S. Embassy Kigali 2008).

Many Hutus who gained positions of power in the executive branch of government in the years following the genocide have since been forced out, imprisoned, and even killed in suspicious circumstances, some for raising issues related to ethnicity and inequality. For example, in a meeting on August 23, 1995, Twagiramungu criticized Kagame because out of 145 bourgmestres (mayors) he had appointed 117 Tutsis, "clearly overstepping the unspoken agreement never to mention ethnicity in the cabinet in an aggressive way" (Prunier 2008, 45). This criticism was not unwarranted—evidence suggests that in February and March 1995, Kagame's nominations for administration officials at the local level were over 95 percent Tutsi, with a significant proportion of them consisting of "foreign" Tutsis, or Tutsi returnees from Uganda (Prunier 1995). Within three days of the end of that meeting, by August 29, 1995, both Sendashonga and Twagiramungu were pushed out, according to U.S. ambassador to Rwanda Robert Gribbin, "because they dared push for a greater role for Hutu—that is, more democracy in the system" (Gribbin 2005, 156–57). Rwanda's official news agency called them "Hutu supremacists" (Kinzer 2008, 192). In addition, Kagame fired the ministers of justice and information, both Hutus. The minister of communications, a Tutsi, was fired as well; however, scholars have suggested that her firing was to provide cover to indicate that the dismissals were not exclusively Hutus, another nod to the idea that Kagame cared to some extent about legitimacy and against the argument that his hegemony is so complete that he can do whatever he wants (Prunier 2008; for additional information on these firings, see Reyntjens 2013).

Data collected by a group at the University of Antwerp (de Roeck et al. 2016) shows the share of executive positions held by the RPF has increased relatively steadily with time and that while nearly 40 percent of executives are Hutus, Tutsis far outnumber them, especially in prestigious positions. Only a small number of positions go to Tutsis who are not part of the RPF. Based on extensive fieldwork in rural areas, development and conflict scholar Bert Ingelaere (2010) makes a homologous argument about "twinning" of Tutsis with Hutus at the local level, wherein the highest-level local officials are generally RPF Tutsis transplanted from elsewhere by the central government, and unpaid elected positions, with little real power, are held by local Hutus.

Similar arguments are levied against the security sector. A group of government defectors charges that "the Tutsi dominate the command of the military and security institutions" (Gahima et al. 2010) and, moreover, that this imbalance is clearly intentional. According to Joel Mutabazi, Kagame's bodyguard for twenty years, "All of the soldiers in his bodyguard were Tutsi. If you married a Hutu woman, you were kicked out," he told London's *Times* as he fled charges of supporting an exiled general and sought refuge in Uganda, a statement independently corroborated by another member of the force (quoted in Starkey 2012).

According to many scholars and observers, the non-recognition, ethnicity-blind strategy, is, in reality, a mask for an intentional consolidation of power among representatives of the Tutsi minority (Bradol and Guibert 1997; Reyntjens 2013). A cable from the U.S. embassy in Kigali assesses that "while the Rwandan government (GOR) presents itself as a champion of national unity and equal opportunity, de-emphasizing ethnic identity and ostensibly opening positions throughout society to those of skill and merit, political authority in the country does not yet reflect this ideal" (2008). In Reyntjens's assessment, "Of course, the elimination of ethnicity was a worthwhile goal, shared by many Rwandans, but this objective was manipulated as a tool for the monopolization of power in the hands of a small group," a strategy reminiscent of 1950s Rwanda and of Burundi from 1965 to 1988 (Reyntjens 2013, 19; see also Lemarchand 1996). Ordinary Rwandans, too, regularly question the motives of the government's efforts at social engineering. As one released prisoner told Rwanda scholar Susan Thomson, "If I thought these strategies of reconciliation were really designed to keep us together and living in peace, I would support it" (2012, 96).

The overall assessment from those who have done in-depth, on-the-ground fieldwork with Rwandans is that the non-recognition strategy has not yet resulted in the transcendence of ethnic identity. While many of the citations in this section are dated, the continued salience of ethnicity and mistrust are confirmed by more recent publications (Eramian 2014; Goehrung 2017; Russell and Carter 2018), as well as by personal communications we had with scholars currently in the field and others who have conducted fieldwork quite recently and not yet published their findings. Research into these issues in Rwanda is becoming more and more difficult to do (Thomson 2018).

Ethnicity remains important in Rwanda. As one Rwandan indicated to us (all quotes from King 2014, 141–142), just after claiming that ethnicity did not exist, "It's that there are physical traits upon which you can say that this one is Hutu and that one is Tutsi . . . despite everything, children can usually tell from first sight, yes, he is this, she is that [ethnicity]." Others we met over the course of research in the late 2000s described how one's circumstances and experiences lead to widespread continued private use of ethnic categories. "You ask if you have a father, 'no,' you know it's a Tutsi. If you see scars, surely you know. Or someone says they don't have a father, nor a mother, no sisters, and they tell you the whole story. Where they were, what they saw, like that. You get ideas and it [ethnicity] comes out very easily." Another explained to us, "Do you think that one with an imprisoned father isn't known as a Hutu? That a child that is paid by FARG [a scholarship program for genocide survivors] isn't recognized as a survivor [i.e., Tutsi]?." Buckley-Zistel concluded that "today (ethnic) group identity is meaningful (arguably even more than before the genocide)" (2006, 12).

Moreover, people find it useful to know one another's ethnic identity because distrust remains pervasive, especially along ethnic lines. As one Rwandan woman explained to us: "That is the policy [that ethnicities do not exist], but the daily reality is that we know that ethnicity cannot be erased like that, all in one shot. It still exists in our hearts. Everyone knows who is there and when you are sitting there and you see a Hutu, you know it is a Hutu. There are conversations you can't have in the presence of a Hutu. There are conversations that Hutus can't have in the presence of a Tutsi." Such inability to discuss issues across ethnic groups confines people to discussions within their networks. This stands in contrast to the approach in Burundi, where there are even radio programs that explicitly discuss ethnic issues. RPF members told Reyntjens that even RPF Hutus could not be trusted fully given doubts about where their loyalties lay (Reyntjens 2013).

That the non-recognition strategy is being implemented (or at the very least perceived to be being implemented) alongside hidden preference for Tutsis is central to the continued salience of ethnicity and mistrust, as well as important horizontal inequalities along ethnic lines. That is, ordinary Rwandans' everyday reality signals to them that ethnicity still matters, even though they are repeatedly told all are Rwandans and ostensibly equal. Here we see a disconnect between de jure and de facto experiences. As one man told us, "We say that we have reconciliation and unity, we sing it in the radios, in the *ingandos*, everywhere, and in the radio we hear this, but in practice it is lacking. That's the problem." In his study drawing on four hundred life histories of ordinary Rwandans, Ingelaere (2010) reports that Hutu respondents recounted experiencing more prejudice under the current regime and, not surprisingly, Tutsi respondents indicated perceptions of fewer prejudices. Anthropologist Larissa Begley similarly reports respondents' opinions that "the government says that everyone has the same identity, but when it comes to getting better jobs or benefits, the better identity is Tutsi" (2011, 158). In earlier research, we find that a scholarship for genocide survivors is perceived by other Rwandans to entrench ethnicity alongside entitlement and thereby unfairly prioritize Tutsi. Interview participants identified other groups in need, including Hutus who lost their parents during the war, who were not eligible for the scholarship (King 2014). Since grievances cannot be articulated along ethnic lines, the RPF has denied Hutus recourse to complain about their exclusion. The pre-genocide president, Habyarimana, and today's president, Kagame, can both be accused of "manipulat[ing] ethnicity, the former by scapegoating and eventually exterminating the Tutsi, the latter by discriminating against the Hutu under the guise of ethnic amnesia" (Reyntjens 2013, 25).

The government contends with an important contradiction inherent in the pairing of its non-recognition approach with the ways in which it has sought maintenance of power and ostensible legitimacy. The RPF legitimates its rule domestically and internationally on a narrative of having stopped the genocide of the Tutsis (Pottier 2002; Reyntjens 2004). As a result, it needs to keep alive the ideas of a Hutu threat and Tutsi victims, collectivizing Hutus and Tutsis as perpetrators and survivors, respectively. At the same time, therefore, the government espouses the contradictory positions that ethnicity no longer matters—a foundation of its non-recognition approach—and draws on a highly ethnicized narrative of Tutsi victimhood and hidden preference for Tutsis. The implications of this contradiction inform Rwanda's future.

Prospects

As Kinzer—who authored a positive biography of Kagame—opined about him and his policies in a recent interview, "Some think he is laying the foundations for peace, others think the opposite" (quoted in Pilling and Barber 2017). Those who side with Kagame and his non-recognition approach might argue that he is building a positive peace by promoting meaningful economic development. While the peace being built would not be in the liberal democratic mold, some contend that the model could still be successful. The key debate with regard to Rwanda, though, is whether a focus on the economic, to the exclusion of democracy and social space for discussion, including conversations about ethnicity, can be a route to sustainable peace. As Thomson writes, "The RPF's expectation is that Rwandans will be willing to exchange justice for the benefits of economic growth." And while she expects no imminent return to mass violence, she deems the current situation a "precarious peace" (2018, 9, 13).

Critics may argue that the economic pie is not growing sufficiently quickly for distributional issues, including along ethnic lines, not to matter. Moreover, in Rwanda, we observe a paradox of non-recognition. That is, while one may assume that the salience of ethnicity would decline with non-recognition, in Rwanda ethnicity continues to command importance. There are some who contend that it is the very non-recognition strategy of outlawing ethnicity and discussions surrounding it that is sustaining social exclusion and the maintenance of boundaries. Insofar as this is the case, and leaving recognition issues as they are, the paradox of non-recognition is such that the way non-recognition is being implemented is sustaining the cleavage that threatens to undermine the state and peace-building project.

Of course, even twenty-five years is a short amount of time to see identity change. Yet Kagame faces a "dilemma of recognition," and since he does not assure with recognition, he needs a way—characterized by surveillance, intimidation, and the suppression of dissent (Freedom House 2018)—to keep the citizenry in line and to mitigate against the mobilization effects. As a *Financial Times* article noted, "Even admirers wonder whether [Kagame] might be Rwanda's equivalent of General Josip Tito, who kept Yugoslavia together only for it to shatter after he was gone" (Pilling and Barber 2017). It is not so easy, though, to say that the regime should switch to ethnic recognition as Burundi has done because, in doing so, the current situation would become all the more visible for Hutus and would likely inspire efforts to overthrow the regime.

The case of Ethiopia may allow us additional insight into this question by drawing on the analytical leverage that comparison offers. Like Rwanda, Ethiopia's key contemporary constitutional moments occurred under minority leadership. But, unlike Rwanda, Ethiopia's government adopted recognition. What can we learn by comparing these two minority regimes that adopted different approaches to conflict management in similarly ethnically divided societies?

8

Ethnic Recognition Under Minority Rule in Ethiopia

In the aftermath of mass violence in Ethiopia through the 1970s and 1980s, Ethiopia's new president, Meles Zenawi, adopted recognition in the early 1990s. He argued, "We cannot ignore that Ethiopia is a diverse country. Previous attempts to do that have led to wars" (quoted in McWhirter and Melamede 1992, 33). Similarly, a Western diplomat commented at the time that Ethiopia's government was "recognizing ethnicity for what it is—a very powerful issue" (quoted in Lorch 1995). Both, though, also acknowledged the risks inherent in the new approach to diversity and recognition. The diplomat continued, "They are sitting on an ethnic time bomb. They have come up with an impossible solution, which is to tackle it pre-emptively. It is a frightening experiment. Will it work? I don't think anybody knows" (quoted in Lorch 1995). Meles was similarly measured in his assessment of prospects: "If Ethiopia breaks apart, then it wasn't meant to be" (quoted in McWhirter and Melamede 1992, 33).

That Meles, a minority Tigrayan leader, chose ethnic federalism diverges from our theoretical prediction that would see a minority leader opt for nonrecognition, as in post-genocide Rwanda. Indeed, up until that time, minority Amharic leaders, from the second-largest ethnic group, had built Ethiopia around an Amharic cultural and linguistic identity that denied ethnic diversity. The switch to recognition, with the 1994 constitution going so far as to enshrine the right to self-determination for ethnic groups, thus represents a dramatic shift in strategy and entails the thickest example of ethnic recognition in Africa. (This is sometimes called the 1995 constitution since that is when it came into force.) This institutional mismatch—recognition under minority leadership—persisted until 2018, when a leader from the plurality Oromo group became prime minister. What explains the adoption of recognition by Ethiopia's minority leader? Do ethnic power configurations come into play in this case, as our theory proposes? Furthermore, what is the effect of recognition on peace and conflict?

Diversity, Violence, and Recognition. Elisabeth King and Cyrus Samii, Oxford University Press (2020). © Oxford University Press.
DOI: 10.1093/oso/9780197509456.003.0001

The Ethiopian case allows us to consider recognition under minority leadership. Furthermore, Ethiopia has many more ethnic groups than Burundi and Rwanda, and there is a smaller difference in the population share between the plurality and second-largest ethnic groups in Ethiopia. Conflicts have also had an ethnonational component. These distinguishing features allow us to consider the generality of our theory.

This chapter follows a similar structure to the previous two. First, we review the Ethiopian context and nature of the conflict, illustrating a history of ethnically based inequality, mistrust, and violence that constitute the basic conditions underlying our theory. Second, we present an overview of Ethiopia's historic approach to non-recognition and concentrate on the details of the recognition strategy in contemporary Ethiopia, as enshrined in the constitution and materialized in institutions. Third, we consider the adoption of recognition through the lens of our theory, with sections focusing on the importance of leaders' interests and ethnic power configurations, then considering the assuring and mobilizing effects of recognition. We show that the ruling Tigrayan People's Liberation Front (TPLF) had a keen understanding of its minority position and understood the assuring benefits of recognition. We argue that the minority TPLF leadership was, as expected, worried about mobilization against them. Yet since the TPLF needed to harness the power of ethnic mobilization in order to overthrow the previous regime, path dependency toward ethnic recognition was fostered thereafter. The fourth part of the chapter turns to the on-the-ground implementation of ethnic federalism and its mixed effects on peace. Concentrating on the period up until 2018, we consider the strategies the minority government deployed to mitigate the risks of mobilization against them, including using ethnic federalism as a smokescreen for Tigrayan consolidation of power and advancing authoritarianism. We close the chapter with a consideration of the 2018 change in leadership to a plurality Oromo leader for the first time in Ethiopian history and Ethiopia's future prospects.

Context and nature of the conflict

Ethiopia is, in many ways, different from the tiny central African states upon which we focused in Chapters 6 and 7. Ethiopia is the second-most-populous country in sub-Saharan Africa, after only Nigeria, with a population roughly eight times as large as that of Burundi or Rwanda. It is one of only two sub-Saharan African countries never to have experienced European colonialism, although it was occupied by the Italians in 1936. The country holds an important place in the subcontinent; it is, for instance, the seat of the African Union.

Ethiopia is home to more than eighty ethnic groups, resulting in a high ethnic fractionalization score, although a handful of ethnic groups dominate the state. Oromos are the most numerous group, at about 35 percent of the population, and Amharas, the second-largest group, represent approximately 27 percent of Ethiopians, reflecting one of the measures of demographic dominance we introduced in Chapter 4, a low level of ethnic difference. Together, these two groups account for more than half of Ethiopia's population. Tigrayans, the third- or fourth-largest ethnic group (depending on census), represent roughly 6 percent of the population, less than half of the minority Tutsis' share of the Rwandan population.

The issues of ethnicity, mistrust, and violent conflict, at the core of this book, have long existed and been intertwined in Ethiopia. The state was historically held by one ethnic group—Amharas—whose rule included oppression, efforts at assimilation, violence, and exclusion of others (Young 1996a). While recorded Ethiopian history goes back to the tenth century BC, Ethiopia's modern history begins in the 1850s with a process of state expansion from the north by the Shoan Amhara branch of the Abyssinian nobility. In its efforts to centralize a feudal state, the nobility commonly dispossessed people of their land, including through the conquest of groups such as the Sidama, Gurage, and western Oromo people. The process of state consolidation also marginalized northern Tigray, whose people felt this loss particularly acutely. While Tigrayans share with dominant Amharas a legacy that traces back to the foundation of the Ethiopian state in Tigray and the Abyssinian family, Tigrayans felt excluded from power by Amharas, specifically Amharas from the Shoa region, as Tigrayan traditional authorities were overtaken and Amharic imposed as the state language. After the liberation of Ethiopia from Italian occupation, the process of state consolidation intensified further. Widespread discontent vis-à-vis the Amhara elite arose. Under the rule of Emperor Haile Selassie (1930–36, 1941–74), peasants and pastoralists who rebelled against the feudal land-holding system were massacred. The emperor also used violence to clamp down on armed rebellions that arose in Ogaden, Tigray, and Eritrea, among other places, in objection to his policy of Amhara ethnic domination (Tegegn 2012).

Violence persisted under the regime that followed. In 1974, students led a revolution against imperialism that resulted in the overthrow of Haile Selassie and brought to power the ideologically communist Derg (short for the Provisional Military Administrative Council, as well as Amharic for "council"), under the leadership of its chairman Mengistu Haile Mariam. Mengistu led the country with an iron fist, implementing restrictions on freedom of assembly, the press, and political action. In response, the regime faced numerous challenges nearly from its inception, including from the Amhara-based Ethiopian People's

Revolutionary Party (EPRP) and the All-Ethiopia Socialist Movement (Meison), of largely Oromo membership. Tigrayans, Somalis, and others also took action against Mengistu's repressive Amhara-dominated regime. The peak of violence is a period known as the Red Terror (1976–78) wherein arbitrary arrests, torture, and massacres ostensibly targeted against the EPRP became routine for any opposition and all who were not part of the Derg's party. Violence persisted thereafter, and Ethiopia endured civil war through 1991. There was also widespread government-fostered famine that researcher Alex De Waal describes as "one of the most systematic uses of mass murder by the state ever witnessed in Africa" (1991, 101). In all, an estimated 1.4 million were left dead during Mengistu's rule (Tegegn 2012; Toggia 2012).

In response to ongoing violence, exclusion, and oppression, many actors organized insurgencies across Ethiopia. The most prominent were the TPLF, who sought to overthrow the Derg and to become the new leadership of Ethiopia, and the Eritrean People's Liberation Front (EPLF), who also wished to overthrow the Mengistu regime, but with an end goal of secession of Eritrea. In contrast to the Derg's socialist focus on class, the TPLF, drawing in part on Stalinist principles, believed that national/ethnic struggle was the most appropriate basis of organization for the opposition. Sarah Vaughan, who has long studied and worked in Ethiopia and the Horn of Africa, argues that the leaders chose nationalities as the basis of organization because it was the easiest way to mobilize people against "uneven development" under the Derg (1994, 57), consistent with our discussion of the mobilization dimension in Chapter 2. The TPLF allied with, and even fostered the creation of, other ethnically based movements to form the Ethiopian People's Revolutionary Democratic Front (EPRDF). Together, the TPLF-led EPRDF and the Eritrean EPLF militarily defeated the Derg, and the TPLF came to power in 1991. Its leaders formed a transitional government and adopted a national charter to serve as an interim constitution, the first of the two constitutional moments in our dataset. Meles, the leader of the TPLF transitional government, became prime minister and was thrice reelected to the position (in 2000, 2005, and 2010)—albeit in what is described as a "semi-authoritarian" regime (Aalen 2006), "electoral authoritarianism" (Aalen and Tronvoll 2009), or "one-party" regime (Lyons 1996)— serving in this role until his death in 2012. Indeed, our colleagues who work in Ethiopia often remarked that our on-the-ground research experience under an authoritarian government in Rwanda (King 2009) well prepared us for the dynamics and challenges of research in Ethiopia.

The EPRDF and its TPLF leadership continued to dominate politics in Ethiopia until 2018 under Hailemariam Desalegn, despite his identifying as part of the Wolayta ethnic group, the second-largest group from the Southern Nations, Nationalities, and People's Region (SNNPR) (Mills 2018). In 2018,

Abiy Ahmed, from Ethiopia's largest Oromo ethnic group, was appointed prime minister on a wave of protest. In late 2019, Abiy formed the Prosperity Party out of the EPRDF, which he claimed was associated with oppression and human rights abuses (Yibeltal 2019). At the time of writing, the Prosperity Party included all of the EPRDF's constituent parties except the TPLF, and also included a wider set of ethnic groups that previously held lesser status within the state.

Recognition over time

Non-recognition under the emperor (1930–1974)

The ethnic federalism that characterizes Ethiopia today is a dramatic departure from the non-recognition regimes that have predominated historically. Under Emperor Haile Selassie and those who came before him, Ethiopia was built around a strongly centralized non-recognition regime wherein Ethiopians were to assimilate into an Amharic identity. Unlike most countries in Africa, the concepts of state and nation were not imposed by colonial powers (Clapham 1988). The Ethiopian state has long been multiethnic—for example, both Haile Selassie and his father, Ras Makonnen, were of mixed Oromo-Amhara parentage—but, consistent with Ethiopian dynastic tradition, Haile Selassie imposed a strict cultural assimilationist policy, with Amharic as the sole language and Abyssinian Orthodox Christianism as the official religion of the ruling elite. As one Oromo student leader wrote in a 1969 publication:

> Ask anybody what Ethiopian culture is? Ask anybody what Ethiopian language is? Ask anybody what Ethiopian music is? Ask about what Ethiopian religion is? Ask about what the national dress is? It is either Amhara or Amhara-Tigre!! To be a "genuine" Ethiopian one has to listen to Amharic music, to accept the Amhara-Tigre religion, Orthodox Christianity, to wear the Amhara-Tigre shamma in international conferences. In some cases, to be an "Ethiopian" you will even have to change your name. In short, to be an Ethiopian, you will have to wear an Amhara mask (to use Fanon's expression). (Quoted in De Waal 1991, 68)

While focusing on non-recognition through cultural assimilation, Haile Selassie was also cognizant of ethnically based discontent in the provinces. To ward off unrest, he used informal recognition to appoint provincial elites to the senate in Addis, thereby geographically distancing regional elites from their power bases (Gashaw 1993).

Non-recognition and transition under the Derg
(1974–1991)

The Derg, under Mengistu's military dictatorship, continued a non-recognition regime, again centralized under an Amharic identity. Ethiopia's "scientific socialism" focused on organizing people into groups around economic or social categories and did not legitimate ethnicity as a politically relevant organizing principle (Keller and Smith 2005). According to scholar and political analyst John Young, "The Derg also strove to forge a totally centralized state and, therefore, it refused to share power with either the politically conscious middle classes or the emerging regional and ethnic elites, and ensured that the state retained its predominately Amhara character" (1996a, 534). In fact, the regime endeavored to homogenize the people and destroy subnational movements (Spears 2010). These policies were said to be especially challenging for Oromos, the "largest and most amorphous of Ethiopian ethnic groups" (Clapham 1998, 196).

Nonetheless, during this period we also observe some movement along the continuum from non-recognition toward recognition in ways that ultimately facilitated the implementation of recognition after the civil war. The Derg initially acknowledged Ethiopia's ethnic diversity, proclaimed equality of all cultures, and gave lip service to the use of languages beyond Amharic. The government allowed for Muslim holidays in addition to the usually observed Christian holidays, it added radio programming in multiple languages, and education officials discussed the possibility of local language learning. In the mid-1980s, it established the Institute of Nationalities with the goal of studying Ethiopia's ethnic makeup and drafting a type of federal structure for the country. The 1984 census included unprecedented details about ethnicity and language (Smith 2013). The constitution of 1987 even included five autonomous regions: Eritrea, Dire Dawa, Tigray, Assab, and Ogaden, although the devolved powers were strictly limited and not constitutionally protected (Aalen 2006).

Recognition (1991–present)

When the Tigrayan-led EPRDF achieved a military victory over the Derg in 1991, as an alliance of several ethnically based groups, its leadership adopted ethnic federalism, described as a "radical programme of decentralizing state power to ethnic-based units" (Young 1996a, 531). The principle first articulated in the 1991 national charter and then formalized in the constitution that took effect in 1995 is that "every Nation, Nationality and People in Ethiopia has an unconditional right to self-determination, including the right to secession" (Article 39.1). The constitution also identifies that each "Nation, Nationality and People" has specific rights to language, culture, the preservation of history and self-government (Article 39.2). Clearly in contrast to the two previous regimes, the EPRDF coalition sought to promote and institutionalize ethnic diversity in Ethiopia through ethnic federalism and what has often been called "unity in diversity" (see, i.e., Ministry of Foreign Affairs of Ethiopia 2016).

The constitution defines a "Nation, Nationality or People" as "a group of people who have or share large measure of a common culture or similar customs, mutual intelligibility of language, belief in a common or related identities, a common psychological make-up and who inhabit an identifiable, predominantly contiguous territory" (Article 39.5). The Amharic word for nations, *beher*, also translates as "ethnic groups" (Smith 2007, 588).

The transitional government of Ethiopia (TGE) held an inclusive conference soon after assuming the leadership and produced the first document that we include in our dataset. At this conference, it settled the Eritrea issue, agreeing to uphold the results of a referendum that later, in April 1993, led to Eritrean independence. The resulting loss of the port of Assab, the country's only seaport, to Eritrea emerged as a major grievance of many Ethiopians, particularly Amharas. Moreover, despite early inclusivity, one-party rule was already beginning to be established (Lyons 1996).

As part of the system of ethnic federalism, Ethiopia is divided into nine ethnolinguistically based regions (*kilil*), or states, most having one majority ethnic group that lends the state its name, but each containing multiple ethnicities. In addition to the regions, there are two autonomous cities, Addis Ababa and Dire Dawa. There is a strong population concentration around a handful of regions. Upward of 90 percent of Ethiopia's people live in Addis Ababa or one of four regional states: Tigray, Amhara, Oromia, and the SNNPR (Lyons 2019). Regional governments were granted the power to create their own constitutions as a way to limit the central power of the federal government. This federal structure is based on a 1991 map and Proclamation 7/1992 establishing the "national self-governments."

In the ethnic federal structure, the executive branch consists of the prime minister, the head of government, the council of ministers (akin to a cabinet), and the president, the head of state. The legislature has a bicameral structure. The House of People's Representatives, the legislative lower house, has 547 seats directly elected through a first-past-the-post system in each electoral district. Per the constitution, at least twenty seats must be reserved for minority ethnicities, although the constitution does not provide guidelines as to which ethnicities count as minorities. The House of Federation, the upper house, has 120 seats with positions elected by the state councils per their own rules. According to the constitution, there must be one representative from each ethnicity, plus one additional representative for every one million members of that population or ethnic group. The House of Federation has no legislative power and convenes just twice per year (Aalen 2006). Its main function is said to be to ensure harmony and coexistence of the different federal states (Ashenafi 2003). Table 8.1 provides a contemporary overview of this and the other domains of recognition.

The principle of ethnic recognition also extends to additional state institutions, as Table 8.1 illustrates. In regard to the civil service, for instance, there are references to quotas and affirmative action to ensure proportionality among Ethiopia's nations and nationalities (Vaughan and Tronvoll 2003). However, how ethnic representativeness is supposed to work in the civil service remains unclear (Mengistu and Vogel 2006). There are also requirements for representation of ethnic minorities in the armed forces. The Ethiopian constitution states that "the composition of the national armed forces shall reflect the equitable representation of the Nations, Nationalities and Peoples of Ethiopia" (1995, art. 87), however, there is little evidence that such representation has been implemented.

The judicial system in Ethiopia is made up of the federal courts, nine regional court systems, and two municipal systems in Addis Ababa and Dire Dawa (Plummer 2012). While there is no constitutional requirement for representation in the federal courts, state governments are obligated to guarantee balanced ethnic representation among the judicial arms of their government bodies (Fessha and Van Der Beken 2013). The Ethiopian constitution also permits the establishment of religious and customary courts, thus far implemented in some parts of the country as sharia courts, which apply Islamic law. The Ethiopian government reported that there have been informal efforts to guarantee equitable representation of all nations, nationalities, and peoples in all law enforcement

Table 8.1 **Implementation of ethnic recognition policies in seven government and public sector domains in Ethiopia**

Implementation following 1994 constitution	
Executive	Partial
Legislative	Yes
Security	Partial
Justice	Yes
Civil Service	Yes
Education	Yes
Language	Yes

Source: Authors' implementation dataset, described in Chapter 5.

entities, including prosecutors and judges (Committee on the Elimination of Racial Discrimination 2009).

The 1995 Ethiopian constitution also made significant changes to language policies in Ethiopia, outlining groups' rights to "cultural identity, including to right to speak, write and develop their language." The focus on group-based language rights is especially significant since, alongside descent, the Ethiopian state defines ethnic identity based on language. While the official language in Ethiopia remains Amharic and the federal government works in Amharic, the federal court system can also choose between using Ge'ez (Ethiopic) script (same as written Amharic) or a non-Ethiopian script (Habtu 2004). Moreover, regional governments can choose their own working languages in all state-level affairs.

Education is a particularly important sector where ethnic recognition plays out. First, under the government's ethnic recognition strategy, educational content (curricula and textbooks) should reflect regional context and "concrete local conditions" (Egne 2014). Each of Ethiopia's nine regions was granted educational autonomy, allowing the regional governments the opportunity to adapt their curricula and teaching materials to the needs of their citizens. At the same time, the Ministry of Education in Ethiopia produced a set of national education policies and standards that the regional governments are expected to uphold, and the federal government monitors the performance of the regional governments (Mitchell 2015; Zimmermann-Steinhart and Bekele 2012). Second, after the longtime requirement of Amharic as the language of instruction, the nine regional governments are now tasked with choosing the language of instruction in primary schools for their own regions. They select the language of instruction for primary school based upon the ethnic majority in each region with the idea of using mother tongues (secondary school is in English), but they can also choose to use Amharic, and some, such as the Gurage, have done so (Semela 2014; Smith 2013).

Overall, ethnic federalism in Ethiopia set an ambitious program seeking to enshrine ethnic groups throughout institutions of the state. As Young wrote in 1996, "No [other] government on the continent has devolved powers on an ethnic basis; nor has any government explicitly granted its constituent parts the legal right to secede" (1996a, 531). What explains the adoption of this most extreme recognition strategy?

The adoption question: assessing the theory

A number of scholars of Ethiopia endeavor to answer the question of "the EPRDF's rationale for introducing ethnic federalism" (Aalen 2006; see also Aalen 2011; Kefale 2013; Lyons 2019; Vaughan and Tronvoll 2003; Young

1996a). Terrence Lyons, an international relations scholar with specialization in the region, describes the war-to-peace transition and the choice of recognition as an "endogenous process," akin to that in Rwanda, where military victors set post-conflict priorities (2019, 50). Indeed, explanations for the rationale converge on two principal factors, both of which are internal to Ethiopia's history and politics. First, ethnic federalism is seen as a response to a history of ethnic domination and marginalization. Second, and related, the way in which the TPLF conducted the revolution and came to power, in a relatively "fragile political position" (Bélair 2016), required support and legitimation from other groups and concessions to these groups. This may be a case of leaders recognizing ethnic identities and correspondingly sharing power when they must, as we discussed in Chapter 2. We observe little support for the other, external explanations for the adoption of recognition: since Ethiopia was never colonized, its decision to adopt recognition is counter to the prevailing African norm of non-recognition, and the international community was not strongly involved in the Ethiopian transition. (Kefale [2013] does point to the uniquely Stalinist principle of self-determination that influenced revolutionary ideology in Ethiopia.)

What might the our theory add to this literature and to our broader understanding of the adoption of recognition? Ethiopia's 1995 constitution was adopted under a minority government, leading us to expect, all else being equal, non-recognition. Even though this case diverges from our theoretical predictions on adoption, we show that viewing the two prevailing explanations for the adoption of recognition in Ethiopia through the lens of our theory (the first explanation as assuring effects, and the second as mobilization effects), and especially highlighting the importance of the ethnic power configuration, provides additional insights into why Ethiopia's leadership chose ethnic recognition and the subsequent challenges and opportunities that Ethiopia faces in building peace.

The Ethiopian case also allows us to consider the moderating effects of ethnic fractionalization and ethnic difference. We can first assess the differences in strategic calculations in circumstances where there is a larger number of ethnic groups. Theoretically, we expected that adoption under minority rule is more likely in more ethnically fractionalized states such as Ethiopia. We can also investigate our earlier proposition that a smaller "ethnic difference," as in Ethiopia, should dampen the effects of minority rule. In the end, the way the Ethiopian case unfolds is consistent with the moderating scope conditions that we introduce earlier in the book.

Leaders' interests and ethnic power configurations

The Tigrayan leadership is credited with having well understood the implications of its ethnic minority status and is described as "shrewd" in its consequent calculations (Spears 2010, 78). Demographic factors are an important part of the reason that the TPLF took the approach that it did, both in terms of overthrowing the Derg and coming to power and in terms of its adoption of recognition. As Yemane Ghebreab, a senior official in Eritrea's ruling party, said, "The ethnic politics and the constitution . . . were not arrived at with the overall interests of Ethiopia in mind, with the belief that this was the best way to maintain Ethiopian unity. It was essentially a form of self-preservation [for the minority leadership]. That was the agenda" (quoted in Spears 2010, 83). In fact, as Lyons explains, "the victorious rebel movement's position on national self-determination [a key feature of Ethiopian ethnic federalism] was anathema to many Ethiopian nationalists" (2019, 49). We illustrate the importance of ethnic power configurations in the two effects of recognition.

The assuring effects

The EPRDF explanation for its commitment to ethnic recognition is akin to that of present-day Burundian leadership, presenting it as the pathway to peace. A ninth-grade civic and ethical education student textbook explains it this way: "The major purpose of the FDRE [Federal Democratic Republic of Ethiopia] government is to secure the peaceful co-existence of Nations, Nationalities and Peoples who consented to live together on the basis of equality and other principles of democracy. These principles and values . . . are designed to protect not only individual members but also the rights of all Nations, Nationalities and Peoples of Ethiopia as a whole" (cited in Smith 2013, 44).

More strongly than in the cases of Burundi or Rwanda, though, demands for ethnically based recognition were a key part of the war, and thus the assuring effects take on special importance. Meles himself explained about the conference to bring about the transitional charter that

> what we were trying to do was to stop the war, and start the process of peaceful competition, peaceful expression of political opinion, and so forth. The key cause of the war all over the country was the issue of nationalities. Any solution that did not address them, did not address the issue of peace and war. . . . People were fighting for the right to use their language, to use their culture, to administer. So without guaranteeing these rights [it] was not possible to stop the war, or prevent another one from coming up. (Quoted in Vaughan 1994, 56)

Africanist scholars Edmond J. Keller and Lahra Smith (2005) concur that much of the Ethiopian population viewed the decentralization inherent in ethnic federalism as assurance of social equity and democracy. Lyons (1996) assesses that the charter appeared especially designed in this regard to win over the support of the plurality Oromo and other southern groups.

As in Burundi and Rwanda, and per the prevailing scholarship on Ethiopia, legacies of the previous regimes also weighed heavily on the new leadership and on the groups making claims upon them. Young argues that while policies of centralized non-recognition have long been dominant in the Horn of Africa, "continuing problems of ethnic conflict and economic stagnation made clear the failure of these approaches and the theories on which they are based" (1996a, 541). Smith likewise argues that "there is little doubt that the roots of the question of nationalities . . . lay directly in the attempted imposition of cultural and political identities that did not resonate with the newly conquered peoples" (2013, 67; see also Lyons 1996). Dawit Yohannes, one of Meles's legal advisors, argued, "We say there is no country called Ethiopia, no state that defends the interests of this multi-ethnic community grouped under the name Ethiopia. That's why we've been immersed in wars for the last 30 years. So we must start again, from scratch" (quoted in Lyons 1996, 124).

Ethnic recognition offered important assurances to opposition ethnic groups with whom the TPLF had allied to overthrow the Derg. Smith assesses the self-determination clauses, in particular, as having "intense symbolic power" (2013, 83), and recognition through ethnic federalism also offered important group-differentiated rights. Fulfilling early promises of recognition and making assurances to other ethnic groups was a key part of building legitimacy for the new minority leadership.

There were also important demands by the minority Tigray for recognition and group-differentiated rights. Per political scientist Ian Spears, "The contemporary idea of Woyane [an uprising in Tigray that began in 1943] was about making Tigray safe from economic and cultural oppression that arose as a consequence of Amhara (and then Derg) domination centered in Addis Ababa. Controlling power in the capital—even if in conjunction with other ethnic representatives—afforded the TPLF the best protection for the small region it inhabited within Ethiopia" (2010, 94). The TPLF had also long claimed the right to recognition and even secession for Tigrayans, and this was instrumental to their popular support in Tigray. The 1983 TPLF constitution provided an early articulation of these aspirations: "The TPLF, which is the direct outcome of the decades of oppression of the people of Tigray and which reflects their aspirations, is the vanguard of the revolution. . . . Since our people have been victims of national domination, they are also struggling to free themselves of this domination and thereby safeguard their national rights, dignity and the right to self-determination" (TPLF 1983, 1). Given their long-standing platform of ethnically based rights and self-determination, upon coming to power the TPLF was not in a position to be able to deny these rights through non-recognition. In this sense, the leadership needed to assure its own constituency. Given their ge-ographic concentration, Tigrayan leaders may have also seen self-determination and secession as a fallback or "escape hatch" (Spears 2010, 65) in the event that the TPLF was unable to dominate Ethiopia. In short, non-recognition does not appear to have been a choice compatible with the minority TPLF coming to power—not only in terms of assuring effects, but also intertwined with preventing ethnic mobilization against them.

The mobilization effects

Alongside the assuring effects of recognition—and consistent with our theory—the power of ethnic mobilization also weighed heavily on the regime, although in a different way than our theory predicts. Our theoretical chapter presumes the possibility for ethnic mobilization to increase with recognition, and for this to be a risk for minority leaders. Meanwhile, our theory takes for granted that this choice, and the follow-on effects, are concentrated in the post-conflict period and that the leader in question is making a choice about stability for the future rather than the immediate present. In contrast, due to its minority status and Ethiopia's diversity, the TPLF harnessed the power of ethnic mobilization *prior* to the overthrow of the Derg, and indeed used ethnic mobilization to help bring about this overthrow. These actions made it such that their options in the post-conflict period were limited to a continuation of recognition. We argue that mobilization was a key concern, but in a different way than we discuss earlier in the book: The TPLF was worried that it would be impossible to rule—other parties would mobilize against them at that mo-ment, continuing the war—if it did not grant ethnic recognition. This made the two sides of the dilemma of recognition pull more strongly toward recogni-tion rather than in opposite directions, as we theorize is more typically the case under minority leadership.

In order to really challenge the Derg, the TPLF realized that, as a minority in ethnically fragmented Ethiopia, it needed a "pan-Ethiopian framework." The strength of rebel movements is often weak in highly fractionalized states since groups are limited by their inability to move beyond their own ethnic group's interests (Gates 2002). Thus, as a minority, the TPLF created the EPRDF, going so far as to construct allied constituent units rather than co-opting and including preexisting ones. The EPRDF political program states, for instance, that "since Ethiopia is a multi-national country, the way to guide its different nationalities and peoples together for the struggle should be through a Front made up of multi-national member organizations, and not in an organizational framework of individuals" (EPRDF 1991, art. 4.9). One of the EPRDF's political objectives was that "nations and nationalities could secure a better organizational leadership and political participation when they are in struggle under the leadership of nations and nationality organizations of their own" (EPRDF 1991, art. 2a). The program further stated that "the formation of organizations of nations and nationalities that are governed by the democratic objectives which foster fraternity and unity among different organizations is fundamental. The formation of nations and nationality organizations under one revolutionary democratic Front will be the better choice to realize this objective" (EPRDF 1991, art. 2b). Consistent with our analysis, Jon Abbink, a political anthropologist with expertise in the Horn of Africa, argued that "this new model was dictated by necessity—how could an ethnoregional minority from Tigray suddenly rule a large, diverse country without secure 'ethnic allies'?" (2011, 597).

The TPLF harnessed, and simultaneously stemmed, Oromo mobilization by creating its own ethnic organization, the Oromo People's Democratic Organization (OPDO), as a key part of the EPRDF. Mobilization by ethnic Oromos has long been a threat because of their plurality position and their feeling of holding "second-class status" in Ethiopia. According to one scholar writing not long after the adoption of the recognition strategy, "The Oromo national movement is seen as a dangerous political trend by those Ethiopians who are in power and by those who oppose them" (Jalata 1993, 381). As another explained, "A deep-seated fear of 'the Oromo threat' as the powder-keg upon which the Ethiopian state is poised, rises quickly at times of political change or instability—so quickly as to suggest its cultivation as a useful rallying point by successive governments" (Vaughan 1994, 35–36). The TPLF thus sought to gain from ethnic mobilization and also had to address it.

The EPLF mobilization against the Derg for secession of Eritrea likewise invoked both opportunities and challenges for the TPLF. While they were strong militarily, the TPLF stemmed from a minority population, and the Eritreans built one of Africa's strongest rebel movements (Young 1996b; Spears 2010). The Derg also had important Soviet backing, and the TPLF would have had a hard time facing it alone on the battlefield. Working with the EPLF was strategically important and required concessions to post-Derg secession of Eritrea. In fact, agreement on ethnic recognition and a secession provision was not just part of the post-Derg ethnic institutionalization; rather, it had been a deal struck between the TPLF and EPLF as early as 1975 (Branch and Mampilly 2015). As Young opined, "Some key policies of the present Eritrean and Ethiopian governments can only be understood in light of positions established in the course of their revolutionary struggles over the past 2 decades" (Young 1996b, 120).

In sum, the TPLF had allied with other groups in order to win a military victory and needed to take these groups' concerns into account in the constitution. Having committed to recognition as part of its road to power, the regime then had to figure out how to ensure its survival as a minority, with the risks we typically see for minorities in terms of the possibility that other groups mobilize against them. The concepts we raise throughout this book—ethnic power configurations and the dilemma of recognition—thus also help us to better understand the Ethiopian case.

The effects question: implications and consequences

We now turn to the implications and consequences of Ethiopia's post-war recognition strategy, focusing on the period until 2018, under minority rule. Consistent with the quotes by Meles and a foreign diplomat in this chapter's opening paragraph, scholars early described ethnic federalism as perhaps "the only approach that could ensure the unity and survival of the Ethiopian state into the twenty-first century," while also noting that "it is a high risk strategy, and its success is far from certain" (Young 1996a, 532).

The indicators of peace that we examined in the cross-national chapters suggest a story quite like that of Rwanda. Ethiopia, like Rwanda, embraced the idea of a developmental state and grew exponentially at a macroeconomic level, as Figure 8.1 shows (see also Lyons 2019, chapter 7). Significant economic growth represents one of Ethiopia's greatest achievements. However, growth came through a focus on infrastructure rather than on poverty alleviation for ordinary Ethiopians (Branch and Mamphilly 2015) and, as we discuss later in this chapter, it has been unequal—one of the primary complaints of protesters from 2016 onward.

On the assuring side, ethnic federalism resulted in group-based identity and rights being more prominent and respected in Ethiopia than has ever been the case in the past. Figure 8.1 illustrates that ethnic exclusion declined upon the adoption of ethnic federalism in 1991. Language policy is one of the areas in which we observe a dramatic shift following the implementation of ethnic federalism (Smith 2013). For example, twenty-eight regional and local languages came to be used in primary education, in the media, in regional governments, and for signage in public spaces. Many of these languages were previously only used orally. Of course, critiques remain. Some are concerned that most of these languages are regionally dominant languages, meaning that minority linguistic groups remain marginalized (Lanza and Woldemariam 2014). Others contend that using regional languages will inhibit future social mobility across the state (Shohamy and Gorter 2008), possibly a deliberate strategy of the TPLF-led central government. Yet many previously marginalized minorities have been able to assert language, education, and local governance rights in a way that has assured them of their place in the state.

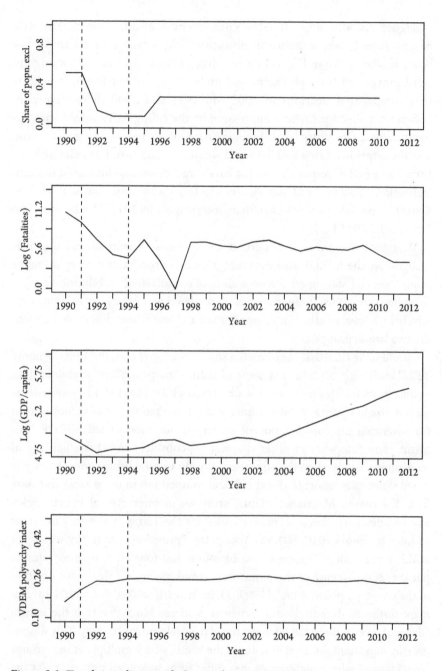

Figure 8.1 Trends in indicators of ethnic exclusion, negative peace, and positive peace in Ethiopia.

Figure 8.1 also illustrates the consequences of an authoritarian style of governance, where political indicators hold steady at a relatively low score similar to Rwanda's and do not, like in Burundi's case, show any upward movement through the period under study. When Ethiopia held its first competitive elections in 2005—in 1995 and 2000 there were noncompetitive elections where oppression by the ruling party paired with opposition party boycotts left Ethiopians with little choice—the government, and the opposition that had garnered significant support, both claimed victory. The EPRDF responded with a harsh crackdown and increased the centralization of power, and subsequent elections were non-competitive. The EPRDF won 100 percent of parliamentary seats in 2015 (Addis Standard 2015; BBC 2015).

Alongside and through important and meaningful cultural and linguistic recognition, the EPRDF also used recognition as a mechanism for splitting the opposition and staving off the possibility of consolidated mobilization against the minority regime. These strategies are rendered more viable by Ethiopia's relatively high level of ethnic fractionalization and low ethnic difference between the two largest groups.

At the same time that they enacted some assuring effects, the EPRDF under TPLF leadership took further steps to reduce the possibility of mobilization against them, which a minority that adopts recognition has to find a way to do, as we theorize in Chapter 2. First, ethnic federalism often served as a smokescreen for advancing the consolidation of power for the minority-led EPRDF. This might constitute what in other chapters we consider a Machiavellian use of recognition. Many view the strategic rationale in establishing nine ethnically based states as an effort to direct political competition to these areas and away from the center. Makau wa Matua, professor of international human rights and law, describes this as a "masterstroke" for the Tigrayan minority in power (quoted in Spears 2010, 80). Per Young, this "provided a means by which the TPLF, representing Tigrayans who constitute just four percent [most sources put this at 6 percent] of the population, could maintain a dominant position in the country's political life" (1999, 3). In the early 2000s, the central government furthered decentralization wherein it offered block grants at the *woreda* (district) level, widely considered a positive development strategy. This was especially important for diverse states in the south, where multiple ethnic groups coincide, and where preferences may differ from state-level priorities. Yet the EPRDF also intended the decentralization process to push political competition further and further away from the center and keep it in the dominant position (Keller and Smith 2005). Indeed, the EPRDF simultaneously promoted Tigrayan interests through control of the army, the security forces, and the economy in the center. As our cross-national analysis suggests, regimes are most likely to grant meaningful recognition in the "soft" cultural sphere rather than in "hard" political and security domains.

In fact, as part of its consolidation of power, the EPRDF simultaneously made non-recognition-like efforts to minimize ethnic diversity in the central government and to obscure ethnically based information that would have lain bare the extent of Tigrayan dominance. Keller and Smith assess ethnic federalism in mid-2000s Ethiopia as "more of an aspiration than a reality," noting that "what is billed as a unique form of ethnic federalism in Ethiopia operates very much like a centralized, unitary state, with most power residing at the center" (2005, 291, 289). Viewing the EPRDF in a manner reminiscent of past authoritarian regimes, Freedom House, the Committee to Protect Journalists, and Amnesty International documented the ways in which freedom of expression throughout Ethiopia was seriously restricted, particularly as it applied to dissent against the government. As Spears opines (consistent with our focus on ethnic power configurations), "In the end, and despite their rhetoric, democracy is an unattractive option if, as a minority, it jeopardizes their hegemony or if, as victors in an epic struggle [like the RPF in Rwanda], they believe they have a greater entitlement to rule" (2010, 96). All of the ruling party's strategies, save for recognition, were also reminiscent of the current Rwandan minority government's strategies under a non-recognition regime. The non-democratic practices kept a firm grip on power and entitlement for a Tigrayan minority that would likely have been lost through more open democracy. The situation echoes Kaufmann and Haklai's (2008) analysis of how minority ethnic rule and democracy, in addition to recognition, uneasily coexist.

A second strategy that the EPRDF employed to stem mobilization against them, and therein minimize the instability that can come from minority adoption of recognition, was to further split the opposition. For example, the National Elections Board of Ethiopia recognized seventy-nine registered political parties. Most of these were regional parties, with fewer than 30 percent of them having a country-wide identity (Abate 2013). With, on average, each ethnic group having its own political party, the EPRDF government managed the ability of groups to work together to mobilize against them. A relatively recent example of the TPLF-led government's efforts to split the opposition relates to violence along the Oromia-Somali border, which some Oromos believed the EPRDF was instigating so as to keep Oromos weak and unable to mobilize (Gardner 2017). Another lies in post-2005 efforts of the central government to reach into even university campuses. At the University of Addis Ababa, the government is reported to have endeavored to "ethnicize" student politics and fracture student groups into regionally based units to prevent consolidated protest (Branch and Mampilly 2015). Moreover, the government framed Ethiopia's organization as one in which all ethnic groups have equal standing, and charged those who complained about marginalization with "being 'anti-Ethiopian'—promoting their own self-interest above what's best for all" (Tesfaye 2014). Simultaneously, the TPLF insisted on internal unity, fearing that demographically larger groups, such as the Oromo, would be able to challenge a fractured minority party (Spears 2010).

The regime even went so far as presenting those who opposed ethnic recognition—such as the main opponent in the 2005 elections, the Coalition for Unity and Democracy (CUD), a party that supports federalism but not ethnic federalism—as "the Interahamwe of Ethiopia," referencing the notorious bands who carried out killings during the genocide in Rwanda. Drawing a further parallel to the Rwandan genocide, the Meles regime claimed that *failing to recognize* ethnic groups would be "akin to genocide" and that Tigrayans, like Tutsis, would be eradicated if the CUD were to become the government (Aalen 2006, 254, 261). This position provides a fascinating contrast to the Rwandan government's claim that it is *recognition* that may lead to future violence against the minority Tutsis.

The regime also used the ongoing presence of ethnic mobilization to justify repression. Like in Rwanda, the government claimed that its repression was necessary to keep peace in a multiethnic state. When it faced credible threats to its maintenance of power in the 2005 elections, the most open in the country's history, the result was a harsh crackdown and outlawing of opposition. Ethiopia's information minister contended that had it not been for the regime's actions in this instance, people might have turned to violence that "might have made the Rwandan genocide look like child's play" (Spears 2010, 90). The government launched a "re-ideologization" campaign that polarized groups, according to participants, and it argued that without EPRDF leadership, Ethiopia would fall into upheaval (Tronvoll 2011). According to Beza Tesfaye, an NGO-based researcher, "Though the EPRDF envisioned ethnic federalism as a means of maintaining control over an ethnically-diverse state, when groups assert their autonomy, the government's response to ethnic mobilization around political grievances—similar to its response to any type of political opposition—has been harsh and swift" (2014). Yet the regime was loath to have Ethiopia considered "conflict-affected." In a study that we conducted with UNICEF, the government would not allow a "conflict analysis" to take place, since it claimed the country was not in conflict (Monaghan and King 2015). The regime simultaneously, and in contradiction, touted the success of ethnic recognition—much as the Rwandan government touts the success of non-recognition—and pointed to ongoing ethnic conflicts as a foundation for its authoritarian stance.

Rather than the paradoxical effects of recognition that transcend ethnicity that we argue are emerging in Burundi, in Ethiopia ethnic federalism has been implemented in such a way as to entrench ethnicity as the *only* manner of accessing state power and resources. This has even resulted in more groups claiming separate ethnic identities and ethnically defined administrative structures. For example, the Siltie people had long been considered a subclan of the Gurage ethnic group, but in 2001 they sought recognition as a separate ethnic group (Smith 2007). Silties voted that they constitute a distinct ethnic group, and by doing so they gained both symbolic recognition and the group-differentiated rights and share of power laid out in the constitution. Over the last few years, demonstrators from ethnic groups that do not have their own ethnic majority states have advocated for statehood (Abdu 2018, 2019). As we completed final edits on this book in late 2019, a referendum among Sidama people (Ethiopia's fifth largest ethnic group) led to the creation of a tenth ethnically-based regional state (Paravicini 2019). Another manifestation of the ethnic lens through which Ethiopian politics is refracted is that conflicts that are not ethnically based, such as land disputes, are often reframed in ethnic terms, since ethnicity provides the most traction for disputants (Aalen 2006, 259). Some argue, consistent with scholars who oppose ethnic recognition as a conflict management strategy, that ethnic federalism has pitted different ethnic groups against one another (Aalen 2011; Abbink 2011; Bélair 2016; Regassa 2010). Identity was already salient, but the recognition strategy heightened ethnic identity for many groups (Lyons 2019). The experience of recognition since 1991 confirms many of the fears of liberals and other opponents of group-based recognition who worry about the freezing of static ethnic identities and the entrenchment of these ethnicities as the lines of cleavage.

Ethnic rivalry and mistrust have continued to influence politics in important ways, and complaints over inequality rose to prominence. As we discussed in Chapter 2, when recognition serves to make inequalities more visible, groups may resort to violence to address their grievances. In 2015, mass protests arose among Oromos in response to plans to expand the boundaries of the capital, Addis Ababa, into Oromia. Amharas then launched protests in their region in rejection of the TPLF's "disproportionate economic and diplomatic power" (Kestler-D'Amours 2018). Further protests developed based on generalized silencing of dissent, lack of democracy, and economic deprivation along, but also across, ethnic lines. Important group-based inequalities remained in areas such as education (Tesfay and Malmberg 2014) and access to healthcare and health-related outcomes (Bobo et al. 2017; Federal Democratic Republic of Ethiopia 2017), but not all of Ethiopia's inequality is ethnically based. Ethiopia's Gini co-efficient, considered a measure of economic inequality or income distribution among a population, grew from 30 in 1999 to nearly 40 at last measure in 2015, after an initial post-war decline between 1995 and 1999 (World Bank 2015).

The state brutally cracked down on protest and issued two states of emergency in 2016 and 2017. Hailemariam Desalegn, first Meles's deputy prime minister and then Prime Minister from 2012 to 2018, ultimately resigned over this mass protest and unrest. Hailemariam was from the Southern Ethiopian

People's Democratic Movement faction of the EPRDF, which he himself called the weakest of the four factions in the ruling party; it is also the most divided, with fifty-six different ethnic groups represented therein. In an interview after his resignation, Hailemariam said that he was unable to move forward with reforms that he and the other non-TPLF factions desired, claiming that the TPLF effectively stymied change during his tenure in an effort to maintain dominance (Mills 2018). At the time of their writing in 2015, with a negative peace maintained through repression, Branch and Mampilly (2015) reported despair and loss of hope in the possibility of peaceful change. Mains (2011) entitled his book on youth and the future in Ethiopian cities *Hope Is Cut*.

The recognition strategy may, in the end, have had important implications for the survival of the TPLF-led regime. While other factors were also important in prompting protest, the recognition strategy itself likely enabled ethnically based protest, not only in providing a nudge to mobilization but also in facilitating contestation along ethnic lines through which underrepresented groups could make credible claims of marginalization. The International Crisis Group assessed in 2009 that ethnic federalism "has failed to accommodate grievances" but "has powerfully promoted ethnic self-awareness among all groups" (2009, ii). Lyons (2019) characterizes the tension in Ethiopian politics and ethnic federalism as between, on one hand, the idea of empowering decentralized ethnic groups, and on the other, authoritarianism and the centralization of power.

Prospects

In April 2018, Abiy Ahmed came to power as the new leader of the EPRDF. While the EPRDF coalition survived, the leading faction therein has changed. That Abiy is the first Oromo leader of the country and that Oromos are the plurality group in Ethiopia are central features of much of the news reporting surrounding this event (BBC 2018; Boko 2018; Burke 2018; Mules 2018; Sengupta 2018; World Politics Review 2018), pointing to the importance not only of ethnic politics in Ethiopia but also of the ethnic power configurations that we highlight in this book. Abiy came to power amid more than three years of powerful protests, led principally by youth in the Oromia region, with grievances centered on the long-standing marginalization of Oromos by the minority leadership. Reporting suggests that there were widespread fears that without an Oromo leader, the country was at risk of breaking apart (Marsh 2018; Sengupta 2018). Oromo nationalism has been called "one of the most potent forces in Ethiopia today" (World Politics Review 2018). News reports indicate the transition was rooted in Oromo protest of their political, economic, and cultural marginalization, and in the EPRDF's desire to quell ethnic tensions therein and more broadly (BBC

2018; Maasho 2018; Sengupta 2018). As we saw in Chapter 2, if recognition provides visibility but not sufficient redistribution, conflict can increase. Those who worry about the ways in which recognition can facilitate the ease and effectiveness of calls for mobilization along ethnic lines may wonder if the salience of ethnic politics would be less powerful today had the EPRDF chosen non-recognition in the early 1990s, however unlikely this would have been in terms of adoptability. At the same time, we could speculate that such a leader from a previously marginalized group may not have emerged were it not for the implementation of various forms of recognition over the prior twenty-five years.

While Abiy is expanding political freedoms and reducing the dominance of the security sector, ultimately aiming, he says, to move toward multiparty democracy, grievances along ethnic lines have surfaced (Burke 2018; International Crisis Group 2018; Schemm 2018). The number of violent protests has declined, but interethnic violence in Ethiopia has increased, with some reports that Oromos are seeking to settle old scores with attacks against minorities such as Tigrayans and Somalis, other attacks relating to long-standing land disputes, and still other violence by Qeerroo Oromo youth who judge change to be insufficient (International Crisis Group 2018; Maasho 2018; Schemm 2018). Ethnic mobilization for justice and equality more broadly is reported to have increased significantly since Abiy took power, and the mobilization of ethnic militias is also on the rise (Mamdani 2019). Internal displacement has long been high in Ethiopia, and more than 1.4 million people are reported to have become internally displaced in 2018 due largely to ethnic conflicts—the highest internal displacement of all countries in that year (Internal Displacement Monitoring Center 2018). Scholar Mahmood Mamdani (2019) expresses concerns that Abiy's reforms are clashing with the recognition regime in ways that could promote more interethnic violent conflict.

There is now, however, no longer the institutional mismatch that existed under the minority regime, leaving, per our theory, more room for creative maneuvering. Abiy is engaging in multiple efforts to promote reconciliation (Mules 2018), through such efforts as calling on Ethiopians to build cross-ethnic bridges (Marsh 2018), being more inclusive of other ethnic identities in the cabinet (Capel 2018), delivering speeches in multiple languages (Maasho 2018), and visiting the Tigray region (Schemm 2018). Abiy has also effectively put an end to twenty years of conflict with Eritrea and reopened the border. He was awarded the 2019 Nobel Peace Prize in recognition of these efforts. Through his rhetoric, Abiy asserts that all Ethiopians should benefit from a national identity but that they need not sacrifice their differences (Giorgis 2018; Gardner 2018). While self-identifying as Oromo, his complex personal identity has also allowed for somewhat wider appeal: his father was Muslim Oromo, his mother was Amhara Christian, he now self-identifies as Pentecostal Christian, and he is fluent in Oromo, Amharic, Tigrinya, and English. The challenge for peace, according to the International Crisis Group, is the government's success in managing tensions, inclusive rhetoric, and responses to violence (Mules 2018). President Abiy carefully balanced power among different ethnic groups in his first EPRDF government, although many of the most important positions went to members of the OPDO, including those of prime minister, foreign minister, defense minister, and attorney general. Most of the National Security Council members were also Oromos (Soliman 2018). Another consideration is that while Abiy is a plurality leader, the size of his group is not so large in comparison to the next-largest group, Amharas, in contrast to the much greater demographic difference between Hutus and Tutsis in our other two cases.

Thinking through the lens of our theory, the challenge for Abiy is likely to be different from what it was under TPLF leadership of the EPRDF. In contrast to Rwanda's effort to transcend ethnic identity through an inclusive Rwandanness that overrides ethnic identity, Ethiopia since the overthrow of the Derg has, at least rhetorically, aimed for "unity in diversity." The idea of ethnic federalism is that groups can maintain their ethnic identities while also being part of a united Ethiopia. How citizens weigh these identities—"Ethiopia First" versus the primacy of ethnic identity—is contested (Mengie 2015), and some argue that the TPLF-led EPRDF inadequately strove to build a national identity that would be key to peace (Aalen 2006). If diversity comes to come at the expense of unity, as it did under Meles and Hailemariam, groups may be more likely to mobilize along ethnic lines against each other and the state (mobilization effects), renewing conflict. If unity comes at the expense of diversity, groups may hold or even increase their grievances, thereby not achieving the assuring effects of recognition, and further opening the regime to conflict. Former prime minister Hailemariam raised further challenges of balancing individual and group-based rights:

> One of the flaws in our current system . . . is the contradiction between a group right and a citizen right. We were skewed in favour of recognising group rights, of an ethnic identity over a national identity. While in theory these rights should be two sides of the same coin, in practice this does not do so. The TPLF but also the Oromo are major beneficiaries of this practice. How this is resolved depends on how Abiy presents himself and how we deal with the tension between these rights. (Quoted in Mills 2018)

The elections due in May 2020 (just after this book goes to press), though they are risking delay due to ethnically based violence, will be especially important in assessing the success of these efforts and further possibilities for post-ethnic politics.

PART IV

CONCLUSIONS

9

The Promise of Recognition

This book examines the choices that leaders face in trying to manage violent intergroup conflicts. While every conflict is different, as leaders endeavor to bring conflict to an end they face common challenges in regard to (re)establishing security, political institutions, economic development, justice, and reconciliation. Recurrent in all of these challenges is the key decision that leaders need to make regarding ethnic diversity: whether or not to publicly recognize ethnic groups in state institutions. Their choice reflects a long-standing and ongoing academic debate waged on both philosophical and practical grounds.

Why do some leaders of conflict-affected countries formally recognize different ethnic identities among their citizens while others do not? How does ethnic recognition affect the course of peace in those countries? These are questions of high theoretical interest to social scientists studying democracy, peace, and development—and of great practical relevance to policymakers engaged in making these concepts a reality around the world.

Indeed, as we discussed in Chapter 2, recent years have seen an increasingly strong commitment to recognition among the norms-defining documents of the UN and regional bodies such as the European Union, particularly for minorities and other historically underrepresented groups. We note, however, that these commitments are based more on hopes than on evidence.

This book focused on providing such evidence. Bringing together literatures on institutional origins, peace agreements, and conflict management, we proposed the concept of ethnic recognition and made the case for its importance. We then brought systematic evidence to debates over recognition through a mixed-methods study that combines quantitative cross-national analysis of original datasets and qualitative case study approaches. Through a systematic mapping, we found that recognition is adopted about 40 percent of the time. Ours constitutes the first such mapping of ethnic recognition in peace processes globally. Moreover, when ethnic recognition is adopted, we found overall positive effects on peace in the short or medium term. While we embarked on this project without knowing what type of story we would ultimately be telling, in

Diversity, Violence, and Recognition. Elisabeth King and Cyrus Samii, Oxford University Press (2020). © Oxford University Press.
DOI: 10.1093/oso/9780197509456.003.0001

the end ours is a rather optimistic account of at least one strategy with potential to promote post-conflict peace, in contrast to the pessimistic analyses that dominate scholarship on peace and conflict today.

We proposed a theoretical lens that offers insight into the variation in the adoption of recognition and its effects. In a peace- and state-building landscape that focuses so often on the international community, we shed light on the important role of national leaders and the domestic strategic conditions they encounter on the ground. We examined the merits and risks of publicly recognizing ethnic groups in state institutions compared to not doing so with respect to an oft-overlooked factor: ethnic power configurations. Our theory posited trade-offs between two types of effects for a leader intent on political survival. First, the assuring effects of recognition help mitigate mistrust across ethnic cleavages through symbolic recognition, visibility that allows groups to assess how they are doing, and group-differentiated rights, which may seek to address accumulated inequalities and grievances that can be at the root of conflict. Second, the mobilization effects follow from the fact that ethnic recognition licenses and potentially facilitates collective action along ethnic lines. For plurality leaders, the two effects push in the same direction, favoring recognition. Minority leaders, however, face a dilemma of recognition since the benefits of the assuring effects must be weighed against the threats of mobilization by larger groups. We found that our lens illuminates important factors overlooked by other internal and external explanations of the institutional origins of ethnic recognition.

Drawing on global data, we found important and systematic differences between adoption rates and effects for leaders from minority and plurality groups that give credence to our theory. We found that in conflict-affected contexts, plurality leaders adopt recognition about 60 percent of the time, whereas minority leaders do so much less often, in about 25 percent of cases, representing a difference of 35 percentage points.

We likewise found differences in the effects of recognition on peace that are suggestive of the interplay of the assuring and mobilization effects central to our theory. For plurality leaders, we found that recognition leads to heightened political inclusiveness, reduced violence, increased economic vitality, and stronger democracy. For minority leaders, while recognition does not substantially worsen these outcomes, we do not find evidence of positive effects.

As such, we found no singular effect of recognition, but instead effects that are contingent upon ethnic power configurations. Consideration of these conditional effects of ethnic recognition on adoption, and on positive and negative peace, can advance the study of conflict management more widely with the potential to reconcile the often contradictory findings in existing literature.

Our case studies of Burundi, Rwanda, and Ethiopia also lent support to our observations and the mechanisms we posited. In all three of the cases, we showed that in considering whether or not to recognize ethnic groups, leaders were reacting to ethnic demographics and their place in the ethnic power configuration. We also demonstrated that in each of the cases, the assuring and mobilization effects featured in leaders' decision-making. Moreover, the way that recognition affected peace outcomes in these cases is indicative of the relevance of these two mechanisms to peace.

Additional insights from case studies

Taken together, the case studies suggest four elaborations. These are points that we did not anticipate initially and were difficult to observe in the cross-national analysis. They represent ways that the case studies enriched the logic we developed. First, while in our cross-national analysis we coded recognition in binary terms, our case studies in fact demonstrate that recognition strategies operate more as a continuum. Recognition regimes emerge through gradual steps and admit a range of policy options. In Burundi, the non-recognition regime instituted in the 1992 constitution nonetheless built on consultation processes that employed informal quotas. This experience informed the deliberations that led to the 2000 Burundian Arusha Accords that instituted ethnic quotas. In Rwanda, during the latter years of the Habyarimana regime (prior to the genocide) and during the Rwandan civil war, we witness the beginning of movement from a recognition regime to non-recognition on some dimensions, such as the proposal to eliminate ethnicity on identity cards. The 1993 Rwandan Arusha Accords used a power-sharing approach that did not name ethnic groups but intended to distribute power along ethnic lines, thereby presenting an institutional arrangement that stood between the explicit recognition of the prior Habyarimana regime and the non-recognition of the Kagame regime that would follow. In Ethiopia, despite the Derg's strong ideological opposition to ethnicity as a politically relevant category and its attempts to stamp out its importance, it nonetheless began to study and make a census of ethnicity and explored possibilities for the use of different ethnic languages, both of which paved the way for the ethnic federal regime the EPRDF instituted when it came to power. Insofar as we want to track recognition around the globe, thinking about recognition as a continuum may inform a more refined assessment that allows for more incremental movement and suggests trends.

Second, recognition policies often emanate from minority group demands, but not exclusively so, and they are not always the result of minority demands for protection. In Burundi, for example, proposals for ethnic quotas originated in both minority Tutsi leaders' concerns about tyranny of the majority as well as majority Hutu leaders' desire to win favor with potential Tutsi constituents.

The Hutu leaders in this case came from a party whose standing among Hutus was slipping, so their strategic interest in quotas was based on wanting to be seen as the party that brought peace and could therefore serve the interests of Tutsis as well as Hutus. In Ethiopia, the recognition regime was ushered in under the stewardship of the minority Tigray leadership, rooted in part in long-standing Tigrayan demands, although equally as a response to demands from Eritreans and members of larger—but long-marginalized—ethnic groups such as Oromos. Proposals for recognition can involve a much more complex set of interests than what is captured in Tajfel's description of a "world-wide push towards differentiation originating from minorities" (1981, 316), which we discussed in Chapter 2.

Third, recognition and non-recognition can have paradoxical effects. While critics of recognition policies often worry about it entrenching ethnicity as an axis of political contention, we find that recognition can sometimes work toward the depoliticization of ethnic identities (Raffoul 2018). This is an insight we drew from the Burundi case. After the adoption of recognition, political polarization along ethnic lines decreased, and the ethnic quotas allowed for new cross-ethnic factional coalitions. This suggests that recognition institutions can be designed to generate assuring effects that help to mitigate the mobilization effects. These paradoxical effects begin to challenge at least one of the concerns of opponents of recognition: worry about recognition freezing ethnic identity. Through the paradox of recognition, ethnic recognition strategies can also be consistent with the constructivist premise that the salience of ethnic identity is fluid.

Of course, the paradox of recognition is not an automatic outcome. The Ethiopian case is one of intensified ethnic mobilization under the recognition regime. Two important factors distinguish the Ethiopian case from Burundi. The first is that the ethnic federation is not based on the same types of integrative institutions as Burundi's quota system. The second is Ethiopia's minority group leadership following the adoption of recognition, in contrast to plurality group leadership in Burundi. Either of these differences could prevent the types of paradoxical effects from emerging in Ethiopia. Later in this conclusion we will propose that future research should investigate the mechanisms that depoliticize ethnicity. By the same turn, non-recognition does not necessarily result in depoliticizing ethnicity. Rather, and again paradoxically, it can sustain ethnic polarization insofar as it offers no direct assurances and, by barring open discussion, confines people to discussing grievances within their ethnic networks, as occurs in Rwanda, reinforcing the identities and bases of mistrust.

Finally, we should not idealize recognition as a strategy, as it also offers instruments for a Machiavellian "menu of manipulation" (Schedler 2002). In our case studies, we see examples of the ways in which recognition can be instrumentalized for purposes of exclusion that are subtler than other strategies of "recognition to exclude," such as apartheid, that we reviewed in Chapter 2. In Burundi, for example, the ruling Hutu-dominated party used ethnic quotas to co-opt Tutsi leaders who were willing to go along with their authoritarian program and as a way to delegitimize the standing of the traditionally Tutsi-dominated parties. In Ethiopia, recognition served to enable the minority power holder to concentrate authority in the capital while diffusing conflict to the regions that had been recognized. Since claims on the state must be channeled through recognized ethnic identities, the question of who may legitimately make these claims becomes a major point of conflict. This dynamic shifts attention into the regions and away from the center. In the same way that recognition can be used to subtly exclude, non-recognition can be used as a smokescreen for policies of ethnic favoritism. In Rwanda, despite an ostensible commitment to non-recognition, the distribution of power and opportunities within key institutions reflects favoritism toward members of a Tutsi inner circle. So while this book ultimately demonstrates the promise of recognition, recognition is, like others, a strategy open to manipulation.

Overall, our findings suggest important implications for policy and scholarship, as well as a larger research agenda that could continue to push forward our knowledge about diversity, violence, and recognition.

Implications for policy

Consider a group coming together today at a peace negotiation or constitutional moment in the context of violent conflict where ethnicity has been an important cleavage. We might imagine negotiations or constitutional processes in Myanmar, Syria, or Yemen, among other places. What, based on the findings of this book, might we recommend to participants in such a process? We draw out four implications from our analysis that we hope may be instructive.

First, in facing the challenges of dealing with ethnic identity in the aftermath of violence, policymakers should understand that they are not alone. Many leaders around the world have contended with the dilemma of recognition. Moreover, observers and policymakers ought to consult this history to derive lessons. Our theory, with its emphasis on the ethnic power configuration, provides guidance for determining which countries' histories would be most informative for the case at hand. For example, in Myanmar, the majority Bamar ruling elite might draw lessons from the experience of cases such as Burundi, which implemented recognition policies under majority ethnic rule. For a country such as Syria, where, at the time of writing, political authority remained subject to ongoing contestation, the legacy of long-standing minority Alawite political domination is a crucial feature of the context and will continue to be so as long as the Alawite elites remain in power. Policymakers with the goal of peace-making will have to understand the dilemma of recognition that such minority-dominated regimes face, finding ways to address the leaders' concerns over ethnic mobilization. Cases such as Rwanda or Ethiopia may provide valuable insights.

Second, while the particularities of the ethnic power configuration may inform the road forward, overall the historical record suggests that recognition tends to promote peace in contexts of ethnic division. As a result, our findings suggest that—in the short to medium run at least—recognition is worth serious consideration as a foundation for peace-building. In cases of plurality rule, the assuring effects of recognition can contribute to stability, and the mobilization effects present relatively little threat. In cases of minority rule, our theory and findings would suggest that successful implementation of recognition requires complementary strategies to address fears of mobilization on the part of the minority leadership.

Third, there are many ways through which recognition might be tailored to a given context, with varying emphasis on different state sectors. We saw great variation in the implementation of recognition policies across domains such as the executive, the security sector, and language. Recognition provides a basic analytical concept and a foundation for institutional design. It may enable policymakers to think in concert about action across different policy spheres that they would usually think about in isolation from one another. Zooming out from a specific policy to the more aggregate concept of ethnic recognition allows policymakers a more global picture of an interacting set of opportunities.

Finally, participants in peace processes and constitution-making are well aware of the difficulties of their endeavors, and our study of recognition highlights the many challenges inherent in social engineering in ethnically divided contexts in particular. Addressing identity and reshaping society in a way that builds peace is highly constrained by political—and, we add, ethnic—power configurations. The challenges of social engineering also include the fact that institutional effects can be paradoxical. For example, non-recognition may actually sustain the salience of ethnic identity by relegating discussions of interethnic inequalities to the private sphere, contributing to suspicion and mistrust.

Implications for scholarship

This book also offers implications for the scholarly literature. First, we illustrate the value of the high-level concept of ethnic recognition and the general idea of assuring effects and mobilization effects. Ethnic recognition allowed us to consider eighty-six constitutional moments side by side, and relating recognition to the assuring and mobilization effects enabled us to think about them in common strategic terms. These concepts offer guidance in finding commonalities as well as meaningful distinctions across contexts that differ in precise institutional details. Coding for the concept of ethnic recognition had empirical value in allowing us to home in on the importance of ethnic power configurations, something that likely would not have come to light using narrower concepts such as ethnic quotas or ethnic federalism. It also allowed us to consider side by side institutional domains, such as the legislature and justice sectors, which would typically be studied in isolation. It further enabled us to identify the interplay between domains or sectors and the way that leaders prioritize across them in relation to recognition. Based on this experience, we hope that other scholars take up the concept of ethnic recognition in trying to analyze issues related to diversity and violence around the world.

Using the concept of ethnic recognition also provided insights into the relevance of ethnic politics today. By applying the concept, we were able to see more clearly how contestation over questions of ethnic identity is playing out the world over. What we see is tremendous variation in the adoption of ethnic recognition and that conflict-affected countries are split almost evenly between adoption and non-adoption. Moreover, even in cases where recognition is not adopted, it is naive to think that the salience of ethnicity has disappeared. Group identity remains important, and non-recognition—through its paradoxical effects—may actually contribute to sustaining it. These findings contrast with such findings as those of Lieberman and Singh (2012), for instance, in part because we focus not on historic, or first, institutionalization of ethnic identity but rather on recognition during or after contemporary conflict that has increased the importance of ethnicity. Our findings also contrast with liberal arguments proposing that recognition entrenches ethnic divisions in a way that sustains conflict and that non-recognition offers the surest route to transcending ethnic divisions (Connor 1972; Deutsch 1966; Snyder 2000).

Our analysis further highlighted the value of studying institutional origins along with institutional effects. This contributes to the broader research agenda on the origins of contemporary institutional orders (Acemoglu and Robinson 2012; North, Wallis, and Weingast 2009). Following others (Brancati and Snyder 2011, 2013), we appreciated the need to study origins to disentangle origins from effects. Moreover, what we have also shown is that an understanding of the etiology of institutions helps us to better understand the conditional nature of their effects. For recognition, we find that forces very similar to those that determined the adoption of the institutions shaped the effects of these same institutions.

Finally, we have offered a corrective to the tendency to think about recognition versus non-recognition, or other related institutions, as choices having a universal and consistent effect. We show that one cannot think about recognition in simple either/or terms or in a manner that is detached from key features of the political context. While our findings overall lend support to those who argue for recognition (Cederman et al. 2017; Lijphart 1977; McGarry and O'Leary 2006), we also find that the strength of the effect is contingent on important moderating factors. Moreover, we identified what we think is a key factor—ethnic power configurations—and developed a theory, hinged on two mechanisms, that allows us to understand why these effects on peace may vary.

These contributions represent an important step forward in the enduring debate over institutional design to manage diversity in conflict-affected contexts that continues in scholarship and practice (McGarry, O'Leary, and Simeon 2008; see also Kuperman 2015; Reilly 2001; Reynolds 2011). Furthermore, this book contributes empirical evidence to inform more philosophical debates over the value of recognition (Barry 2001; Kymlicka 1995; Taylor 1992). Our findings also speak to those who object to recognition because it seems to contradict the liberal emphasis on individual rights. In Chapters 1 and 2, we raised the possibility that sole consideration of individual rights may reproduce inequalities, prejudices, and mistrust along ethnic lines. Recognition allows for addressing these challenges head-on. The evidence presented here suggests that recognition can be a crucial bridge from circumstances of ethnic polarization to more inclusive and peaceful societies.

An agenda for further research

In addition to this book's implications for policy and existing scholarly debates, we intend this work as a contribution to developing a broader research program on institutional strategies to address ethnic conflict. A number of questions take off from where this book ends. Here we raise four groups of questions we think ought to be the subject of further research.

The first set of questions concerns the long-term effects of recognition and non-recognition, and the evolution of recognition regimes. Our quantitative and case study analyses are limited to the first decade or decade and a half following institutional choices. But recognition policies shape identities, and identity change is likely to occur slowly, over generations. Do such processes carry through in a linear fashion into the future? Why might such processes stall or reverse? Extending the period of study would allow scholars to assess whether short-term contributions to peace from recognition or non-recognition may contribute to sustainable peace or be offset by long-term contributions to new conflict and violence. Theorizing the intergenerational processes through which these types of longer-term processes occur could provide insights into how institutions should be designed or reformed over time, as well as insights into moderating factors other than the ethnic power configuration.

The second set of questions concerns the mechanisms that relate recognition and non-recognition to the political salience of ethnicity. Consider the paradox of recognition, whereby (at least in the case of Burundi) the institutionalized group-based guarantees enabled by recognition have begun to reduce the need for ethnic groups to mobilize actively to pursue group interests. What aspects of a recognition regime cause such depoliticization? In Burundi, recognition-based institutions ensure that each of the main ethnic groups gets a share of the distribution of power, resources, and opportunities. Yet the recognition regime also involves quota-based ethnic integration of major institutions. Integration requires that members of different ethnic groups work together in prosecuting military campaigns, operating public sector agencies, and so on. Integration increases intergroup contact and creates ties based on profession and political coalition that cut across ethnicity. The social psychological literature shows that such processes can reduce prejudice and promote intergroup cooperation, even in contexts of violent conflict, although these effects depend on institutional factors and level of inequality between the groups (Ditlmann et al. 2017). Recognition regimes that rely primarily on separation, such as Ethiopia's ethnic federal system, also ensure that different groups receive a share. This offers assuring effects, but the question remains as to whether generating paradoxical depoliticization effects requires doing more to encourage intergroup cooperation. If so, this would raise questions about the durability of the peace that separation-based recognition regimes offer.

Consider as well the paradox of non-recognition. In this case, because no public acknowledgment or space is granted for airing grievances about interethnic inequalities or vulnerabilities, ethnic identities remain salient in the private sphere, possibly lurking as a strong basis for political mobilization should the moment arise. Will such significance fade over time as new generations grow up without having their ethnic identity—and their connection to the history associated with their identity—being reinforced through state institutions? Perhaps non-recognition can deliver on the promise to remove ethnicity as a relevant cleavage for future generations if it is coupled with broad-based economic growth, as generous interpretations of dynamics in Rwanda propose (Kinzer 2008). That said, this book is concerned with cases in which ethnic identity is tied to past injustice and violence, creating focal points of group victimization shared across generations (Petersen 2001). In such cases, can processes that sustain ethnic cleavages be disrupted by state policies that steer attention away from such cleavages and rely primarily on creating economic opportunities? Can theories of identity recategorization that examine when groups abandon ethnic identities in favor of a superordinate identity (Gaertner and Dovidio 2000) or theories of strategic identity choice that examine how individuals choose among their multiple identities (Penn 2008; Sambanis and Shayo 2013) be fruitfully applied to such cases?

Third, having theorized the basic strategic dynamics associated with recognition, we now have a foundation for considering institutional details. Thus we can ask, for example, whether specific institutional arrangements may help to mitigate mobilization effects that can threaten to overwhelm the assuring effects and undermine progress toward peace. In Burundi, for example, parties cannot be formed to explicitly pursue ethnic aims, and ethnic quotas require that each party put forward both Hutu and Tutsi candidates. These measures constrain parties in their ability to pursue extreme ethnic interests, lest such party leaders fail to attract any out-group candidates and thereby fail to meet the quota requirement. This distinguishes Burundi's party system from that of Ethiopia, where ethnic parties predominate. Or perhaps there are policies that produce assuring effects while falling short of recognition at the constitutional level. To take an example outside of our set of three cases, the management of the Kurdish conflict in Turkey is anomalous with respect to our theory, given that successive majority-Turkish governments have acted to repress Kurds in their pursuit of Kurdish-specific rights. Over recent decades, governments have extended certain rights to allow Kurdish-language education and media (Somer 2010). As a form of symbolic recognition as well as group-differentiated rights, time will tell whether or not such actions create "paradox of recognition" effects, whereby limited recognition works to address a wider set of grievances that currently contribute to ethnic mobilization. Our suggestion is that as scholars move forward to consider institutional details, they look across domains, rather than simply within them, to think about recognition as an interacting complex system.

Finally, our theory of recognition may offer useful considerations for analyzing conflicts beyond the types of ethnically charged civil wars that have been the focus of this book. For instance, the lens of our theory may help to uncover important dimensions of political conflicts over ethnic inequality and changing demographics in North America and Europe. Consider the currently salient political conflict in North America and Europe over whether accumulated inequalities due to past discrimination, slavery, or colonization today require recognition-based strategies for redress. Or consider contestation over policies for addressing cultural diversity introduced by immigration. Affirmative action and minority rights proponents often highlight the same kinds of assuring effects that our theory emphasizes (Weisskopf 2004). A predominant basis for popular criticism of such policies is the intention to preserve majority-group status. Some propose that such self-serving defenses are themselves the perverse outcome of recognition-based policies. Political scientist Francis Fukuyama (2018), for example, proposes that recognition-based initiatives in the West have triggered ethnic identification dynamics that gave rise to contemporary white identity movements. Such dynamics resemble the mobilization effects our theory emphasizes. However, these critical accounts do not consider the possibility of longer-term paradoxical depoliticization effects. We encourage further research on how recognition and non-recognition strategies might be applied in addressing a wider range of conflicts than what this book covers.

Concluding remarks

Having previously conducted extensive research in Burundi and Rwanda, we began this book skeptical but open-minded about the effects of recognition strategies on peace. Rwanda was a context in which recognition was followed by genocide, and where non-recognition was subsequently established in an effort to build peace. Burundi was a context where the opposite pattern unfolded. The existing literature and available evidence were inadequate to answer the questions we asked of ourselves in trying to make sense of these institutional choices as well as their likely consequences. We thus undertook the research we detail throughout this book.

We were surprised to find that the evidence spoke rather clearly: recognition policies tend to be associated with stronger progress toward peace. Of course, this is not the case everywhere, and the road from adoption to effects is neither straightforward nor easy. But we end this book cautiously optimistic. The cases we consider are high-stakes conflict-affected contexts, and recognition is a foundational issue in processes of building peace. We hope this book will inspire policymakers and scholars alike to take a fresh look at recognition strategies for managing conflict.

Appendix

STATISTICAL TABLES

This appendix extends the analyses in Chapters 4 and 5, offering more detailed presentation of the statistical relationship between minority ethnic rule and the adoption and effects of recognition.

Determinants of the adoption of recognition

We begin with our analysis of the determinants of the adoption of recognition, as discussed in Chapter 4. Table A.1 reproduces the main results table from King and Samii (2018) with the addition of new control variables for whether the conflict involved secessionist demands and colonial history. For details on the sources of control variables, see King and Samii 2018 and especially the supporting information for that paper. The coefficients in the table are on the scale of marginal effects—that is, changes in the probability of adopting recognition for a unit change in a given variable, holding all other variables to their means. The first estimate simply presents what we saw in Table 4.2—namely, that minority-led regimes are 36 percentage points less likely to adopt recognition than plurality-led regimes. The next estimates to the right (columns 2 and 3) incorporate variables to control for ethnic relations in the country, including whether the country had been under minority ethnic rule (as per the codings based on Fearon et al. 2007) prior to the onset of violence, the level of ethnic fractionalization, whether the violence was part of an ethnic conflict, the share of the population that is part of an ethnic group subject to systematic exclusion, and whether the country hosts ethnic groups that are regionally concentrated. These additional variables come from the Ethnic Power Relations dataset of Cederman, Wimmer, and Min (2010) and the ethnic conflict dataset of Esteban, Mayoral, and Ray (2012), as well as our extensions (up to the year 2012) of these datasets based on the respective authors' coding criteria, using sources such as

Table A.1 **Effects of minority ethnic rule on the adoption of ethnic recognition, controlling for potential confounding factors (logistic regression marginal effect coefficients)**

Model	Logistic regression marginal effects: Outcome is ethnic recognition in constitution or settlement (0/1)										
	1	2	3	4	5	6	7	8	9	10	11
Minority leader (d)	-0.36***	-0.32**	-0.33**	-0.46***	-0.46***	-0.55***	-0.51**	-0.22	-0.30*	-0.15	-0.55**
	(0.11)	(0.14)	(0.16)	(0.17)	(0.18)	(0.15)	(0.22)	(0.29)	(0.16)	(0.14)	(0.23)
Pre-violence minority leader (d)		-0.06	-0.06	0.05	0.03	-0.15	-0.07	0.02	0.12	-0.66	0.11
		(0.16)	(0.18)	(0.23)	(0.23)	(0.19)	(0.36)	(0.22)	(0.21)	(0.57)	(0.20)
Ethnic fractionalization			-0.15	-0.53	-0.54	-0.47	-0.38	-0.51	0.72	1.17	0.80
			(0.37)	(0.50)	(0.48)	(0.46)	(0.69)	(0.44)	(0.54)	(1.56)	(0.54)
Ethnic conflict (d)			0.25	0.15	0.17	0.25		0.31	0.09		-0.05
			(0.15)	(0.18)	(0.21)	(0.15)		(0.20)	(0.15)		(0.22)
Excluded proportion			0.10	0.51*	0.57**	0.84***	0.77***	0.55*	0.46	1.09	0.50
			(0.26)	(0.27)	(0.28)	(0.30)	(0.42)	(0.29)	(0.40)	(0.89)	(0.42)
Regionally concentrated groups (d)			0.15	0.34**	0.37***	0.38***	0.34	0.37***	-0.17	-0.99***	-0.28
			(0.29)	(0.15)	(0.12)	(0.12)	(0.23)	(0.12)	(0.50)	(0.02)	(0.58)
Territorial or secessionist demands (d)				-0.10	-0.08	-0.05	0.18	-0.13	-0.12	1.00***	-0.08
				(0.19)	(0.21)	(0.24)	(0.38)	(0.22)	(0.23)	(0.02)	(0.22)
log(GDP/capita)				0.01	-0.01	-0.08	-0.12	-0.02	-0.15	-0.16	-0.16
				(0.09)	(0.08)	(0.11)	(0.11)	(0.08)	(0.14)	(0.18)	(0.13)
Freedom House "partly free" (d)				0.11	0.20	0.08	0.37*	0.15	0.17	0.57**	0.23
				(0.17)	(0.18)	(0.19)	(0.22)	(0.19)	(0.15)	(0.25)	(0.15)
log(mountain percent)				0.22**	0.25*	0.20*	0.15	0.23**	0.14	0.09	0.15
				(0.10)	(0.11)	(0.10)	(0.11)	(0.10)	(0.10)	(0.13)	(0.10)

	(1)	(2)	(3)	(4)	(5)	(6)	(7)	(8)	(9)	(10)
log(fatalities + 1)			0.01	0.01	0.01	0.01	0.01	0.01	0.04	0.01
			(0.03)	(0.03)	(0.03)	(0.03)	(0.03)	(0.02)	(0.03)	(0.02)
PITF atrocities historical max			−0.07	−0.08	−0.06	−0.09	−0.07	−0.07*	−0.20	−0.09*
			(0.05)	(0.06)	(0.05)	(0.09)	(0.06)	(0.04)	(0.20)	(0.05)
Military victory (d)			−0.18	−0.23	−0.19	−0.15	−0.21	−0.16	−0.03	−0.17*
			(0.15)	(0.14)	(0.16)	(0.17)	(0.15)	(0.11)	(0.07)	(0.10)
Previous powersharing (d)				−0.04	0.17	0.23	−0.04	−0.24	0.50	−0.23
				(0.21)	(0.21)	(0.28)	(0.22)	(0.26)	(0.42)	(0.26)
Multilateral engagement (d)				0.21	0.12	0.37	0.17	0.14	0.98***	0.20
				(0.15)	(0.18)	(0.23)	(0.15)	(0.16)	(0.10)	(0.18)
Ethnic conflict X Minority leader (d)							−0.34			0.37
							(0.24)			(0.25)
Region dummies	N	N	N	N	Y	Y	N	Y	Y	Y
Colonial dummies	N	N	N	Y	Y	N	N	N	N	N
Year trend (linear + quadratic)	N	N	Y	Y	Y	Y	Y	Y	Y	Y
Observations	86	81	75	75	75	54	75	65	42	65
Omitted observations	None	No excl. prop.	No excl. prop. FH "free"	No excl. prop. FH "free"	No excl. prop. FH "free"	No excl. prop. FH "free" Non-eth. conf.	No excl. prop. FH "free"	No excl. prop. FH "free" Europe	No excl. prop. FH "free" Non-eth. conf. Europe	No excl. prop. FH "free" Europe

Notes: Logistic regression marginal effect coefficients measure differences in probability of adoption for a unit change in each regressor variable.
Standard errors in parentheses. Standard errors account for clustering by country.

* $p < 0.10$, ** $p < 0.05$, *** $p < 0.01$.

(d) for discrete change of dummy variable from 0 to 1.

"No excl. prop." refers to cases omitted due to missing "excluded proportion" data: Djibouti 1994 and 2001; Pakistan 2011; Sierra Leone 1999; Sudan 2011.

"FH 'free'" refers to cases coded as "free" by Freedom House. These predict recognition perfectly and so they are dropped from models 4–10.

The dummy variable for Europe predicts recognition perfectly and so these cases are dropped from models 8–10.

"Non-eth. conf." refers to cases that are not coded as "ethnic conflicts" in the Wimmer et al. 2009 dataset.

the CIA World Factbook. Column 4 adds control variables for key structural conditions, including income per capita, the Freedom House scores, ruggedness of terrain (which is a known predictor of the onset of new violent conflicts), fatality levels prior to negotiation of a settlement, and whether the settlement was brought about through military victory. Column 5 adds controls pertaining to the negotiation context, including a variable for whether the country had previously experienced power-sharing and strong international engagement. Even after incorporating all of these controls, the estimated effect of minority leadership remains at around 40 percentage points. Column 6 shows results after controlling for indicators as to whether the country was part of the British, French, Spanish, or Ottoman Empires (coefficients omitted to save space) based on the codings from the Issues Correlates of War Colonial History Data Set (Hensel 2018). Incorporating such controls actually yields a larger (55 percentage point) estimated effect for minority leadership. We do not retain these variables in the rest of the analysis because they force us to drop many perfectly predicted cases when we look at the subsample of ethnic conflicts, and because they are highly collinear with region, for which we control (discussed later).

In columns 7 and 8, we show how the effects of minority leadership are moderated by whether the conflict in question is an ethnic conflict, on the basis of a coding of conflicts by Cederman, Wimmer, and Min (2010). We find that the effects of minority leadership in conditions of ethnic conflict are stronger, reducing the probability of recognition by 55 percentage points.

Columns 9, 10, and 11 provide evidence regarding heterogeneity across regions. In our dataset, all of the ten cases in Europe (including the Balkan cases, the Russian Federation, cases in the Caucasus, and the UK/Northern Ireland) are cases of plurality ethnic rule and ethnic recognition. This 100 percent rate of adoption is in line with our theory—although, as discussed in Chapter 2, it may also be the case that other factors peculiar to Europe explain it. This also raises the question as to whether the apparent effect in the pooled data is driven primarily by these European cases. The estimates in columns 9, 10, and 11 show what happens when we omit Europe from the analysis, while still controlling for the various confounders described earlier and also including indicators for the other regions. The estimates in columns 9 and 10 are smaller than the estimates from the pooled data (columns 5 and 6)—although, interestingly, in non-European cases, the effect is stronger for cases without ethnic conflict. That the strength of the effect is smaller is due to the fact that we have dropped ten European cases that perfectly conform to the expected pattern. Nonetheless, the resulting point estimate is a decrease in the rate of adoption by around 20 percentage points for minority-led regimes. Given the small sample size that we are left with, the estimates are noisy, but the key point is that the estimated effects are still quite large.

Tables A.2 and A.3 present the estimates regarding the moderating effects of ethnic fractionalization, ethnic difference, military victory, and autocracy versus freedom as per Freedom House coding. The ethnic fractionalization estimates were used to produce Figure 4.1, which shows that in countries with very low ethnic fractionalization, minority- and plurality-led regimes differ very strongly in the rates at which they adopt recognition. But in places with high fractionalization, we estimate no substantial difference across minority- and plurality-led regimes. A similar pattern holds for ethnic difference: the effect of minority rule increases as the difference between the largest ethnic group population share and next-largest group share increases. For military victory, the regression result is undefined because all minority regimes with military victories adopted recognition. As such, we cannot fit the logistic regression (this is known as a "separation problem"). That said, this pattern, and the patterns in the raw data displayed in Table A.3, show that military victory and minority rule tend always toward non-recognition in their combination, although the number of cases is small. Finally, for autocracy, the regression results exclude "free" countries, as these adopt recognition 100 percent of the time. Among "partly free" and "not free"/autocratic regimes, we find that the effect of minority rule is intensified in "not free"/autocratic cases. Indeed, the regression results suggest that once we control for the other potential confounders, the negative effect of minority rule occurs exclusively among the "not free"/autocratic regimes. Of course, this also implies that "not free"/autocratic plurality regimes tend to choose recognition.

The effects of recognition

We turn now to our analysis of the effects of recognition. As discussed in Chapter 5, we use a difference-in-differences approach, which regresses our peace outcome variables on indicators for whether or not we are in a year following the passing of a new constitution or settlement, whether that constitution or settlement adopts recognition, and then fixed effects indicators for each country and year. We also control for a quadratic trend in the number of years since the observation enters the sample. This effectively controls for the number of years for which the observation has been affected by violent conflict. The coefficient on the "recognition" indicator measures the value of adding recognition to a constitution or comprehensive political settlement.

In the main text, Figures 5.4 and 5.5 focus on results coded as ethnic conflicts by the Ethnic Power Relations dataset (Cederman et al. 2010). Recall that our dataset also includes conflict-affected countries whose conflicts are not considered to be ethnic. For full transparency, we present here results for both

Table A.2　**Interaction effects for ethnic fractionalization (eth. frac.), ethnic difference (eth. dif.), military victory, and autocracy in modifying the effect of minority ethnic rule on the adoption of ethnic recognition (logistic regression marginal effect coefficients)**

Logistic regression marginal effects: Outcome is ethnic recognition in constitution or settlement (0/1)

	(1)	(2)	(3)	(4)
Minority leader (d)	−0.70**	−0.30	−0.42**	−0.06
	(0.30)	(0.27)	(0.20)	(0.27)
Min. leader X Eth. frac.	0.68			
	(0.92)			
Min. leader X Eth. dif.		−0.36		
		(0.55)		
Min. leader X Military victory			−0.17	
			(0.38)	
Min. leader X Autocracy (d)				−0.53***
				(0.13)
Observations	75	75	71	75
Control variables	Y	Y	Y	Y

Notes: Logistic regression marginal effect coefficients measure differences in probability of adoption for a unit change in each regressor variable

Standard errors in parentheses. Standard errors account for clustering by country.

* $p < 0.10$, ** $p < 0.05$, *** $p < 0.01$.

(d) for discrete change of dummy variable from 0 to 1.

All specifications include the same sample and control variables as column 5 in Table A.1; the coefficients on the control variables are omitted to save space.

the full set of cases as well as the ethnic conflict cases. Patterns tend to be stronger for the ethnic conflict cases.

Table A.4 shows the results of the difference-in-differences analysis. The coefficient estimates for the "post-settlement" variable capture how trends differ after a constitution or settlement is agreed upon. Then the coefficient estimates for the "recognition" variable capture the added value of recognition in such constitutions or settlements. We show results for effects on fatalities (presented on the natural logarithmic scale to account for high skew in the distribution of this outcome variable), an indicator for whether there is any significant political violence in a given year (reaching at least 25 deaths), gross domestic product

Table A.3 **Relationships between minority ethnic rule on the adoption of ethnic recognition for negotiated settlements versus military victories and then for free, partly free, and not free/autocratic regimes**

	No recognition	Recognition
Negotiated settlements		
Plurality leader	16	22
	42%	58%
Minority leader	27	9
	75%	25%
Total	43	31
Military victories		
Plurality leader	2	5
	29%	71%
Minority leader	4	1
	80%	20%
Total	6	6
Free regimes		
Plurality leader	0	4
	0%	100%
Minority leader	0	2
	0%	100%
Total	0	6
Partly free regimes		
Plurality leader	11	13
	46%	54%
Minority leader	14	6
	70%	30%
Total	22	19
Not free/autocratic regimes		
Plurality leader	7	10
	41%	59%
Minority leader	17	2
	89%	11%
Total	23	11

Note: Raw counts and row percentages displayed.

Table A.4 **Effects of constitutions or political settlements and the added value of recognition in such constitutions or settlements on violence, economic vitality, and democracy (least squares difference-in-differences coefficient estimates)**

	1	2	3	4	5	6
	All cases	*Eth. conf.*	*All cases Min. ldr.*	*All cases Plur. ldr.*	*Eth. conf. Min. ldr.*	*Eth. conf. Plur. ldr.*
Log(Fatalities)						
Post-settlement	−0.37	−0.40	−0.90	−0.01	−0.87	0.27
	(0.51)	(0.59)	(0.79)	(0.45)	(0.92)	(0.32)
Recognition	−0.19	0.01	−1.14	−0.57	−0.49	−1.02*
	(0.64)	(0.69)	(0.94)	(0.61)	(0.79)	(0.47)
Violence						
Post- settlement	−0.06	−0.06	−0.13	−0.00	−0.13	0.10*
	(0.07)	(0.09)	(0.12)	(0.08)	(0.14)	(0.05)
Recognition	−0.02	−0.02	−0.12	−0.08	−0.09	−0.22**
	(0.09)	(0.10)	(0.14)	(0.10)	(0.12)	(0.07)
Log(GDP per capita)						
Post- settlement	−0.08	−0.07	−0.11	−0.06	−0.10	−0.02
	(0.05)	(0.07)	(0.06)	(0.07)	(0.06)	(0.10)
Recognition	0.14	0.14	0.01	0.17	−0.11	0.16
	(0.08)	(0.11)	(0.10)	(0.10)	(0.09)	(0.13)
VDEM Polyarchy Index						
Post- settlement	0.04	0.04	0.08*	−0.04	0.05	−0.06*
	(0.03)	(0.04)	(0.04)	(0.02)	(0.04)	(0.03)
Recognition	0.02	0.04	−0.05	0.11**	−0.04	0.14**
	(0.04)	(0.05)	(0.06)	(0.04)	(0.08)	(0.04)
N (country-years)	1666	1096	600	1061	415	678

Notes: All estimates are based on linear least squares regressions that include two-way fixed effects (for year and country).

Robust standard errors clustered by country are shown in parentheses.

All estimates also control for a quadratic trend in the number of years that the country is in the sample.

* $p < 0.05$, ** $p < 0.01$.

(GDP) per capita (also on the natural logarithmic scale), and the VDEM polyarchy index to measure democracy. Column 1 shows results when we pool all of the data, and so we are not limiting the analysis to ethnic conflicts or splitting the sample on the basis of whether the case is under ethnic minority or plurality rule. When we lump all of the cases together in this way, we do not find any strong patterns—our interpretation is that effects are watered down in this sample. Column 2 looks only at ethnic conflict cases, but then lumps minority and plurality rule cases together. Again, average relationships are weak. Columns 3 and 4 pull the sample apart by whether cases are minority leadership or plurality leadership cases. Here some more revealing patterns start to emerge. Finally, Columns (5) and 6 present results for ethnic conflict, separating the analysis by whether the country is under minority or plurality leadership. Here the patterns become very clear. As anticipated by our theory, recognition reduces fatality rates, reduces the probability of any violence, increases gross domestic product per capita, and increases the extent to which politics are democratic. The results in columns 5 and 6 are the basis of Figures 5.4 and 5.5 in Chapter 5.

REFERENCES

Aalen, L. 2006. "Ethnic Federalism and Self-Determination for Nationalities in a Semi-Authoritarian State: The Case of Ethiopia." *International Journal on Minority and Group Rights* 13, nos. 2/3: 243–61.

Aalen, L. 2011. *The Politics of Ethnicity in Ethiopia: Actors, Power and Mobilisation Under Ethnic Federalism*. Leiden: Brill.

Aalen, L., and K. Tronvoll. 2009. "The End of Democracy? Curtailing Political and Civil Rights in Ethiopia." *Review of African Political Economy* 36, no. 120: 193–207.

Abate, T. 2013, March 30. *Ethnic-Based Politics in Ethiopia*. Available from: https://www.lawethiopia.com/images/ethnic%20politics%20in%20ethiopia/Ethnic-based-politics.pdf.

Abbink, J. 2011. "Ethnic-Based Federalism and Ethnicity in Ethiopia: Reassessing the Experiment After 20 Years." *Journal of Eastern African Studies* 5, no. 4: 596–619.

Abdu, B. 2018. "Sidama's Quest for Statehood." *The Reporter* (Addis Ababa), November 10. Available from: https://www.thereporterethiopia.com/article/sidamas-quest-statehood.

Abdu, B. 2019. "Demonstration Rocks Wolayita." *The Reporter* (Addis Ababa), May 18. Available from: https://www.thereporterethiopia.com/article/demonstration-rocks-wolayita.

Acemoglu, D., and J. Robinson. 2012. *Why Nations Fail: The Origins of Power, Prosperity and Poverty*. New York: Crown.

Addis Standard. 2015. "A Historic 100% Win for Ethiopia's Ruling EPRDF." *Addis Standard*, June 22. Available from: http://addisstandard.com/breaking-a-historic-100-win-for-ethiopias-ruling-eprdf.

African Peer Review Mechanism. 2005. *Country Review Report of the Republic of Rwanda*. Available from: https://www.eisa.org.za/aprm/pdf/Countries_Rwanda_APRM_Report.pdf.

Alesina, A., A. Devleeschauwer, W. Easterly, S. Kurlat, and R. Wacziarg. 2003. "Fractionalization." *Journal of Economic Growth* 8, no. 2: 155–94.

Ali, T., and R. O. Matthews. 2004. *Durable Peace: Challenges for Peacebuilding in Africa*. Toronto: University of Toronto Press.

Anderson, B. 2003. *Imagined Communities*. London: Verso.

Angrist, J. D., and J. Pischke. 2009. *Mostly Harmless Econometrics: An Empiricist's Companion*. Princeton: Princeton University Press.

Ansoms, A. 2009. "Re-Engineering Rural Society: The Visions and Ambitions of the Rwandan Elite." *African Affairs* 108, no. 431: 289–309.

Appiah, K. A. 2005. *The Ethics of Identity*. Princeton: Princeton University Press.

Appiah, K. A. 2018. *The Lies That Bind: Rethinking Identity*. New York: W. W. Norton.

Arusha Accords. 1993. *Peace Agreement Between the Government of the Republic of Rwanda and Rwandese Patriotic Front*. Available from: https://peaceaccords.nd.edu/sites/default/files/accords/Rwanda_Peace_Accord.pdf.

Arusha Peace and Reconciliation Agreement for Burundi. Available from: https://peaceaccords. nd.edu/sites/default/files/accords/Arusha_Peace_Accord____.pdf. Accessed March 17, 2017.

Ashenafi, M. 2003. "Ethiopia: Process of Democratization and Development." In *Human Rights Under African Constitutions*, edited by A. A. An-Na'im, 29–51. Philadelphia: University of Pennsylvania Press.

Autessere, S. 2010. *The Trouble with the Congo: Local Violence and the Failure of International Peacebuilding*. Cambridge: Cambridge University Press.

Bah, A. 2017. "Seeking Democracy in Côte d'Ivoire: Overcoming Exclusionary Citizenship." Global Centre for Pluralism (Ottawa). Available from: https://www.pluralism.ca/wp-content/uploads/2018/01/CotedIvoire_EN.pdf.

Banting, K., and W. Kymlicka, eds. 2003. *Multiculturalism and the Welfare State: Recognition and Redistribution in Contemporary Democracies*. Oxford: Oxford University Press.

Barkey, K. 2008. *Empire of Difference: The Ottomans in Comparative Perspective*. Cambridge: Cambridge University Press.

Barkhof, S. 2011. "Playing the Ethnic Card: Liberal Democratic and Authoritarian Practices Compared." In *Routledge Handbook of Ethnic Conflict*, edited by K. Cordell and S. Wolff, 311–21. New York: Routledge.

Barry, B. 2001. *Culture and Equality: An Egalitarian Critique of Multiculturalism*. Cambridge, MA: Harvard University Press.

Basedau, M., and A. Moroff. 2011. "Parties in Chains: Do Ethnic Party Bans in Africa Promote Peace?" *Party Politics* 17, no. 2: 205–22.

Bates, R. 1983. "Modernization, Ethnic Competition, and the Rationality of Politics in Contemporary Africa." In *State Versus Ethnic Claims: African Policy Dilemmas*, edited by D. Rothchild and V. A. Olorunsola, 152–71. Boulder, CO: Westview.

BBC. 1989. "Burundi Prime Minister Says Social Justice Will Solve Country's Problems." BBC Summary of World Broadcasts, April 20.

BBC. 1990. "Burundi: Buyoya Rejects Idea of Multi-Party System." BBC Summary of World Broadcasts, March 17.

BBC. 1992a. "Burundi: Buyoya Warns Against Destabilization Attempts; Hutus Arrested." BBC Summary of World Broadcasts, August 17.

BBC. 1992b. "Burundi President Says Africans Not Mature Enough to Understand Democracy." BBC Summary of World Broadcasts, December 17.

BBC. 2008. "Rwanda Still Teaching Genocide." BBC News, January 17.

BBC. 2015. "Ethiopia Election: EPRDF Wins All 547 Seats in Poll." BBC News, June 22.

BBC. 2018. "Abiy Ahmed: Ethiopia's Prime Minister." BBC News, September 14.

BBC International Monitoring Reports. 2001. "Burundi: Rebel Group Rejects Document on Arusha Negotiators (from *NetPress*)." December 9.

BBC International Monitoring Reports. 2004. "Burundi: Former Rebel Official Speaks on Pretoria Talks on Elections. (Burundi Radio Publique Africaine)." July 20.

Begley, L. 2011. "'Resolved to Fight the Ideology of Genocide and All of Its Manifestations': The Rwandan Patriotic Front, Violence and Ethnic Marginalisation in Post-Genocide Rwanda and Eastern Congo." D.Phil. thesis, University of Sussex.

Bekken, N. 2011. "Rwanda's Hidden Divisions: From the Ethnicity of Habyarimana to the Politics of Kagame." Beyond Intractability. Available from: http://www.beyondintractability.org/casestudy/bekken-rwandas-hidden-divisions.

Bélair, J. 2016. "Ethnic Federalism and Conflicts in Ethiopia." *Canadian Journal of African Studies* 50, no. 2: 295–301.

Belmont, K., S. Mainwaring, and A. Reynolds. 2002. "Introduction: Institutional Design, Conflict Management, and Democracy." In *Architecture of Democracy: Constitutional Design, Conflict Management, and Democracy*, edited by A. Reynolds, 1–11. Oxford: Oxford University Press.

Bentley, K., and S. Southall. 2005. *An African Peace Process: Mandela, South Africa and Burundi*. Cape Town: HSRC Press.

Berman, A. 2016. "Dictator in Disguise." *Harvard Political Review*, April 22. Available from: http://harvardpolitics.com/world/your-friendly-neighborhood-dictator.

Blumer, H. 1958. "Race Prejudice as a Sense of Group Position." *Pacific Sociological Review* 1: 3–7.

Bobo, F. T., E. A. Yesuf, and M. Woldie. 2017. "Inequities in Utilization of Reproductive and Maternal Health Services in Ethiopia." *International Journal for Equity in Health* 16, no. 105: 1–8.

Bobo, L., and F. D. Gilliam Jr. 1990. "Race, Sociopolitical Participation, and Black Empowerment." *American Political Science Review* 84, no. 2: 377–93.

Bogaards, M., M. Basedau, and C. Hartmann. 2010. "Ethnic Party Bans in Africa: An Introduction." *Democratization* 17, no. 4: 599–617.

Boko, H. 2018. "Abiy Ahmed: Ethiopia's First Oromo PM Spreads Hope of Reform." France24 News, July 30. Available from: https://www.france24.com/en/20180730-abiy-ahmed-spreads-hope-reform-ethiopia.

Borman, N. C., L. E. Cederman, S. Gates, B. Graham, S. Hug, K. Strom, and J. Wucherpfennig. 2019. "Power Sharing: Institutions, Behavior, and Peace." *American Journal of Political Science* 63, no. 1: 84–100.

Brabant, S., and T. Vircoulon. 2015. "Burundi: Unraveling the Peace." *Notes de l'institut francais des relations internationals.* https://www.ifri.org/en/publications/enotes/notes-de-lifri/burundi-unravelling-peace

Bradol, J. H., and A. Guibert. 1997. "Le temps des assassins et l'espace humanitaire, Rwanda, Kivu, 1994–1997" [The time of assassins and the humanitarian space, Rwanda, Kivu, 1994–1997]. *Hérodote* 86/87: 116–49.

Brancati, D. 2006. "Decentralization: Fueling the Fire or Dampening the Flames of Ethnic Conflict and Secessionism?" *International Organization* 60, no. 3: 651–85.

Brancati, D., and J. L. Snyder. 2011. "Rushing to the Polls: The Causes of Early Post-Conflict Elections." *Journal of Conflict Resolution* 55, no. 3: 469–92.

Brancati, D., and J. L. Snyder. 2013. "Time to Kill: The Impact of Election Timing on Post-Conflict Stability." *Journal of Conflict Resolution* 57, no. 5: 822–53.

Branch, A., and Z. Mampilly. 2015. *Africa Uprising: Popular Protest and Political Change.* London: Zed Books.

Brass, P. 1991. *Ethnicity and Nationalism: Theory and Comparison.* Thousand Oaks, CA: Sage Publications.

Brown, G. K., and A. Langer. 2010. "Horizontal Inequalities and Conflict: A Critical Review and Research Agenda." *Conflict, Security and Development* 10, no. 1: 27–55.

Buckley-Zistel, S. 2006. "Remembering to Forget: Chosen Amnesia as a Strategy for Local Coexistence in Post-Genocide Rwanda." *Africa* 76, no. 2: 131–50.

Burke, J. 2018. "Women Win Half of Ethiopia's Cabinet Roles in Reshuffle." *The Guardian*, October 16.

Buyinza, J. 2007. "Rwanda: Damning Revelations." *The New Times* (Kigali), December 11. Available from: https://allafrica.com/stories/200712120024.html.

Capel, C. 2018. "Ethiopian Prime Minister Abiy Ahmed Appoints New Finance Minister." *The National*, October 16.

Cederman, L. E., and L. Girardin. 2007. "Beyond Fractionalization: Mapping Ethnicity onto Nationalist Insurgencies." *American Political Science Review* 101, no. 1: 173–85.

Cederman, L. E., K. S. Gleditsch, and H. Buhaug. 2013. *Inequality, Grievances, and Civil War.* New York: Cambridge University Press.

Cederman, L. E., K. S. Gleditsch, and J. Wucherpfennig. 2017. "Predicting the Decline of Ethnic Civil War: Was Gurr Right and for the Right Reasons?" *Journal of Peace Research* 54, no. 2: 262–74.

Cederman, L. E., A. Wimmer, and B. Min. 2010. "Why Do Ethnic Groups Rebel? New Data and Analysis." *World Politics* 62, no. 1: 87–119.

Chandra, K. 2004. *Why Ethnic Parties Succeed.* Cambridge: Cambridge University Press.

Chandra, K. 2006. "What Is Ethnic Identity and Does It Matter?" *Annual Review of Political Science* 9: 397–424.

Chandra, K. 2009. "Designing Measures of Ethnic Identity: The Problems of Overlap and Incompleteness." *Qualitative Methods Newsletter* 7, no. 1 (Spring): 36–41.

Chandra, K. 2012. *Constructivist Theories of Ethnic Politics*. Oxford: Oxford University Press.

Chauchard, S. 2017. *Why Representation Matters: The Meaning of Ethnic Quotas in Rural India*. Cambridge: Cambridge University Press.

Cheeseman, N. 2015. *Democracy in Africa: Successes, Failures, and the Struggle for Political Reform*. Cambridge: Cambridge University Press.

Chrétien, J. P. 1995. "Jean Chrétien on Recognition of Quebec as a Distinct Society." November 29. Available from: https://openparliament.ca/debates/1995/11/29/jean-chretien-1/only.

Chrétien, J. P. 2003. *The Great Lakes of Africa: Two Thousand Years of History*. Translated by Scott Straus. New York: Zone Books.

Chrétien, J. P., and J. F. Dupaquier. 2007. *Burundi 1972: Au bord des genocides*. Paris: Karthala.

Chua, A. 2003. *World On Fire: How Exporting Free Market Democracy Breeds Ethnic Hatred and Global Instability*. New York: First Anchor Books.

Cinalli, M. 2005. "Below and Beyond Power Sharing: Relational Structures Across Institutions and Civil Society." In *Power Sharing: New Challenges for Divided Societies*, edited by I. O'Flynn and D. Russell, 172–87. London: Pluto.

Clapham, C. 1988. *Transformation and Continuity in Revolutionary Ethiopia*. Cambridge: Cambridge University Press.

Cochrane, F. 2008. *Ending Wars*. Cambridge: Polity Press.

Collier, P., V. L. Elliott, H. Hegre, A. Hoeffler, M. Reynal-Querol, and N. Sambanis. 2003. *Breaking the Conflict Trap: Civil War and Development Policy*. Washington, DC: World Bank and Oxford University Press.

Collier, P., and A. Hoeffler. 2004. "Greed and Grievance in Civil War." *Oxford Economic Papers* 56, no. 4: 563–95.

Collier, P., and N. Sambanis. 2002. "Understanding Civil War." *Journal of Conflict Resolution* 46, no. 1: 3–12.

Committee on the Elimination of Racial Discrimination. 2009. "Consideration of Reports Submitted by States Parties Under Article 9 of the Convention." *United Nations International Convention on the Elimination of all Forms of Racial Discrimination*.

Connor, W. 1972. "Nation Building or Nation Destroying." *World Politics* 24, no. 3: 319–55.

Constitution of the Tigrayan Peoples Liberation Front (TPLF). 1983. Adopted at the Second Organizational Congress of the Tigray People's Liberation Front (TPLF). Available from: http://ciml.250x.com/africa/ethiopia/tplf_constitution_may_1983.pdf.

Coppedge, M., J. Gerring, S. I. Lindberg, S. E. Skaaning, J. Teorell, D. Altman, M. Bernhard, M. S. Fish, A. Glynn, A. Hicken, C. H. Knutsen, A. Lührmann, K. L. Marquardt, K. McMann, V. Mechkova, P. Paxton, D. Pemstein, L. Saxer, B. Seim, R. Sigman, and J. Staton. 2017. *Varieties of Democracy (V-Dem) Codebook v7.1*. Gothenburg: University of Gothenburg, V-Dem Institute.

Coser, L. A. 1956. *The Functions of Social Conflict*. New York: Free Press.

Csergő, Z., P. Roseberry, and S. Wolff. 2017. "Institutional Outcomes of Territorial Contestation: Lessons from Post-Communist Europe, 1989–2012." *Publius: The Journal of Federalism* 47, no. 4: 491–521.

Cunningham, C. D., G. C. Loury, and J. D. Skrentny. 2002. "Passing Strict Scrutiny: Using Social Science to Design Affirmative Action Programs." *Georgetown Law Journal* 90, no. 4: 835–82.

Curtis, D. 2012. "The International Peacebuilding Paradox: Power Sharing and Post-Conflict Governance in Burundi." *African Affairs* 12, no. 446: 72–91.

Dallaire, R., and B. Beardsley. 2004. *Shake Hands with the Devil: The Failure of Humanity in Rwanda*. London: Arrow.

Daly, S. Z. 2013. "State Strategies in Multi-ethnic Territories: Explaining Variation in the Former Soviet Union and Eastern Bloc." *British Journal of Political Science* 44, no. 2: 381–408.

Davenport, C. 2007. *State Repression and the Domestic Democratic Peace*. Cambridge: Cambridge University Press.

De Ferranti, D., G. Perry, F. Ferreira, and M. Walton. 2004. *Inequality in Latin America: Breaking with History?* Washington, DC: World Bank.

De Roeck, M., F. Reyntjens, S. Vanderginste, and M. Verpoorten. 2017. "Special Data Feature: Institutions in Burundi and Rwanda: A 20-Year Data Overview (1995–2016)." In *L'Afrique des Grands Lacs: Annuaire 2015–2016*, 9–50.

De Waal, A. 1991. "Evil Days: Thirty Years of War and Famine in Ethiopia." New York: Human Rights Watch.

Des Forges, A. 1999. *Leave None to Tell the Story.* New York: Human Rights Watch.

Deutsch, K. W. 1966. *Nationalism and Social Communication: An Inquiry into the Foundations of Nationality.* Cambridge, MA: MIT Press.

De Zwart, F. 2005. "Targeted Policy in Multicultural Societies: Accommodation, Denial, and Replacement." *International Social Science Journal* 57, no. 183: 153–64.

Ditlmann, R., C. Samii, and T. Zeitzoff. 2017. "Addressing Violent Intergroup Conflict from the Bottom Up?" *Social Issues and Policy Review* 11, no. 1: 38–77.

Diamond, L. 2005. *Squandered Victory: The American Occupation and the Bungled Effort to Bring Democracy to Iraq.* New York: Henry Holt.

Duflo, E. 2005. "Why Political Reservations." *Journal of the European Economic Association* 3, no. 2: 668–87.

Dunning, T. 2010. "Do Quotas Promote Ethnic Solidarity? Field and Natural Experimental Evidence from India." Unpublished manuscript, Yale University.

Eck, K., and L. Hultman. 2007. "One-Sided Violence Against Civilians in War: Insights from New Fatality Data." *Journal of Peace Research* 44, no. 2: 233–46.

The Economist. 2016. "Census and Sensibility." *The Economist*, November 5.

Eisenberg, A., and W. Kymlicka. 2011. "Bringing Institutions Back In: How Public Institutions Assess Identity." In *Identity Politics in the Public Realm: Bringing Institutions Back In*, edited by A. Eisenberg and W. Kymlicka, 1–30. Vancouver: University of British Columbia Press.

Egne, R. M. 2014. "Representation of Ethiopian Multicultural Society in Secondary Teacher Education Curricula." *Journal of Teacher Education for Sustainability* 16, no. 1: 54–75.

Elkins, Z., T. Ginsburg, and J. Melton. 2007. "Baghdad, Tokyo, Kabul: Constitution Making in Occupied States." *William and Mary Law Review* 49: 1139–78.

Elkins, Z., T. Ginsburg, and J. Melton. 2010. "Chronology of Constitutional Events, Version 1.1." Comparative Constitutions Project. Available from: http://www.comparativeconstitutionsproject.org.

EPRDF. 1991. *EPRDF Program.* Available from: https://zelalemkibret.files.wordpress.com/2011/11/eprdf-program.pdf.

Eramian, L. 2014. "Ethnicity Without Labels? Ambiguity and Excess in 'Postethnic' Rwanda." *Focal: Journal of Global and Historical Anthropology* 2014, no. 7: 96–109.

Esteban, J., L. Mayoral, and D. Ray. 2012. "Ethnicity and Conflict: An Empirical Study." *American Economic Review* 102, no. 4: 1310–42.

Fanon, F. 1963. *The Wretched of the Earth.* Paris: Présence Africaine.

Fearon, J. D. 2003. "Ethnic and Cultural Diversity by Country." *Journal of Economic Growth* 8, no. 2: 195–222.

Fearon, J. D., K. Kasara, and D. D. Laitin. 2007. "Ethnic Minority Rule and Civil War Onset." *American Political Science Review* 101, no. 1: 187–93.

Federal Democratic Republic of Ethiopia. 2017. *Health Sector Transformation Plan-I: Annual Performance Report EFY 2009* (Version 1). Addis Ababa: Ministry of Health and Italian Agency for Development Cooperation.

Fessha, Y. T., and C. Van Der Beken. 2013. "Ethnic Federalism and Internal Minorities: The Legal Protection of Internal Minorities in Ethiopia." *African Journal of International and Comparative Law* 21, no. 1: 32–49.

Finnemore, M., and K. Sikkink. 1998. "International Norm Dynamics and Political Change." *International Organization* 52, no. 4: 887–917.

Forum of Federations. n.d. "Introduction to Federalism." Forum of Federations: The Global Network on Federalism and Devolved Governance. Available from: http://www.forumfed.org/federalism/introduction-to-federalism.

Fraser, N. 1995. "From Redistribution to Recognition? Dilemmas of Justice in a Post-Socialist Age." *New Left Review* 1, no. 212: 68–93.

Freedom House. 2016. *Methodology: Freedom in the World 2016.* Freedom House. Available at https://freedomhouse.org/report/freedom-world-2016/methodology.

Freedom House. 2018. *Freedom in the World, 2018: Rwanda Profile.* Freedom House. Available from: https://freedomhouse.org/report/freedom-world/2018/rwanda.

Fryer, R. G., and C. G. Loury. 2005. "Affirmative Action and Its Mythologies." *Journal of Economic Perspectives* 19, no. 3: 147–62.

Fukuyama, F. 2018. *Identity: The Demand for Dignity and the Politics of Resentment.* New York: Farrar, Straus and Giroux.

Gaertner, S. L., and J. F. Dovidio. 1986. "The Aversive Form of Racism." In *Prejudice, Discrimination, and Racism,* edited by S. L. Gaertner and J. F. Dovidio, 61–89. San Diego: Academic Press.

Gaertner, S. L., and J. F. Dovidio. 2000. *Reducing Intergroup Bias: The Common Ingroup Identity Model.* New York: Routledge.

Gagnon, V. P. Jr. 1994. "Ethnic Nationalism and International Conflict: The Case of Serbia." *International Security* 19, no. 3: 130–66.

Gahima, G., K. Nyamwasa, T. Rudasingwa, and P. Karegeya. 2010. *Rwanda Briefing.* https://francegenocidetutsi.org/RwandaBriefingAugust2010NyamwasaEtAl.pdf

Galtung, J. 1969. "Violence, Peace, and Peace Research." *Journal of Peace Research* 6, no. 3: 167–91.

Gardner, T. 2017. "Ethiopia's Tense Ethnic Federalism Is Being Tested Again." *Quartz Africa,* September 15.

Gardner, T. 2018. "Abiy Ahmed Is Not a Populist." *Foreign Policy,* December 5.

Gashaw, S. 1993. "Nationalism and Ethnic Conflict in Ethiopia." In *The Rising Tide of Cultural Pluralism: The Nation-State at Bay,* edited by C. Young, 138–57. Madison: University of Wisconsin Press.

Gashugi, O. A. 2013. "Clearer Genocide Ideology Law to be More Lenient." *Rwanda Focus,* August 5.

Gates, S. 2002. "Recruitment and Allegiance: The Microfoundations of Rebellion." *Journal of Conflict* 46, no. 1: 111–30.

Gellner, D. N. 2007. "Caste, Ethnicity and Inequality in Nepal." *Economic and Political Weekly* 42, no. 20: 1823–8.

Gellner, E. 1983. *Nations and Nationalism.* Oxford: Blackwell.

George, A. L., and A. Bennett. 2004. *Case Studies and Theory Development in the Social Sciences.* Cambridge, MA: MIT Press.

Gilligan, M. J., E. Mvukiyehe, and C. Samii. 2013. "Reintegrating Rebels into Civilian Life: Quasi-Experimental Evidence from Burundi." *Journal of Conflict Resolution* 57, no. 4: 598–626.

Giorgis, H. 2018. "Abiy Ahmed Meets the Ethiopian Diaspora." *The Atlantic,* August 4. Available from: https://www.theatlantic.com/entertainment/archive/2018/08/abiy-ahmed-meets-the-ethiopian-diaspora/566591.

Gleditsch, N. P., P. Wallensteen, M. Eriksson, M. Sollenberg, and H. Strand. 2002. "Armed Conflict 1946–2001: A New Dataset." *Journal of Peace Research* 39, no. 5: 615–37.

Goehrung, R. 2017. "At Issue: Violence, and the Narrative of Genocide: The Dangers of a Third-Term in Rwanda." *African Studies Quarterly* 17, no. 1: 79–98.

Gourevitch, P. 1998. *We Wish to Inform You That Tomorrow We Will Be Killed with Our Families.* New York: Picador USA.

Gribbin, R. E. 2005. *Aftermath of Genocide: The U.S. Role in Rwanda.* New York: iUniverse.

Guichaoua, A. 2015. *From War to Genocide. Criminal Politics in Rwanda, 1990–1994.* Madison: University of Wisconsin Press.

Gurr, T. R. 1993. "Why Minorities Rebel: A Global Analysis of Communal Mobilization and Conflict Since 1945." *International Political Science Review* 14, no. 2: 161–201.

Habtu, A. 2004. "Ethnic Pluralism as an Organizing Principle of the Ethiopian Federation." *Dialectical Anthropology* 28, no. 2: 91–123.

Habyarimana, J., M. Humphreys, D. N. Posner, and J. M. Weinstein. 2007. "Why Does Ethnic Diversity Undermine Public Goods Provision?" *American Political Science Review* 101, no. 4: 709–25.

Harbom, L., S. Högbladh, and P. Wallensteen. 2006. "Armed Conflict and Peace Agreements." *Journal of Peace Research* 43, no. 5: 617–31.

Harden, B. 1988. "Burundi Killings' Roots Lie in Tribal Hatreds." *Washington Post*, August 21.

Hartzell, C., M. Hoodie, and D. Rothchild. 2001. "Stabilizing the Peace After Civil War: An Investigation of Some Key Variables." *International Organization* 55, no. 1: 183–208.

Hensel, P. R. 2018. "ICOW Colonial History Data Set, Version 1.1." Available at http://www.paulhensel.org/icowcol.html.

Hoben, S. J. 1989. *School, Work, and Equity: Educational Reform in Rwanda.* Boston: African Studies Center, Boston University.

Högbladh, S, 2011. "Peace Agreements 1975–2011—Updating the UCDP Peace Agreement Dataset." In *States in Armed Conflict*, edited by T. Pettersson and L. Themnér, 39–56. Uppsala: Department of Peace and Conflict Research, Uppsala University.

Horowitz, D. L. 1985. *Ethnic Groups in Conflict.* Berkeley: University of California Press.

Horowitz, D. L. 1991. *A Democratic South Africa? Constitutional Engineering in a Divided Society.* Berkeley: University of California Press.

Horowitz, D. L. 2000. *Ethnic Groups in Conflict*, 2nd ed. Berkeley: University of California Press.

Horowitz, D. L. 2001. *The Deadly Ethnic Riot.* Berkeley: University of California Press.

Horowitz, D. L. 2014. "Ethnic Power Sharing: Three Big Problems." *Journal of Democracy* 25, no. 2: 5–20.

Howard, L. M., and A. Stark. 2018. "How Civil Wars End: The International System, Norms, and the Role of External Actors." *International Security* 42, no. 3: 127–71.

Huntington, S. P. 2004. *Who Are We? The Challenges to America's National Identity.* New York: Simon and Schuster.

Hutt, R. 2016. "5 Things to Know About Rwanda's Economy." *World Economic Forum*, April 7. Available from: https://www.weforum.org/agenda/2016/04/5-things-to-know-about-rwanda-s-economy.

Ingelaere, B. 2009. *Living Together Again: The Expectation of Transitional Justice in Burundi—A View from Below.* Antwerp: University of Antwerp Institute of Development Policy and Management.

Ingelaere, B. 2010. "Peasants, Power and Ethnicity: A Bottom-Up Perspective on Rwanda's Political Transition." *African Affairs* 109, no. 435: 273–92.

Internal Displacement Monitoring Center. 2018. *Ethiopia Tops Global List of Highest Internal Displacement in 2018.* Available from: https://reliefweb.int/report/ethiopia/ethiopia-tops-global-list-highest-internal-displacement-2018.

International Crisis Group. 2000. *The Mandela Effect: Prospects for Peace in Burundi.* International Crisis Group. Available at https://www.crisisgroup.org/africa/central-africa/burundi/mandela-effect-prospects-peace-burundi.

International Crisis Group. 2009. *Ethiopia: Ethnic Federalism and Its Discontents.* International Crisis Group. Available from: https://www.crisisgroup.org/africa/horn-africa/ethiopia/ethiopia-ethnic-federalism-and-its-discontents.

International Crisis Group. 2017. *Burundi: The Army in Crisis.* International Crisis Group. Available from: https://www.crisisgroup.org/africa/central-africa/burundi/247-burundi-army-crisis.

International Crisis Group. 2018. *Crisis Watch: Latest Updates (November): Ethiopia.* International Crisis Group. Available from: https://www.crisisgroup.org/crisiswatch/november-2018.

International Crisis Group. 2019. June 20. *Running Out of Options in Burundi.* Available at: https://www.crisisgroup.org/africa/central-africa/burundi/278-running-out-options-burundi.

International Panel of Eminent Personalities. 2000. *Rwanda: The Preventable Genocide.* Kigali: African Union. Available from: https://www.refworld.org/docid/4d1da8752.html.

Ishiyama, J. 2009. "Do Ethnic Parties Promote Minority Ethnic Conflict?" *Nationalism and Ethnic Politics* 15, no. 1: 56–83.

Ismail, A. 2017. "Prof. Yash Ghai Reading Sri Lankan Minds on Federalism States 'There Seems to be a Phobia in Your Country.'" *Daily Mirror*, November 9.

Jackson, T. 2000. *Equal Access to Education: A Peace Imperative for Burundi*. London: International Alert.

Jalata, A. 1993. "Ethiopia and Ethnic Politics: The Case of Oromo Nationalism." *Dialectical Anthropology* 18, nos. 3/4: 381–402.

Jarstad, A. 2001. "Changing the Game: Consociational Theory and Ethnic Quotas in Cyprus and New Zealand." Ph.D. dissertation, Uppsala University.

Jervis, R. 1976. *Perception and Misperception in International Politics*. Princeton, NJ: Princeton University Press.

Johns, M. 2003. "'Do as I Say, Not as I Do': The European Union, Eastern Europe and Minority Rights." *East European Politics and Societies* 17, no. 4: 682–99.

Jones, B. D. 1999. "The Arusha Peace Process." In *The Path of a Genocide: The Rwanda Crisis from Uganda to Zaire*, edited by H. Adelman and A. Suhrke, 131–56. New Brunswick, NJ: Transaction.

Jones, B. D. 2001. *Peacemaking in Rwanda: The Dynamics of Failure*. Boulder, CO: Lynne Rienner.

Joshi, M., and J. Darby. 2013. "Introducing the Peace Accords Matrix (PAM): A Database of Comprehensive Peace Agreements and Their Implementation, 1989–2007." *Peacebuilding* 1: 256–74.

Kagame, P. 2014. "Kagame Speaking at Brandeis University in Boston" [video], April 23. Available from: https://www.youtube.com/watch?v=KaBF5etmrXM.

Kalyvas, S., and L. Balcells. 2010. "International System and Technologies of Rebellion: How the End of the Cold War Shaped Internal Conflict." *American Political Science Review* 104, no. 3: 415–29.

Kauffman, C. 1996. "Possible and Impossible Solutions to Ethnic Civil Wars." *International Security* 20, no. 4: 136–75.

Kauffman, E. 2011. "The Demography of Ethnic Conflict." *Journal of Ethnopolitics* 3, no. 4: 367–68.

Kauffman, E., and O. Haklai. 2008. "Dominant Ethnicity: From Minority to Majority." *Nations and Nationalism* 14, no. 4: 743–67.

Kefale, A. 2013. *Federalism and Ethnic Conflict in Ethiopia*. Abingdon: Routledge.

Keller, E., and L. Smith. 2005. "Obstacles to Implementing Territorial Decentralization: The First Decade of Ethiopian Federalism." In *Sustainable Peace: Power and Democracy After Civil Wars*, edited by P. Roeder and D. Rothchild, 265–91. Ithaca, NY: Cornell University Press.

Kertzer, D., and D. Arel, eds. 2002. *Census and Identity: The Politics of Race, Ethnicity and Language in National Censuses*. Cambridge: Cambridge University Press.

Kestler-D'Amours, J. 2018. "Ethiopia Mass Protests Rooted in History." Al-Jazeera, February 20.

Khadiagala, G. 2002. "Implementing the Arusha Peace Agreement on Rwanda." In *Ending Civil Wars: The Implementation of the Peace Agreements*, edited by E. M. Cousens, S. J. Stedman, and D. Rothchild, 463–98. Boulder, CO: Lynne Rienner.

King, C. 2007. "Power, Social Violence, and Civil Wars." In *Leashing the Dogs of War*, edited by C. A. Crocker, F. Osler Hampson, and P. Aall, 115–30. Washington, DC: United States Institute of Peace Press.

King, E. 2009. "From Data Problems to Data Points: Challenges and Opportunities of Research in Post-Genocide Rwanda." *African Studies Review* 52, no. 3: 127–48.

King, E. 2014. *From Classrooms to Conflict in Rwanda*. New York: Cambridge University Press.

King, E. 2017. "What Framing Analysis Can Teach Us About History Textbooks, Peace and Conflict: The Case of Rwanda." In *(Re)Constructing Memory: Education, Identity and Conflict*, edited by M. J. Bellino and J. H. Williams, 23–48. Rotterdam: Sense.

King, E., and C. Samii. 2018. "Minorities and Mistrust: On the Adoption of Ethnic Recognition to Manage Conflict." *Journal of Peace Research* 55, no. 3: 289–304.

Kinzer, S. A. 2008. *A Thousand Hills: Rwanda's Rebirth and the Man Who Dreamed It*. Hoboken: John Wiley and Sons.

Kirisci, K., and G. M. Winrow. 1997. *The Kurdish Question and Turkey: An Example of a Trans-State Ethnic Conflict*. London: Routledge.

Krook, M. L., and D. Z. O'Brien. 2010. "The Politics of Group Representation: Quotas for Women and Minorities Worldwide." *Comparative Politics* 42, no. 3: 253–72.

Kruks, S. 2001. *Retrieving Experience: Subjectivity and Recognition in Feminist Politics*. Ithaca, NY: Cornell University Press.

Kuperman, A., ed. 2015. *Constitutions and Conflict Management in Africa: Preventing Civil War Through Institutional Design*. Philadelphia: University of Pennsylvania Press.

Kymlicka, W. 1995. *Multicultural Citizenship: A Liberal Theory of Minority Rights*. Oxford: Oxford University Press.

Kymlicka, W., and I. Shapiro. 1997. "Introduction." In *Ethnicity and Group Rights*, edited by W. Kymlicka and I. Shapiro, 3–21. New York: New York University Press.

Langer, A. 2013. "Horizontal Inequalities, Ethnic Politics and Violent Conflict: The Contrasting Experiences of Ghana and Côte d'Ivoire." In *Preventing Violent Conflict in Africa: Inequalities, Perceptions, and Institutions*, edited by Y. Mine, S. Fukuda-Parr, and F. Stewart, 66–94. New York: Palgrave Macmillan.

Langer, A., and S. Mikami. 2013. "The Relationship Between Objective and Subjective Horizontal Inequalities: Evidence from Five African Countries." In *Preventing Violent Conflict in Africa: Inequalities, Perceptions, and Institutions*, edited by Y. Mine, S. Fukuda-Parr, and F. Stewart, 208–51. New York: Palgrave Macmillan.

Lanza, E., and H. Woldemariam. 2014. "Multiculturalism and Local Literacy Practices in Ethiopia: Language Contact in Regulated and Unregulated Spaces." *Multilingual Margins* 1, no. 1: 74–100.

Lemarchand, R. 1970. *Rwanda and Burundi*. New York: Praeger.

Lemarchand, R. 1994. *Burundi: Ethnocide as Discourse and Practice*. Washington, DC: Woodrow Wilson Center.

Lemarchand, R. 1996. *Burundi: Ethnic Conflict and Genocide*. New York: Cambridge University Press.

Lemarchand, R. 2009. *The Dynamics of Violence in Central Africa*. Philadelphia: University of Pennsylvania Press.

Lerner, H. 2011. *Making Constitutions in Deeply Divided Societies*. Cambridge: Cambridge University Press.

Levine, R., and D. Campbell, eds. 1972. *Ethnocentrism: Theories of Conflict, Ethnic Attitudes and Group Behaviour*. New York: John Wiley.

Lieberman, E. S. 2005. "Nested Analysis as a Mixed-Method Strategy for Comparative Research." *American Political Science Review* 99, no. 3: 435–52.

Lieberman, E. S., and P. Singh. 2012. "The Institutional Origins of Ethnic Violence." *Comparative Politics* 45, no. 1: 1–24.

Lieberman, E. S., and P. Singh. 2017. "Census Enumeration and Group Conflict: A Global Analysis of the Consequences of Counting." *World Politics* 69, no. 1: 1–53.

Lijphart, A. 1977. *Democracy in Plural Societies*. New Haven: Yale University Press.

Lijphart, A. 1985. "The Field of Electoral Systems Research: A Critical Survey." *Electoral Studies* 4, no. 1: 3–14.

Lijphart, A. 1985. *Power-Sharing in South Africa*. Berkeley: University of California, Institute of International Studies.

Logan, C., and E. Gyimah-Boadi. 2016. "Africa's Largest Public-Opinion Survey Is Under Threat, but Here's What You Can Do About It." *Washington Post*, September 9.

Londregan, J., H. Bienen, and N. van de Walle. 1995. "Ethnicity and Leadership Succession in Africa." *International Studies Quarterly* 39, no. 1: 1–25.

Longman, T. 2010. *Christianity and Genocide in Rwanda*. New York: Cambridge University Press.

Lorch, D. 1995. "Ethiopia Holding Elections in Federal System." *New York Times*, May 7.

Lyons, T. 1996. "Closing the Transition: The May 1995 Elections in Ethiopia." *Journal of Modern African Studies* 34, no. 1: 121–42.

Lyons, T. 2019. *The Puzzle of Ethiopian Politics*. Boulder, CO: Lynn Rienner.

Maasho, A. 2018. "Ethnic Unrest Tarnishes New Ethiopian Leader's Reforms." Reuters, August 24.

Mains, D. 2011. *Hope Is Cut: Youth, Unemployment, and the Future in Urban Ethiopia*. Philadelphia: Temple University Press.

Malley, R. 2018. "10 Conflicts to Watch in 2018." *Foreign Policy*, January 2.

Mamdani, M. 2001. *When Victims Become Killers: Colonialism, Nativism and the Genocide in Rwanda*. Princeton: Princeton University Press.

Mamdani, M. 2019. "The Trouble with Ethiopia's Ethnic Federalism." *New York Times*, January 3.

Manirakiza, M. 2002. *Burundi: Quand le passé ne passe pas (Buyoya I–Ndadaye) 1987–1993*. Paris: Longue Vue.

Marsh, J. 2018. "Why Ethiopians Believe Their New Prime Minister Is a Prophet." CNN, August 29.

Mattes, M., and B. Savun. 2009. "Fostering Peace After Civil War: Commitment Problems and Agreement Design." *International Studies Quarterly* 53, no. 3: 737–59.

Mattes, M., and B. Savun. 2010. "Information, Agreement Design, and the Durability of Civil War Settlements." *American Journal of Political Science* 52, no. 2: 511–24.

McCulloch, A., and J. McGarry, eds. 2017. *Power-Sharing: Empirical and Normative Challenges*. London: Routledge.

McFaul, M. 2007. "Political Transitions: Democracy and the Former Soviet Union." *Harvard International Review* 28: 40–45.

McGarry, J. 2017a. "Centripetalism, Consociationalism and Cyprus: The 'Adoptability' Question." In *Power Sharing: Empirical and Normative Challenges*, edited by A. McCulloch and J. McGarry, 16–35. London: Routledge.

McGarry, J. 2017b. "Conclusion: What Explains the Performance of Power-Sharing Settlements?" In *Power Sharing: Empirical and Normative Challenges*, edited by A. McCulloch and J. McGarry, 268–89. London: Routledge.

McGarry, J., and B. O'Leary. 1993. "Introduction: The Macro-Political Regulation of Ethnic Conflict." In *The Politics of Ethnic Conflict Regulation*, edited by J. McGarry and B. O'Leary, 1–40. New York: Routledge.

McGarry, J., and B. O'Leary. 1999. *Policing Northern Ireland: Proposals for a New Start*. Belfast: Blackstaff Press.

McGarry, J., and B. O'Leary. 2006. "Consociational Theory, Northern Ireland's Conflict, and Its Agreement 2: What Critics of Consociation Can Learn from Northern Ireland." *Government and Opposition* 41, no. 2: 249–77.

McGarry, J., B. O'Leary, and R. Simeon. 2008. "Integration or Accommodation? The Enduring Debate in Conflict Regulation." In *Constitutional Design for Divided Societies*, edited by S. Choudhry, 41–90. Oxford: Oxford University Press.

McWhirter, C., and G. Melamede. 1992. "Ethiopia: The Ethnicity Factor." *Africa Report* 37, no. 5: 33–46.

Melander, E., F. Möller, and M. Öberg. 2009. "Managing Intrastate Low-Intensity Armed Conflict 1993–2004: A New Dataset." *International Interactions* 35, no. 1: 58–85.

Melander, E., T. Pettersson, and L. Themnér. 2016. "Organized Violence, 1989–2015." *Journal of Peace Research* 53, no. 5: 727–42.

Mengie, T. 2015. "Ethnic Federalism and Conflict in Ethiopia: What Lessons Can Other Jurisdictions Draw." *African Journal of International and Comparative Law* 23, no. 3: 462–75.

Mengistu, B., and E. Vogel. 2006. "Bureaucratic Neutrality among Competing Bureaucratic Values in an Ethnic Federalism: The Case of Ethiopia." *Public Administration Review* 66, no. 2: 205–16.

Mgbako, C. 2005. "Ingando Solidarity Camps: Reconciliation and Political Indoctrination in Post-Genocide Rwanda." *Harvard Human Rights Journal* 18: 201–24.

Mhlanga, B. 2013. "Post-Coloniality and the Matebeleland Question in Zimbabwe." In *Nationalism and National Projects in Southern Africa: New Critical Reflections*, edited by S. J. Ndlovu-Gatsheni and F. Ndhlovu, 270–88. Pretoria: Africa Institute of South Africa.

Mills, G. 2018. "Ethiopia's Need for 'Deep Renewal.'" *Daily Maverick* (South Africa), August 14.

Ministry of Foreign Affairs of Ethiopia. 2016. *Ethiopia's Unity in Diversity on Display*. Facebook update, December 14. Available from: https://www.facebook.com/MFAEthiopia/posts/ethiopias-unity-in-diversity-on-displaythe-11th-nations-nationalities-and-people/1563723766988194.

Mitchell, R. 2015. "The Implications of School Improvement and School Effectiveness Research for Primary School Principals in Ethiopia." *Educational Review* 67, no. 3: 328–42.

Monaghan, C., and E. King. 2015. *Civics and Ethical Education for Peacebuilding in Ethiopia: Results and Lessons Learned*. Nairobi: UNICEF.

Mthembu-Salter, G. 2016. "Peace and Peace Agreements in Burundi: When the Right Time Comes." In *Peace Agreements and Durable Peace in Africa*, edited by G. Maina and E. Melander, 47–84. Pietermaritzburg: University of Kwazulu-Natal Press.

Mules, I. 2018. "Ethiopia: Talk of Peace Fails to Quell Ethnic Clashes." DW News, September 24.

Multicultural Policy Index. 2019. Available from: http://www.queensu.ca/mcp.

Newbury, C. 1988. *Cohesion of Oppression: Clientship and Ethnicity in Rwanda, 1860–1960*. New York: Columbia University Press.

Ngaruko, F., and J. Nukurunziza. 2000. "An Economic Interpretation of Conflict in Burundi." *Journal of African Economies* 9, no. 3: 370–409.

Niesen, P. 2010. "Political Party Bans in Rwanda 1994–2003: Three Narratives in Justification." *Democratization* 17, no. 4: 709–29.

Niyonzima, M., G. Kayibanda, I. Ndahayo, C. Nzeyimana, G. Mulindaha, S. Sentama, S. Munyambonera, J. Sibomana, and J. Habyarimana. 1957. "Le manifeste des Bahutus." In *Rwanda Politique 1958–1960*, edited by F. Nkundabagenzi, 20–30. Brussels: Centre de Recherche et d'Information Socio-Politique.

Nkurunziza, P. 2011. "President Pierre Nkurunziza of Burundi, Shares with the World the Goodness of Burundi" [video], May 1. Available from: https://www.youtube.com/watch?v=MmwnEz8iyHg.

North, D., J. J. Wallis, and B. R. Weingast. 2009. *Violence and Social Orders: A Conceptual Framework for Interpreting Recorded Human History*. New York: Cambridge University Press.

O'Donnell, G., and P. G. Schmitter. 1986. *Transitions from Authoritarian Rule: Tentative Conclusions and Uncertain Democracies*. Baltimore: Johns Hopkins.

O'Leary, B. 2005. "Debating Consociation: Normative and Explanatory Arguments." In *From Power-Sharing to Democracy: Post-Conflict Institutions in Ethnically Divided Societies*, edited by S. Noel, 3–43. Toronto: McGill-Queens University Press.

Olson, R. W. 1996. *The Kurdish Nationalist Movement in the 1990s: Its Impact on Turkey and the Middle East*. Lexington: University of Kentucky Press.

Olson Lounsbery, M., and K. DeRouen Jr. 2016. "The Viability of Civil War Peace Agreements." *Civil Wars* 18, no. 3: 311–37.

Paravicini, G. 2019. "Ethiopia's Sidama vote overwhelmingly to form autonomous region." *Reuters*, November 23.

Paris, R. 1997. "Peacebuilding and the Limits of Liberal Internationalism." *International Security* 22, no. 2: 54–89.

Penn, E. M. 2008. "Citizenship Versus Ethnicity: The Role of Institutions in Shaping Identity Choice." *Journal of Politics* 70, no. 4: 956–73.

Perlez, J. 1988. "The Bloody Hills of Burundi." *New York Times Magazine*, November 6.

Petersen, R. D. 2001. *Resistance and Rebellion: Lessons from Eastern Europe*. Cambridge: Cambridge University Press.

Petersen, R. D. 2002. *Understanding Ethnic Violence: Fear, Hatred, and Resentment in Twentieth-Century Eastern Europe*. Cambridge: Cambridge University Press.

Phillips, A. 1995. *The Politics of Presence*. Oxford: Oxford University Press.

Pilling, D., and L. Barber. 2017. "Interview: Kagame Insists Rwandans Understand the Greater Goal." *Financial Times*, August 27.

Pitkin, H. 1967. *The Concept of Representation*. Berkeley: University of California Press.

Plummer, J. 2012. *Diagnosing Corruption in Ethiopia: Perceptions, Realities, and the Way Forward for Key Sectors*. Washington, DC: World Bank.

Posen, B. R. 1993. "The Security Dilemma and Ethnic Conflict." *Survival* 35, no. 1: 27–47.

Posner, D. 2004. "Measuring Ethnic Fractionalization in Africa." *American Journal of Political Science* 48, no. 4: 849–63.

Posner, D. 2005. *Institutions and Ethnic Politics in Africa*. Cambridge: Cambridge University Press.

Pottier, J. 2002. *Re-Imagining Rwanda: Conflict, Survival and Disinformation in the Late Twentieth Century*. Cambridge: Cambridge University Press.

Prunier, G. 1995. *Rwanda: Update to End November 1995*. WRITENET. Available from: http://www.refworld.org/docid/3ae6a6b51f.html. Accessed May 31, 2018.

Prunier, G. 1997. *The Rwanda Crisis: History of a Genocide 1959–1994*. London: C. Hurst.

Prunier, G. 2008. *Africa's World War: Congo, the Rwandan Genocide, and the Making of a Continental Catastrophe*. Oxford: Oxford University Press.

Putnam, R. 2007. "E Pluribus Unum: Diversity and Community in the Twenty-First Century. The 2006 Joan Skytte Prize Lecture." *Scandinavian Political Studies* 30, no. 2: 137–74.

Raffoul, A. W. 2020. "The Politics of Association: Power-Sharing and the Depoliticization of Ethnicity in Post-War Burundi." *Ethnopolitics* 19, no. 1: 1–18.

Regassa, T. 2010. "Learning to Live with Conflicts: Federalism as a Tool of Conflict Management in Ethiopia—An Overview." *Mizan Law Review* 4, no. 1: 52–101.

Reilly, B. 2001. *Democracy in Divided Societies: Electoral Engineering for Conflict Management*. New York: Cambridge University Press.

Republic of Rwanda. 1995. *Document final provisoire: Conférence sur la politique et la planification de l'éducation au Rwanda*. Kigali: Ministère de l'Enseignement Primaire et Secondaire et Ministère de l'Enseignement Supérieur de la Recherche Scientifique et de la Culture.

Republic of Rwanda. 2001. *Law No. 47/2001 on Prevention, Suppression and Punishment of the Crime of Discrimination and Sectarianism*. Available from: https://www.refworld.org/pdfid/4ac5c4302.pdf.

Republic of Rwanda. 2004. *3rd National Summit Report on Unity and Reconciliation*. Kigali: National Unity and Reconciliation Commission.

Republic of Rwanda. 2006. *Rwanda: Genocide Ideology and Strategies for Its Eradication*. Senate Report. Kigali: Republic of Rwanda.

Republic of Rwanda. 2017. *Overview*. National Commission for the Fight Against Genocide (CNLG). Available from: https://www.cnlg.gov.rw/index.php?id=10.

Reynolds, A. 2005. "Reserved Seats in National Legislatures: A Research Note." *Legislative Studies Quarterly* 30, no. 2: 301–10.

Reynolds, A. 2011. *Designing Democracy in a Dangerous World*. Oxford: Oxford University Press.

Reyntjens, F. 1993. "The Proof in the Pudding Is in the Eating: The June 1993 Elections in Burundi." *Journal of Modern African Studies* 31, no. 4: 563–83.

Reyntjens, F. 2004. "Rwanda, Ten Years On: From Genocide to Dictatorship." *African Affairs* 103, no. 411: 177–210.

Reyntjens, F. 2006. "Briefing: Burundi: A Peaceful Transition After Decades of War?" *African Affairs* 105, no. 418: 117–35.

Reyntjens, F. 2013. *Political Governance in Post-Genocide Rwanda*. New York: Cambridge University Press.

Roeder, P., and D. Rothchild. 2005. *Sustainable Peace: Power and Democracy After Civil Wars*. Ithaca, NY: Cornell University Press.

Rothchild, D. 1997. *Managing Ethnic Conflict in Africa: Pressures and Incentives for Cooperation*. Washington, DC: Brookings Institution.

Rubin, B., and H. Hamidzada. 2007. "From Bonn to London: Governance Challenges and the Future of Statebuilding in Afghanistan." *International Peacekeeping* 14, no. 1: 8–25.

Russell, S. G., and P. L. Carter. 2019. "When the Past Is in the Present: The Paradox of Educational Opportunity and Social Inclusion in South Africa and Rwanda." *Sociology of Race and Ethnicity* 5, no. 4: 547–61.

Rwandan Patriotic Front. 1990. *Position on the Current Crisis in Rwanda: Summary Overview and Political Program*. October

Ryan, C. S., J. S. Hunt, J. A. Weible, C. R. Peterson, and J. F. Casas. 2007. "Multicultural and Colorblind Ideology, Stereotypes, and Ethnocentrism Among Black and White Americans." *Group Processes and Intergroup Relations* 10, no. 4: 617–37.

Sambanis, N. 2004. "What Is a Civil War? Conceptual and Empirical Complexities of an Operational Definition." *Journal of Conflict Resolution* 48, no. 6: 814–58.

Sambanis, N., and M. Shayo. 2013. "Social Identification and Ethnic Conflict." *American Political Science Review* 103, no. 2: 294–325.

Samii, C. 2013a. "Who Wants to Forgive and Forget? Transitional Justice Preferences in Post-War Burundi." *Journal of Peace Research* 50, no. 2: 219–33.

Samii, C. 2013b. "Perils or Promise of Ethnic Integration: Evidence from a Hard Case in Burundi." *American Political Science Review* 107, no. 3: 558–73.

Samii, C. 2014. "Military Integration in Burundi." In *New Armies from Old: Military Integration After Civil War*, edited by R. Licklider, 213–28. Washington, DC: Georgetown University Press.

Samii, C., and E. West. 2019. "Repressed Productive Potential and Revolt: Insights from an Insurgency in Burundi." *Political Science Research and Methods* (in press).

Samuels, K. 2006. "Post-Conflict Peace-Building and Constitution-Making." *Chicago Journal of International Law* 6, no. 2: 663–82.

Sasse, G. 2005. "Securitization or Securing Rights? Exploring the Conceptual Foundations of Policies Towards Minorities and Migrants in Europe." *JCMS: Journal of Common Market Studies* 43, no. 4: 673–93.

Schabas, W., and M. Imbleau. 1997. *Introduction to Rwandan Law*. Cowansville, QC: Yvon Blais.

Schedler, A. 2002. "The Menu of Manipulation." *Journal of Democracy* 13, no. 2: 36–50.

Schemm, P. 2018. "After Years of Unrest, Ethiopians Are Riding an Unlikely Wave of Hope. Will It Last?" *Washington Post*, May 6.

Schwartz, S. 2017. "You Can't Go Home Again: Return Migration and Conflict Dynamics in Burundi." Unpublished manuscript, Columbia University.

Scorgie, L. 2004. "Rwanda's Arusha Accords: A Missed Opportunity." *Undercurrent* 1, no. 1: 66–76.

Scott, J. 1995. *Seeing Like A State: How Certain Schemes to Improve the Human Condition Have Failed*. New Haven: Yale University Press.

Seawright, J. 2016. *Multi-Method Social Science: Combining Qualitative and Quantitative Tools*. Cambridge: Cambridge University Press.

Sefa Dei, G. J. 2005. "The Challenge of Inclusive Schooling in Africa: A Ghanaian Case Study." *Comparative Education* 41: 267–89.

Semela, T. 2014. "Teacher Preparation in Ethiopia: A Critical Analysis of Reforms." *Cambridge Journal of Education* 44, no. 1: 113–45.

Sen, A. 2006. *Identity and Violence: The Illusion of Destiny*. New York: W. W. Norton.

Sengupta, S. 2018. "Can Ethiopia's New Leader, a Political Insider, Change It from the Inside Out?" *New York Times*, September 17.

Shohamy, E., and D. Gorter. 2008. *Linguistic Landscape: Expanding the Scenery*. New York: Routledge.

Simonsen, S. V. 2005. "Addressing Ethnic Divisions in Post-Conflict Institution-Building: Lessons from Recent Cases." *Security Dialogue* 36, no. 3: 297–318.

Sisk, T. D. 1996. *Power Sharing and International Mediation in Ethnic Conflicts*. Washington, DC: United States Institute of Peace Press.

Slater, D., and D. Ziblatt. 2013. "The Enduring Indispensability of the Controlled Comparison." *Comparative Political Studies* 46, no. 10: 1301–1327.

Smith, A. D. 1986. *The Ethnic Origins of Nations*. Oxford: Blackwell.

Smith, L. 2007. "Voting for an Ethnic Identity: Procedural and Institutional Responses to Ethnic Conflict in Ethiopia." *Journal of Modern African Studies* 45, no. 4: 565–94.

Smith, L. 2013. *Making Citizens in Africa: Ethnicity, Gender, and National Identity in Ethiopia*. Cambridge: Cambridge University Press.

Snyder, J. 2000. *From Voting to Violence: Democratization and Nationalist Conflict*. New York: Norton.

Snyder, J. L., and R. Jervis. 1999. "Civil War and the Security Dilemma." In *Civil Wars, Insecurity, and Intervention*, edited by B. F. Walter and J. Snyder, 15–37. New York: Columbia University Press.

Soliman, A. 2018. "Ethiopia's Prime Minister Shows Knack for Balancing Reform and Continuity." Chatham House, April 27. Available from: https://www.chathamhouse.org/expert/comment/ethiopia-s-prime-minister-shows-knack-balancing-reform-and-continuity.

Somer, M. 2005. "Failures of the Discourse of Ethnicity: Turkey, Kurds, and the Emerging Iraq." *Security Dialogue* 36, no. 1: 109–28.

Somer, M. 2010. "Turkey's New Kurdish Opening: Religious Versus Secular Values." *Middle East Policy* 18, no. 2:152–65.

Song, S. 2017. "Multiculturalism." in *Stanford Encyclopedia of Philosophy*, edited by E. Zalta, Spring 2017 edition. Available from: https://plato.stanford.edu/archives/spr2017/entries/multiculturalism.

Sowell, T. 2004. *Affirmative Action Around the World: An Empirical Study*. New Haven: Yale University Press.

Spears, I. 2010. *Civil War in African States: The Search for Security*. Boulder, CO: First Forum Press.

Stanton, G. 2009. "The Rwandan Genocide: Why Early Warning Failed." *Journal of African Conflicts and Peace Studies* 1, no. 2: 6–25.

Starkey, J. 2012. "Rwandan Defectors Tell of Life on the Run from Paul Kagame's Assassins." *The Times*, October 8. Available from: http://www.theaustralian.com.au/news/world/rwandan-defectors-tell-of-life-on-run-from-paul-kagames-assassins/news-story/8a8014a5a5a0317a724e4ae6e8ec8a7d.

Stettenheim, J. 2000. "The Arusha Accords and the Failure of International Intervention in Rwanda." In *Words over War: Mediation and Arbitration to Prevent Deadly Conflict*, edited by M. Greenberg, M. E. McGuinness, and J. H. Barton, 213–36. New York: Carnegie Commission on Preventing Deadly Conflict.

Stewart, F. 2002. "Crisis Prevention: Tackling Horizontal Inequalities." *Oxford Development Studies* 28, no. 3: 245–62.

Stewart, F., and G. Brown. 2007. "Motivations for Conflict: Groups and Individuals." In *Leashing the Dogs of War*, edited by C. A. Crocker, F. Osler Hampson, and P. Aall, 219–41. Washington, DC: United States Institute of Peace.

Strand, H., and H. Urdal. 2014. "Hear Nothing, See Nothing, Say Nothing: Can States Reduce the Risk of Armed Conflict by Banning Census Data on Ethnic Groups?" *International Area Studies Review* 17, no. 2: 167–83.

Straus, S. 2006. *The Order of Genocide: Race, Power, and War in Rwanda*. Ithaca, NY: Cornell University Press.

Straus, S. 2015. *Making and Unmaking Nations: War, Leadership, and Genocide in Modern Africa*. Ithaca: Cornell University Press.

Straus, S. 2019. "The Limits of a Genocide Lens: Violence Against Rwandans in the 1990s." *Journal of Genocide Research* 21, no. 4: 504–24.

Sue, C. 2015. "Hegemony and Silence: Confronting State-Sponsored Silences in the Field." *Journal of Contemporary Ethnography* 44, no. 1: 113–40.

Sullivan, R. 1994. "Juvenal Habyarimana, 57, Ruled Rwanda for 21 Years." *New York Times*, April 7.

Sundberg, R., K. Eck, and J. Kreutz. 2012. "Introducing the UCDP Non-State Conflict Dataset." *Journal of Peace Research* 49, no. 2: 351–62.

Tajfel, H. 1981. *Human Groups and Social Categories: Studies in Social Psychology*. New York: Cambridge University Press.

Tajfel, H. 1982. *Social Identity and Intergroup Relations*. New York: Cambridge University Press.

Tambiah, S. J. 1991. *Sri Lanka—Ethnic Fratricide and the Dismantling of Democracy*. 2nd ed. Chicago: University of Chicago Press.

Taub, A. 2016. "A Central Conflict of 21st-Century Politics: Who Belongs?" *New York Times*, July 8.

Taylor, C. 1992. *Multiculturalism and the Politics of Recognition: An Essay with Commentary*. Princeton: Princeton University Press.

Taylor, R. 2001. "Northern Ireland: Consociation or Social Transformation." In *Northern Ireland and the Divided World: Post-Agreement Northern Ireland in Comparative Perspective*, edited by J. McGarry, 36–52. Oxford: Oxford University Press.

Tegegn, M. 2012. "Mengistu's 'Red Terror'." *African Identities* 10, no. 3: 249–63.

Tesfay, N., and L. E. Malmberg. 2014. "Horizontal Inequalities in Children's Educational Outcomes in Ethiopia." *International Journal of Educational Development* 39: 110–20.

Tesfaye, B. 2014. "Let's Talk About Ethnicity and Nationalism in Ethiopia." Africa Is a Country, October 7. Available at http://africasacountry.com/2014/10/lets-talk-about-ethnicity-and-nationalism-in-ethiopia.

Thomson, S. M. 2009. "Ethnic Twa and Rwandan National Unity and Reconciliation Policy." *Peace Review* 21, no. 3: 313–20.

Thomson, S. M. 2012. "Peasant Perspectives on National Unity and Reconciliation: Building Peace or Promoting Division?" In *Rwanda Fast Forward: Social, Economic, Military and Reconciliation Prospects*, edited by M. Campioni and P. Noack, 96–110. New York: Palgrave Macmillan.

Thomson, S. M. 2013. *Whispering Truth to Power: Everyday Resistance and Reconciliation in Postgenocide Rwanda*. Madison: University of Wisconsin Press.

Thomson, S. M. 2018. *Rwanda: From Genocide to Precarious Peace*. New Haven: Yale University Press.

Toggia, P. 2012. "The Revolutionary Endgame of Political Power: The Genealogy of 'Red Terror' in Ethiopia." *African Identities* 10, no. 3: 265–80.

Tronvoll, K. 2011. "The Ethiopian 2010 Federal and Regional Elections: Re-establishing the One-Party State." *African Affairs* 110, no. 438: 121–36.

United Nations. 2015. *About the Sustainable Development Goals*. United Nations. Available at https://www.un.org/sustainabledevelopment/sustainable-development-goals.

U.S. Embassy Kigali. 2008. "Ethnicity in Rwanda: Who Governs the Country?" Ref. Kigali 480, August 5. Available through WikiLeaks, http://wikileaks.org/cable/2008/08/08KIGALI525.html.

Uvin, P. 1999. "Ethnicity and Power in Burundi and Rwanda: Different Paths to Mass Violence." *Comparative Politics* 31, no. 3: 253–71.

Uvin, P. 2002. "On Counting, Categorizing, and Violence in Burundi and Rwanda." In *Census and Identity. The Politics of Race, Ethnicity and Language in National Censuses*, edited by D. Kertzer and D. Arel, 148–75. Cambridge: Cambridge University Press.

Van Evera, S. 1997. *Guide to Methods for Students of Political Science*. Ithaca, NY: Cornell University Press.

Vandeginste, S. 2009. "Power-Sharing, Conflict and Transition in Burundi: Twenty Years of Trial and Error." *Africa Spectrum* 44, no. 3: 63–86.

Vandeginste, S. 2014. "Governing Ethnicity After Genocide: Ethnic Amnesia in Rwanda Versus Ethnic Power-Sharing in Burundi." *Journal of Eastern African Studies* 8, no. 2: 263–77.

Vandeginste, S. 2015. "Burundi's Electoral Crisis: Back to Power-Sharing Politics as Usual?" *African Affairs/Royal African Society London* 114, no. 457: 624–36.

Vandeginste, S. 2016. "In Need of a Guardian Angel: Preserving the Gains of the Arusha Peace and Reconciliation Agreement for Burundi." Institute of Development Policy and Management (IOB) Working Papers, University of Antwerp. Available from: https://www.uantwerpen.be/images/uantwerpen/container2673/files/Publications/WP/2016/01-Vandeginste.pdf.

Vandeginste, S. 2018. "Burundi's Constitutional Referendum: Consolidating the Fait Accompli in the Run-Up to the 2020 Elections." ConstitutionNet. Available at: http://constitutionnet.org/news/burundis-constitutional-referendum-consolidating-fait-accompli-run-2020-elections.

Vandeginste, S., and C. L. Sriram. 2011. "Power Sharing and Transitional Justice: A Clash of Paradigms?" *Global Governance* 17: 489–505.

Varshney, A. 2007. "Ethnicity and Ethnic conflict." In *The Oxford Handbook of Comparative Politics*, edited by C. Boix and S. Stokes, 274–94. Oxford: Oxford University Press.

Vaughan, S., and K. Tronvoll. 2003. "The Culture of Power in Ethiopian Political Life." *Sida Studies* 10: 10–177.

Vaughan, S. 1994. *The Addis Ababa Transitional Conference of July 1991: Its Origin, History and Significance*. Edinburgh: Centre for African Studies, Edinburgh University.

Verkuyten, M. 2005. "Ethnic Group Identification and Group Evaluation Among Minority and Majority Groups: Testing the Multiculturalism Hypothesis." *Journal of Personality and Social Psychology* 88, no. 1: 121–38.

Walter, B. 2010. "Conflict Relapse and the Sustainability of Post-Conflict Peace." World Development Report 2011 Background Paper, World Bank. Available from: http://web.worldbank.org/archive/web site01306/web/pdf/wdr%20background%20paper_walter_0.pdf.

Waugh, C. M. 2004. *Paul Kagame and Rwanda: Power, Genocide and the Rwandan Patriotic Front*. Jefferson, NC: McFarland.

Weber, E. 1976. *Peasants into Frenchmen: The Modernization of Rural France, 1870–1914*. Stanford: Stanford University Press.

Weiner, B. 1983. "Some Methodological Pitfalls in Attributional Research." *Journal of Educational Psychology* 75, no. 4: 530–43.

Weisskopf, T. E. 2004. *Affirmative Action in the United States and India*. London: Routledge.

West, E. A. 2016. "Descriptive Representation and Political Efficacy: Evidence from Obama and Clinton." *Journal of Politics* 79, no. 1: 351–55.

WikiLeaks. 2016. "France/Burundi: Ambassador Moller's August 22 Consultations." Available at http://wikileaks.org/plusd/cables/06PARIS5848_a.html.

Wimmer, A. 2013. *Ethnic Boundary Making: Institutions, Power, Networks*. Oxford: Oxford University Press.

Wimmer, A., L. E. Cederman, and B. Min. 2009. "Ethnic Politics and Armed Conflict: A Configurational Analysis of a New Global Data Set." *American Sociological Review* 74, no. 2: 316–37.

Wolff, S. 2010. "Building Democratic States After Conflict: Institutional Design Revisited." *International Studies Review* 12, no. 1: 128–41.

Wolpe, H. 2011. *Making Peace After Genocide: Anatomy of the Burundi Peace Process*. Washington, DC: United States Institute of Peace.

Wolsko, C., B. Park, and C. M. Judd. 2006. "Considering the Tower of Babel: Correlates of Assimilation and Multiculturalism Among Ethnic Minority and Majority Groups in the United States." *Social Justice Research* 19: 277–306.

World Bank. 2004. *Technical Annex for a Proposed Grant of SDR 22.2 Million to the Republic of Burundi for an Emergency Demobilization, Reinsertion and Reintegration Program*. Washington, DC: World Bank.

World Bank. 2015. "GINI Index (World Bank Estimate): Ethiopia." Available from: https://data.worldbank.org/indicator/SI.POV.GINI?locations=ET.

World Bank and United Nations. 2018. *Pathways for Peace: Inclusive Approaches to Conflict Prevention*. Washington, DC: World Bank.

World Politics Review. 2018. "Can 'Abiymania' in Ethiopia Withstand the Threat of Ethnic Conflict?" *World Politics Review*, October 15. https://www.worldpoliticsreview.com/trendlines/26411/can-abiymania-in-ethiopia-withstand-the-threat-of-ethnic-conflict

Yibeltal, K. 2019. "Ethiopia's Abiy Ahmed Gets a New Ruling Party." *BBC News*, November 22.

Young, I. M. 1990. *Justice and the Politics of Difference*. Princeton: Princeton University Press.

Young, J. 1996a. "Ethnicity and Power in Ethiopia." *Review of African Political Economy* 23, no. 70: 531–42.

Young, J. 1996b. "The Tigray and Eritrean Peoples Liberation Fronts: A History of Tensions and Pragmatism." *Journal of Modern African Studies* 34, no. 1: 105–20.

Young, J. 1999. "Governance in Post–Cold War Ethiopia." Paper presented at the Africa Society Conference, Edmonton, Alberta, February 26–28.

Zimmerman-Steinhart, P., and Y. Bekele. 2012. "The Implications of Federalism and Decentralization on Socio-Economic Conditions in Ethiopia." *Potchefstroom Electronic Law Journal* 15, no. 2: 90–117.

INDEX

Tables and figures are indicated by *t* and *f* following the page number

For the benefit of digital users, indexed terms that span two pages (e.g., 52–53) may, on occasion, appear on only one of those pages.